THE IMAGINATION OF JEAN GENET

Yale Romanic Studies, Second Series, 10

The Imagination of Jean Genet

BY JOSEPH H. MCMAHON

NEW HAVEN AND LONDON: YALE UNIVERSITY PRESS

PARIS: PRESSES UNIVERSITAIRES DE FRANCE

1963

For Kay, Frank, Barbara, and Robert

I am grateful to Henri Peyre, Sterling Professor of French at Yale, who read this book in its early stages and offered valuable suggestions for its improvement; to many students in Yale, especially in Pierson College, whose reaction to Genet's plays frequently served to sharpen my own; and to Lynette Kohn, who read through the manuscript patiently, looking for errors and offering numerous suggestions for improvement. Thomas C. Witherspoon of the Yale University Press read the manuscript with care and patience; its felicities are often the result of his pruning; what remains awkward is exclusively my responsibility.

Genet's various publishers have given permission to quote, and in some cases, to translate his works. Specific acknowledgments are: Librairie Gallimard for the *Oeuvres complètes;* the Arbalète Press for the several essays gathered in *l'Atelier d'Alberto Giacometti;* J.-J. Pauvert for *les Bonnes;* and Grove Press in New York for the quotations from:

The Blacks: A Clown Show by Jean Genet, translated

Preface

by Bernard Frechtman, copyright © 1960 by Bernard Frechtman, published by Grove Press, Inc.

The Balcony by Jean Genet, translated by Bernard Frechtman, copyright © 1958, 1960 by Bernard Frechtman, published by Grove Press, Inc.

The Maids and *Deathwatch* by Jean Genet, with an Introduction by Jean-Paul Sartre, translated by Bernard Frechtman, copyright © 1954 by Bernard Frechtman, published by Grove Press, Inc.

The Screens by Jean Genet, translated by Bernard Frechtman, copyright © 1962 by Bernard Frechtman, published by Grove Press, Inc.

In the case of *les Bonnes* it has been impossible for me to use the Grove Press translation since the illustration of my argument could only be made by referring to the two versions published by J.-J. Pauvert. It should be mentioned that Grove Press plans to publish *Notre-Dame-des-Fleurs* in the fall of 1963 and *Journal du voleur* at a later date; both will be in translations by Bernard Frechtman. George Braziller has also announced the publication in the fall of 1963 of Jean-Paul Sartre's *Saint-Genet, comédien et martyr,* again in a translation by Bernard Frechtman, copyright © 1963.

The Viking Press, Inc., has given permission to quote from Padraic Colum's edition of James Joyce's *Exiles,* copyright © 1951.

All editions referred to in the text are indicated by an asterisk in the Bibliography, and page references given in the text are to those editions. A very small part of this book, in somewhat different form, appeared in *Yale French Studies,* 29.

J.H.McM.

Pierson College
Yale University
May 1963

CONTENTS

Our intent is not to disengage two or more characters or heroes, since everyone here has been picked from a fabled domain, that is, taken from systematically odious fable. A reader would be better off realizing that we are pursuing an adventure which is unfolding in our deepest recesses, in the most nonsocial part of our soul. Then it's clear that it's because he gives life to his creatures—and willingly assumes the burden of all the sins belonging to this world for whose birth he is responsible—that the creator delivers, saves his creatures, and simultaneously places himself either above the realm of sin or else beyond it. Let him escape from sin so that meanwhile the reader, profiting from his function and our word, may discover these heroes emerging from the crouched position they have had within him until he meets them here.

—*Querelle de Brest*

> The act is beautiful if it pro-
> vokes and makes our throats
> quicken to song. Sometimes
> the awareness with which we
> may have thought of some
> supposedly base act, the ex-
> pressive power which should
> signify it, forces us into song.
> —*Journal du voleur*

Introduction

A reader prone to biograph-
ical curiosity and subject to the need to satisfy it before
beginning an author's work could be frustrated even before his initial encounter with Jean Genet's writing. He
would find, for instance, various editions and critical
articles attributing different birthdates to this enigmatic
man, who appears increasingly as the most important,
original, and fertile of contemporary French dramatists.
Yet it seems consistent and consonant with the other
"facts" of his life that contradictory dates should be

1

offered. While these uneven vital statistics place him in the enviable position of being able to select whichever age best conforms with his mood of the day or the demands of the times, they also have a peculiar pertinence. The existence of at least four such possibilities establishes hesitations about accuracy and even about reality, which express better than would any specific information about hour, day, and place the most appropriate way in which to draw near to the reality which is Jean Genet.

Despite the editorial confusion which sets up this generous range of choice, official records, and Jean Genet himself, designate 1910 as the legally recognized date for the event. The city whose lights he first saw was Paris; the place, Genet tells us in his *Journal du voleur,* a maternity hospital, which diligently established that he was not legitimate. His mother abandoned him to the cares of the state, and he spent the early years of his life in a foster home in the Morvan region of France. This sojourn, elements of which are evoked in his first book, *Notre-Dame-des-Fleurs,* was brought to a dramatic and determining end by his arrest for theft and his relegation to a reform school. The end was dramatic because it brought into question—for others at least, since Genet has never openly addressed himself to this aspect of the problem—the over-all wisdom of consigning a young mind to a penal institution at so early an age. It was determining because it was the first step in a lengthy if unselective journey through the major prisons of France and other European countries. Until, roughly, the age of thirty Genet's activities were for the most part criminal; the monotonous result was that his habitat, more often than not, was jail. The locales and his fellow prisoners did change, however, for Genet's travels were international. From them there emerges a pattern where frontier barriers are broken down to create that vast criminal world that becomes the most comfortable and frequent locus of Genet's thinking. He may have stolen cattle in southeastern Europe, smuggled narcotics in Iberia, earned experience as a pickpocket in Central Europe, collaborated with the Germans, joined and quickly deserted the Foreign Legion—but these activities were all of a piece. That piece, inchoate and thus unformed while it happened, was not to receive systematic presentation or definition until the moment when, arrested and imprisoned for a substantial period, Genet could contemplate his past and begin to determine what it all meant. This was in the early forties when, incarcerated in Fresnes prison, he began writing his first novel and a brief, bad poem entitled *le Condamné à mort*.

The fact of having begun to write and so to fix his experience served Genet as a crux in determining the essence of his life. Until that time there had been activity which, because of its consistency, had established orientations and deposited the germs of judgment in Genet's mind. With the act of writing there comes an attitude toward that activity, an attitude which it is the purpose of this study to follow and analyze. It must be followed because it grows and changes and finds new emphases. It must be analyzed because analysis is a bent of the human mind when confronted with something which perplexes and challenges. The writing of *Notre-Dame-des-Fleurs* was a crux in Genet's life not simply because it was a moment for catching breath, but also because it gave his life a public dimension which was bound eventually to change the direction of his career, deflecting him from participation into meditation and, later, to a new level of assault upon the world which would be more sophisticated and, in its way, more consequential than any theft he had committed as a young man.

The deflection was not immediate nor was it lasting.

The Imagination of Jean Genet

While the two early prison works had brought him to the attention of certain literary circles in Paris, they had not brought him to the straight and narrow. In 1947 he was again in prison, once more for theft, and this time it looked as though this particular activity was to be brought to a permanent end. It was his tenth offense in this category and, according to French law, therefore to be the last; for the law, faced with patterns of bad habits, directs that these habits be curtailed by having the habitué spend the rest of his earthly span in jail. By 1947, however, Genet had won a following which, in addition to being distinguished, was also one of the best manifestations of coalition visible in any area of endeavor of postwar France. Sartre, Cocteau, Mauriac, Mondor, and many others forgot their differences and disagreements in order to sign an appeal to the French President, Vincent Auriol, requesting a pardon for the convict. Rather than spending the rest of his life pacing a prison cell or contemplating what can be seen of the sea from the prison colony at Guiana, Genet found himself pardoned and invited to lunch at the Elysée Palace. Such are the ways and power of the literary world in France.

Theorists of human behavior find here a fascinating mixture. Here is the man of talent finally finding his way to genuine and honestly distinguished fame, the victim of society finally receiving redress for the wrongs done him, a triumph of benevolence and integrity in a society which can overlook its usual procedures in order to recognize and encourage merit. Yet each of these statements may lead to a bevy of inaccurate and wrongly stated declarations. No one of them is altogether wrong or totally right, but together they represent something of the situation of Jean Genet as a public and private figure. What happened in the forties was undoubtedly

4

a transformation, but it was not necessarily a radical change: the triumph of good over evil, of society over the criminal. Nor was it necessarily a conciliation between the two designed to produce a better, more realistic synthesis of the various and diverse forces loose in the world. What Genet was discovering in the works that flowed from his pen in those years was a way of finding a particular kind of sense for the life he had lived; and this is quite different from saying that he was finding *the* sense of that experience. What literary figures were discovering was an unmistakably genuine talent, and, even as they discovered it, they were stumbling into the danger of believing it a clearly describable talent whose capacities could be easily detailed and perhaps even circumscribed.

With a greater exposure to Genet's works—and a greater and more diversified number of works to be exposed to—we can have a somewhat different and more accurate perspective; possessed of it, we can look back on the forties as that crux I have mentioned where several factors converged. There was, on the part of Genet, the unleashing of his expressive talent like a torrent notable more for its power than its direction. There was, on the part of the specialized public which first reacted to him, a recognition of that talent and thus, in the nature of the thing, the establishment of possibilities of dialogue between it and the rest of men. What this means is what publication has always meant for any sensibility worth the value we assign to it: a chance to find and then to elaborate its own perspectives; an opportunity to work out ever more clear and accurate representations of the kind of statement one wishes to make; the possibility of having an outside standard against which to measure how well the message is getting across. There is, then—after this essential convergence of author and public has taken place—a growth in Genet. In that growth he finds increasingly more sophisticated methods of working out what it is he wants to say; he finds, too, in the very process of establishing those methods, that what he wants to say in 1962 is quite different from what he was saying in 1943. It is not that he intends now to contradict what he was saying then; rather, it is that he has learned, in the unfolding of his career, that there is an expertise that comes with the practice of art, enabling the practitioner to discover aesthetically more powerful and more convincing ways of putting things. Genet has learned from his art not only a great deal about the diversity art offers to its disciples, but also a great deal about how it is only in art that he can express the various and apparently antagonistic springs which are the mobiles of his experience and the experience of all men, whether considered individually or as members of a community. To the accusation that he was changing his mind and its former evaluations arbitrarily, Genet would probably answer that he was only coming to know it better and, through this deeper knowledge, achieving a fuller understanding of the fullest meaning of his experience.

The purpose of this study is to analyze and quarrel with this growth. I am not here concerned with a biography of Jean Genet as a parable of the criminal's regeneration and his salvation in art; such an interest would not only correspond poorly with the facts, but would also be irrelevant to the more pertinent values of Jean Genet as a writer. Nor am I concerned with the various ironies of his career save as they bear on that kind of phenomenon I am studying in his development. That he has passed from being a ragpicker, homosexual prostitute, and thief to an increasingly renowned and celebrated dramatist is matter for the recorder of the facts and idiosyncrasies of chronological happenings. My concern is with another level of event, a level which, I believe, is well supported and firmer than any area exposed to us by biography. It is Genet's imagination that is most crucially significant because it is the constant and unendingly refurbished generator of his works, and also because his imagination is a door opening onto vistas of even wider significance.

To say that increasing technical virtuosity gives the kind of nourishment best able to bring his imagination to its full powers is to suggest, though perhaps too simply, what is the basis of the sort of presence he represents in contemporary letters. But as a simple description of a process it evokes nothing particularly novel; great artists, as they become more assured, become more audacious. The young Michelangelo, fearing damaging comments on any work he might leave unfinished, would never have abandoned a rough-hewn piece of stone as the best expression of what he could do with the material; the young Molière, torn between a decision to be a tragedian or a comedian, would have rejected the indeterminate but thoroughly appropriate ending of *le Bourgeois Gentilhomme* as a sure sign of youthful incompetence; Racine, in his early career, would have found it folly to furnish a play so sparsely as, later, he was to furnish *Bérénice*. The sense of form grows within a practicing artist until he feels capable of dominating it and identifying his desires with its fullest yield; in the more fruitful cases, *The Tempest* for example, the artist manages to carry the form beyond the level at which he found it. Capable of subjugating the material with which he works because of a thorough awareness of the shape which can be given that material, the artist need no longer be timorous about his capacities, nor need he worry that there is not in the world material enough or genius sufficient to bring his vision of things into some sort of created reality.

The process of individual artistic growth would tend toward monotony were it merely a question of growth into and dominion over forms. It is, of course, more than this; we do not possess, as Plato was to learn in anguish through the dialectics of his later works, a sure sense of what the forms are. We have only those forms which are presented to us by more talented and fertile imaginations and whatever inchoate and unarticulated gropings toward form we possess usually do not quicken until a better developed, more highly endowed sensibility touches ours and leads it toward understanding. When we speak of form, we are speaking of a generic term which in and of itself has no independent existence; it is simply and necessarily a label we need in order to talk of the many forms we come in contact with. The monotony of recurrent encounters with the same sort of thing is avoided because the talent and the vision it conveys never seem repetitious in those cases where we have the impression that the form has some claim either to endurance or our attention.

Genet deserves more than fleeting attention, not simply because his theatrical dexterity is a sure manifestation of a fertile and growing talent, nor indeed because the shape he gives his ideas on the stage represents yet another advance in the growth of form. He deserves attention because he shows both the close relationship between the articulation of ideas and the forms chosen for this articulation, and because, in the midst of the assorted annoyances of the theatre of the absurd, he offers clear evidence that neither the artist nor his art can grow if either is constricted by a priori acceptance of a limited register of expression. The poverty of ideas which has given birth to the absurd in the theatre does not serve well either the exponents of these ideas or their art. The endless repetition of the same theme in Beckett, Audiberti, and Ionesco is saved from engulfing ennui only by the periodic theatrical thrust of their dramatic invention. One is touched by the emotional plight of Vladimir and Estragon in *En attendant Godot,* of Hamm and Clov in *Fin de partie;* one experiences the terror of an encounter with the unknown in *la Leçon* and *Tueur sans gages.* But one is not led to assent to the ideas inspiring these various emotional states nor brought into dialogue with the situation. One watches it, as one watched the bourgeois theatre of the nineteenth century. That one watches it as a manifestation of one's sophistication is perhaps only witness to the fact that sophistication is not without its forms of dogmatism. The dramatic poverty is there and becomes increasingly self-destructive. It is there because the barriers of dogmatism are never broken through; the art does not progress but remains static, like a defective recording where a once powerful phrase repeats itself unto madness and disillusion.

Genet stands curiously, but with increasing artistic authority, in the midst of this. Though he too imbibes his ideas from a restricted spring, he imbibes them with a full grasp of their ramifications as well as with apparently unlimited means for presenting them. There is then a development in the idea, and it is a development which comes from a consistently deeper and more active understanding of the uses and potentialities of artistic forms. Any reasonable study of Genet must consequently keep both these points of growth united in intimate if frequently disputatious marriage, for the ideas cannot be divorced from the form which expresses them; and the form must be kept clearly in view because it gives the ideas their most appropriate shape.

The consequences of this are various. Since it is the

unleashing and development of Genet's imagination which makes the marriage with form possible, attention must be paid simultaneously to the ways in which his imagination matures and the consequences of this kind of maturation on the whole domain of reality. With Genet the notion of any conflict between reality and the imagination, a conflict cherished throughout the history of Western thought, is annulled. The nostalgia of a Gérard de Nerval for an imaginary world which could not be brought within the scope of humdrum terrestrial events, the frustration of a Stéphane Mallarmé who did not quite know what to do with a persistently luminous moon whose existence he had denied—these problems are not Genet's. Indeed, there are, in this sense, no problems which cannot be sifted through the imagination and given their rightful place in a personal world vision. However arbitrary and cavalier the statement of such belief may seem, it is imposing and certainly not irrelevant. Genet has a persuasiveness and at times an accuracy which transcend the sort of artistic petulance we have become accustomed to and to which we allow ourselves an overgenerous tolerance; he has, too, an instinctive cousinship with the thought of some of the more highly considered contemporary philosophers who would have reality proposed, not as a hard, tangible, available thing, but as something continuously to be hunted for, discovered, and defined. In their search Genet offers generous if unanticipated help; his conviction that reality's truest, most consequential domain is in the area of relationship is not very far removed from Heidegger's, though the discerning reader will quickly note that its direction is altogether different.

Jean Genet's art, then, is not a work of silence, designed to convince us of the absence of powers of communication. Nor is it a new installment in the history of romanticism's personal worlds. Quite the contrary, it is possessed of a modernity and an immediacy that make it, despite its capacity for and fascination with shock, one of the more imposing containers for the aesthetic and ideological issues with which we live and over which we fight with varying degrees of graciousness and conviction.

Because of the fluctuating definition of reality which permeates the work, and because of the fluctuating degree of assurance possessed by the mind that seeks to fix its latest apprehension of reality in the most apt form, Genet's works are not prone to tidy discussion. An American critic, first of all, does not have available all the editions which circulate more freely over the pornographer's counter than in libraries and bookstores. But no critic can guarantee what revisions Genet will introduce into those works published in the open market. *Haute Surveillance, le Balcon* and *les Bonnes* have undergone significant revision; the same is true of at least one novel, *Querelle de Brest*. These revisions should come as no surprise since they are sure signs of the quicksilver quality of Genet's mind. No sooner has he uttered a statement than he thinks either of a better, fuller way of putting that statement or else of an entirely new procedure. The first reaction leads to revision, the second to new works. Since my discussion will be very much preoccupied with the process as a process, and also as perhaps the most significant element in the essence of Jean Genet, I have not hesitated to take my citations from whichever available edition most clearly illustrates the process. Other writers have revised quite as copiously, especially in France, where the practice is hallowed by long usage and a fascination with heavily annotated critical editions; but other writers have usually been concerned with giving better shape, more persuasion to their prose. Genet

11

revises in a constant effort to get things right according to the lights of his latest revelation. Since I am concerned with that constant effort, I have assumed that the best analysis of Genet will be that which considers his work as only one manifestation of a larger work—the sum of all the stages through which any particular book has passed. The method may appear haphazard; I hope the perspective it tries to achieve will justify it.

CLAIRE: You're offering me the desolate exile of your imagination? You're taking your vengeance, aren't you?
—*les Bonnes*

The Birth of an Imagination

An earlier age of Western civilization might have learned to live comfortably with Jean Genet by putting him in his place, as it did the Marquis de Sade. It would have done this with the firm intention of protecting the realm of reality from capricious assaults whose ultimate result could only be a reduction of intelligent communication among men. If no age in Western history has lived easily with the imagination's powers to present and persuade, most ages have found some way of grappling with the problem and de-

13

fining standards. The usual result, in the cases of men like Pico della Mirandola, Francis Bacon, and even Giovanni Batista Vico, was the elaboration of a tense relationship which recognized the imagination's fertility and novelty but which simultaneously sought to put bridles on its use. So long as some vestige of rationality could be kept as the essential base for total interpretations of human experience, the imagination could range in carefully selected directions. But there were limits beyond which it should not go, effects it should not seek to create, worlds of insight and apprehension it should leave unexplored. And, usually, there was a strong belief that any effort to make the imagination the only means of attaining knowledge and insight could be nothing other than a deification of folly.

The problem of an earlier age, when confronted with Jean Genet, would not, then, be Genet himself. He could somehow be inserted into a category and, when safely labeled, could presumably be isolated as a value who was not without his threats if ever he should be unleashed in a world deprived of critical standards. As long as Genet might be described as the victim of an uncontrollable demon, he would be able to continue his activities and the age would be able to go on living with its self-assurance. What would surprise an earlier age is the existence of large numbers of people, intelligent and otherwise, who would make of Jean Genet a *philosophe malgré lui,* the jovial bearer of frightfully bad news about what man really is, what man really wants, and how man is in no sense going where he pretends he wishes to go. When messages like Genet's begin to get through and win adherents, the old standards are no longer applicable, the cautions of our forebears go unheeded. There is more than a process of evanescence here, more than the mindless squandering of a solid heritage under the pressure of younger, tougher, and more spendthrift forces. In considering the impact of Jean Genet on the public of our times, we are necessarily studying a radical shift in Western sensibility as it is expressed both in the structure of literary works and in their intentions.

Men like Pico and Bacon or, later, Voltaire and Diderot, could register their hesitations about the free play of imagination and expect to be understood. Though they were not reluctant to be considered iconoclasts, their shattering of idols knew some restraint. Even as they sought what amounts to an essential redefinition of human experience, they attempted to maintain a certain indispensable sanity by insisting on the prevalence of rational processes over visionary insights. The heart of their opposition was not far removed from a desire to maintain the validity of already existing categories, to clear away certain debris accumulated over the years in order to re-establish proper perspectives. They had clear intentions of maintaining a definition of man as a dignified, potentially lofty creature whose energies could shape the world to his most beneficial expectations. Though the universe they discovered was not the universe of medieval man, it offered none the less a world in which man could feel at home and, given the proper disposition of his forces, manage to be powerful.

Jean Genet, living in an age whose radical realism would have shocked the mind of virtually any earlier age, finds no boundaries to rebellion. He has no basic categories, no commitment to the preservation of any structure of values, no interest in breaking off his meditations and explorations at the point where they seem to violate the limits of decency. There is no decency in Genet's world because its activities serve only to point up the futility of using such words. That Genet derives a vast and even appalling cheer from this might not represent a problem, if we could be convinced that his voluntarism in establishing his vision were more arbitrary than that of other men in Western intellectual history. Yet, while we may find his terms at loggerheads with Bacon's and Diderot's, we cannot altogether avoid the impression that his procedures are frequently similar, being rooted in a tensile desire to make things be the way he wants them to be. Jean Genet may set out cautiously, flinging an unseemly gauntlet before a society he regards as the Enemy; but he manages in the process to find courage more than ample to sustain his original conviction. He also discovers much about man's independence, more about his capacity to define what he is, and still more about the powers the imagination can confer. Imagination helps man to accept definitions which, in purely discursive analysis, would have been rejected either out of hand or else out of horror by earlier theorists of the imagination. In doing this Genet leaves us with problems. How do we decide where the limits of human inquiry should be set? How can we decide that reason is a better arbiter than the imagination, when reason's operations frequently have goals as arbitrary as those presented by the most fanciful visions? How can we know why man acts as he does if, in our formulations, we ignore important aspects of his behavior?

Why Genet raises these questions is not immediately clear, despite the efforts of many critics to read some sort of pattern into his motivation and its literary consequences. The most ambitious of these studies is Jean-Paul Sartre's *Saint-Genet, comédien et martyr* (Paris, 1952) which, curiously enough, serves as the first volume of Genet's complete works. Genet's intention is not clear because there is unmistakably present in his work a pattern in which the self-assurance derived from power grows continually stronger, allowing ever more audacious statements, more dogmatic definitions. Where his earlier works make noticeably frequent references to the role of despair in moving him to write (*Pompes funèbres,* p. 35) his later works—the essays and plays written after he had found a public willing to listen to his voice —are given to the formulation of more absolute statements about the thrust of certain men toward immersion in evil. Their will can lead them to this; once immersed in the evil, they find means of protest against the rules of a society which deserves to be detested (*l'Enfant criminel,* p. 157). If there is no contradiction here, there is surely an issue in the implications of the first kind of statement—suggesting the desire of a mind grown articulate in its despair to present the shield of that despair to those whose bottomless resources of hope would give it poignancy—and the later kind of statement, where the men of hope are challenged to justify the honest basis of their hope. One critic, F. C. St. Aubyn, would not agree with this kind of evaluation. In his article, "A Scandalous Success" (*Hopkins Review,* Fall 1951), he writes: "[Genet] seeks no excuses, no justifications. His spirit accepts beings and things, without confusing them, in their equal nudity. And then refuses to clothe them in useless sentiments." This declaration, so obviously at odds with what I have been saying, clearly creates an issue which is resolved perhaps by considering the marked difference between the outlook we encounter in the early works and the remarkably more confident way of putting things we come across in Genet's later dramas.

Genet's growing hostility to the world of supposedly honest men is the result of the understanding he achieves during the process of writing. When it begins it is simply presentational: Genet says this is the way things were, what it was like to be an orphaned ward of the state, to grow into crime, to know and love other criminals. He finds as he writes that this is not the way things were at all. The act of looking back on them changes them, because the lucidity brought on by the act of reflection, which is the prelude to writing, tells the writer things about those past events which he may not have understood at the time (*Pompes funèbres,* p. 148). As the process goes on, the desire merely to present is supplanted by the desire to explain. Added is a growing awareness of the power of art to penetrate the veils of *faux-semblants* and tell us what the universe is really like and what man's place in that real universe is.

One expression of this kind of wavering but none the less dense power attributed to artistic expression can be found early in *Pompes funèbres,* where Genet explains his goal in this way (p. 39): "I am trying to present these individuals to you as they can be seen under the bright light of the love I bear, not to them, but also to Jean; but I am presenting them also so that they will become more especially reflections of that love." This seems clear enough, if we remember that the Jean mentioned is the hero whose death has given birth to the book, though it is not untinged with a certain arbitrary destruction of the true facts of another individual's existence. But, despite its clarity and precisely specified purpose, the observation is transvaluated at a later moment in the same book, when Genet writes (p. 114): "I am quite aware that this book is only literature, but I would have it exalt my sorrow to a point where it will grow beyond itself and cease to be—much as fireworks cease to be after their explosion. . . . My book will perhaps serve for my simplification. I want to make myself simple and that means that I want to be something like a draftsman's design." The real intention behind these apparently mutually exclusive purposes can perhaps be detected in a comment he makes, in a later work, on the sculptures of Alberto Giacometti (*l'Atelier d'Alberto Giacometti*, p. 10): "Giacometti's work has made the world even more unbearable for me, so deep is the impression this artist has given me of having banished from his glance everything that interfered with it in order to discover what would be left of man if all the false masks were removed." What is marked here is the notion that, until one finds assurance or uncovers a sure way of getting things onto paper in the most appropriate way possible, art can serve as a kind of experimental procedure whose steps and processes can and indeed must be changed so that the desired goal may be achieved.

If you start off with the observation that, as a child, you wanted nothing so much as to be a *joli garçon,* you subsequently observe that there are others in the world who have the same kind of desire and notice that this desire is only one indication of how frequently the surface appearances of actions have little to do with the real motives of such actions. From this you can conclude that it is necessary to look below the surfaces in order to see what particularly murky waters swirl there, *but* you also learn of the power of the imagination to help you become (or, more simply, to understand) what you have always wanted to be. You learn also of its power to entangle others in the message it seeks to convey or the conviction it seeks to impose.

A pertinent example of this kind of dual movement between empirical discovery and imaginative intention can be found in the presentation of *Querelle de Brest,* Genet's history of a young sailor-criminal's movement from uncertainty to assurance. A strong hint of the empirical side of the process is given when we read (p. 182): "Little by little we grew aware—in the depths of our flesh—that Querelle was growing, developing himself in our soul, taking his nourishment from us and principally from our despair that it was not we who were in him but he who was in us." Such a process, though it suggests an automatic kind of identification between creator and creature, is neither necessarily spontaneous nor natural; that it has indeed been planned is suggested two pages later: "We would like these reflections, these observations which could not be realized nor formulated by the characters in this book, to allow you to set yourselves up, not as observers, but rather as creators of these characters who, little by little, disengage themselves from *your* movements." Profit is being drawn here from an essential disposition of every sensible reader to go along with the terms of a book until he achieves a sense of where the book wants to go; but the profit being drawn is not of the kind which satisfies itself with understanding, or even with understanding's most frequent by-product, sympathy. The profit to be drawn is dependent on the assertion that something a good deal more compromising than a movement toward understanding is involved; what is involved is a growth of recognition. The object of the recognition is not some formerly unknown character who rises from the pages of a strange book, nor is it the projection of the author's emotional needs. The object of recognition is ourselves.

"If my song be beautiful, dare you say," writes Genet, "its inspiration is vile?" (*l'Enfant criminel,* p. 162). The challenge is made with a resonant sound designed to echo through the sentimental until it becomes generous guilt: a readily available commodity. The challenge, however, has a purpose, a reality and merit beyond the simple shock dealt to the man of sentiment in an effort to wrest false tears from him. It seeks instead to present him with certain facts of human experience designed to erode his commonly and automatically accepted values in order to present him with other values which differ from his only in their emphasis. The structure of individual reaction which leads to them is identical. While Genet may elect the world of the criminal, redolent as it is with the odors of blood, sperm, and sweat, as being at once a world which rejects our world and its laws (*Journal du voleur,* p. 10), he does so merely in order to resolve an ambiguity, a presence of contrary and conflicting forces within him (ibid., p. 199). This process of selection, he would claim, is part of every man's experience.

In his earlier works the opposition between his world and ours is clear; this sense of conflict, like the awareness of choice, is never denied. Genet in these books does not accuse but is satisfied with the kind of challenge contained in a statement like this: "This is what *you* may offer, but this is what *I* have chosen." He recognizes the dichotomy between good and evil, reality and desire, and he does not yet place these words in quotation marks, being content merely to suggest that the structure which leads to the choice is much the same among those who choose good and those who choose evil. Heroism is perhaps the clearest example of this, for until such time as we bring some kind of analysis to it, heroism appears to represent only a good. It is the label we place on those who, vanquishing their gravest hesitations, dispelling the reign of fear and prudence within them, perform those kinds of acts which give body to our ideals and justify their establishment as goods to be pursued. We go along accepting this kind of structure and perhaps fail to realize that the interpersonal attitudes manifested in the structure may be more important, more *informative,* than the correspondence between act and ideal. In brief, we may, in the interests of establishing and defending an

21

abstraction, fail to give the proper emphasis to the emotional situation our apprehension of a heroic action represents. What we admire in the hero is not the abstracted quality of his act so much as the confirmation his act gives to the path of action we have chosen to follow. We admire the act only because the act tells us ours is the virtuous choice and that from adherence to it will come dignity and, frankly, prestige.

The schoolboy brought from his classroom to assist at the national obsequies for a military hero, the soldier participating in a parade held to honor a man who has shown valor in combat, the young law student observing the respect with which the visiting Supreme Court Justice is received by his faculty, the politician noticing the respect given to the President—all these are moments when the spectator finds in the spectacle a justification for the norms taught him by his education and training, but he finds this because the events are stamped with the unquestionable value of success, the profit to be derived from adherence to the norms. As he becomes more sophisticated, the child educated to accept these norms can make even more complex judgments on the meaning of acts, coming to realize that there are different levels of courage. The mantle of heroism, he discovers, can be as rightfully worn by the man of intellectual and moral convictions as by the man of physical audacity.

The delinquent child, even though his training may differ considerably from that given to others, can come to know in his observation of older, more expert criminals the same kind of reaction the "good" child has when confronted with the hero society offers for his contemplation and, it is purposefully hoped, his edification. Genet's reflections at this point are concerned with something more important than a simple recognition of a hierarchy in society. Between the various levels of the hierarchy, each of which may comprise a real community, there are different apprehensions of an unwavering set of procedures sometimes identified as values. What is being implied is that within the human race there are different units, each differently organized about contradictory and sometimes opposed standards, but all adhering to a common dynamism or a common process. No single one is on the surface of things either better or worse than another. That is a question Genet does not yet raise, preoccupied as he is in these early works with establishing the remarkable structural resemblance which exists between the society in which he has reached maturity and the society which is fundamentally and institutionally opposed to that kind of maturation process. He offers very little that is evaluative in this analysis, save that which a discerning reader can uncover in following the analogy of structures. Nor does he make the kind of accusation found in a provocative film like André Cayatte's *Nous sommes tous des assassins,* where the ruling society is brought up short with some startling questions about the deforming consequences of some of the permissive standards it adopts and makes the measure of heroism in time of war. Genet's interest here is simply to show that the delinquent's mind is formed procedurally in much the same way as the good child's.

Like the child who is a prudent and docile member of good society, the delinquent can have his aspirations quickened by the presence of the power detectable in all manifestations of success, seeing success as either the result of powerful drives or a threshold opening the way to them. So a group of young workers in *Querelle de Brest* can sit without protest watching an older man torment one of their colleagues because they find in his actions something which is instructive of the true distribution of forces in the world. Exposed to this situation, but

not immediately involved with it, they can have some ink-
ling of the best way of one day expressing their reality.
A young man can also learn of the benefits of the possession of power by watching the qualified respect with
which the police handle the dangerous criminal, thereby
suggesting that there is in him something even more consequential than whatever force the police themselves possess. As the child's delinquency grows and brings the
inevitable incarceration, he becomes even more clearly
aware that the criminal world has its hierarchy much as
any other. This hierarchy seems in no way to have its
prestige lowered because it is organized either within a
prison or in a world in which the full play of freedom is
always circumscribed by the possibility of jail. Indeed,
one of the bases for placement in the hierarchy of the
criminal world, whether *in vinculis* or not, is whether
one has served time in a children's prison. Mettray, the
children's prison Genet was kept in at various times during his youth, becomes a very definite part of whatever
prestige can be attached to a convict. Simply being in
the Centrale (an adult prison) is not nearly as prestigious
as being in the Centrale as an old boy of Mettray. It is
something like the difference between being Groton *and*
Harvard and being *just* Harvard. The other bases for the
hierarchy are somewhat less real and are well summarized by St. Aubyn (p. 57): "Genet in his prison cell
creates, then, inside himself, an order of chivalry of
which he is the initiator, founder and only knight. For
the heroes to be acceptable in this order it is necessary
to add beauty of face and elegance of body, a taste for
crime, the circumstances which make the criminal, the
moral vigor capable of accepting such a destiny with
its punishment and the cruelty of this punishment, the
intrinsic quality which permits a criminal to shine even
in those shadowy regions of the underworld."

Sartre would probably consider this tendency to establish the criminal world as a perfect parallel to the other, supposedly better world, as part and parcel of Genet's over-all tendency to mythologize things, e.g. assigning to criminals roles and ideas they would be startled to know they possessed. This, Sartre says, is a kind of deceit because it attributes to other criminals roles which, though they might elicit the criminal's fascination, would not evoke any real understanding of a true relationship between the role as defined by Genet and the life the individual criminal had lived. Why, then, does Genet indulge in the almost diabolically intelligent establishment of this kind of parallel? For Sartre, it is because having been named, having been placed by others in a particular slot, Genet has accepted the legitimacy of the process and is now concerned with applying it to others, with finding slots for them. Sartre writes (p. 48): "The basis of his adventure is the fact that he has been named; the result is a radical metamorphosis of his person and his language. Because of this ceremonial naming which transformed him, according to his sights, into a *sacred object,* a starting point was given to that slow progression by which one day he would be made a 'Prince of Thieves' and a poet."

Both analyses, Sartre's and St. Aubyn's, have their pertinence and an explication value; but within each analysis is a suggestion that the kind of comparison Genet wishes to make, the sort of parallel establishment he wishes to point out, is defective either because it is voluntaristic or servile, in either case unrealistic. What each analysis ignores is that Genet is mainly concerned with the resemblance between the two processes, not the results. And in looking at both processes he is firmly convinced that what he has found in his world is what the child of decent society finds in his: a dynamism which, if followed, leads one to the highest point within one's unit. He is equally convinced, however, that there is one initial defect within the delinquent which he must overcome in his movement toward acceptance of the dynamism and its rewards: the absence of any established authority which says that this is indeed the right way.

Since there is no official force to give this situation a stamp of approval, it may take the delinquent child some time to accord it the same respect the "good" child accords to the memory of George Washington or Charlemagne; yet once he passes beyond the state of merely noticing these situations—or, better, once he is aware of how much affected he is by these situations—he can begin to idealize them with their own brand of heroism; what is more important, he is able to see a certain heroic quality in his own acts. The murderer, Yeux-Verts (Green Eyes), of *Haute Surveillance* is not simply a criminal, any more than the astronauts are only men who seek some guarantee of immortality; he is also the embodiment of an ideal and the younger criminal is moved by the ideal Yeux-Verts represents to seek to become more like him. In a similar way, a writer observing the funeral services of a friend can come to know what it is that nations seek to create in bringing all the pomp they are capable of to the obsequies of eminent men (*Pompes funèbres,* p. 136). The young criminal thus comes to know what there is in common between him and those to whom he is supposedly opposed: he and they have the same reactions, though their means of achieving those reactions may be quite different.

The consequences of this observation are quite extraordinary, for once the discovery has been made it unleashes a whole series of further reactions and, with somewhat more disastrous effects, raises some very prickly questions. If what is common to all men is the way they react to situations, the important thing to discover is why some situations are "acceptable" as bases for particular reactions while others are not. The method is quickly, if not clearly, discerned: through an effort of the will, an effort not thoroughly divorced from narcissism. At this point the combat between those who seek to react to "good" and those who seek to react to "evil" is approximately the combat of equals, at least on a comparative ideological level. The forces of good have the illusion of strength, because they are numerous and have a long self-satisfied history of cheering themselves up with the contemplation of the length and range of their ideas; but doom looms large behind them, deriving much of its power from the fact that the forces of good, even though they admit the possibility of some kind of threat, could never expect it to come from the likes of Jean Genet. His attitude, whether because he has no choice or whether because he already has other ideas in mind, is tolerant. Its benevolence—so far as we can have any confidence in his memory—grows from a conviction that both attitudes are based on lies and that the possession of strength or numbers does not keep a lie from being the falsification it is. The only hold the lies have on truth results from the frequency with which they have been repeated and ultimately accepted by large groups of people. Whatever safety exists in these numbers is, then, the consequence of prolonged delusion.

Genet's discovery of this not only gives him a conviction that will be crucial to every manifestation of his later growth, but it also gives him an object whose fascination he cannot escape and whose potentiality for further dazzling variations he never ceases to exploit. He writes in *Querelle de Brest* (p. 328): "What Mario's imagination told him about Querelle was no doubt false, but it was just that falsity which allowed him to get at the truth." In *les Nègres,* he sets up a décor and basic situation that will play on this tendency of "truth" to be nothing but established falsehood and, in being that, to arrive painfully and involuntarily at the real truth. This real truth may, in the final analysis, be no more true; still it does serve to show that the former "truth" is on its own terms (or even on other terms) false. The ultimate value of this discovery lies neither in Genet's conviction nor in his fascination, but in the fact that it leads Genet to an awareness that ideas, though they be false, have consequences and that these consequences are real. This, of course, is not an idea found only in Genet, nor is it one peculiar to modern times. Plato had seen and made much of it, but Plato's interest was in establishing a universal scepticism about the reliability of the senses and a consequent need to pursue and love the forms. Aristotle had seen Plato's interest and therefore approached the problem with the sole desire of straightening out Plato rather than the problem. In both cases the situation was seen in relation to some standard outside the data and consequences of the situation itself. It is here that modern sensibilities quicken and, once quickened, grapple with the role of the false and deceitful in the composition of lived reality that comes to be not the correspondence of situations with some carelessly identified exterior truth, but rather any complex of actions having results. This is at the heart of Lawrence Durrell's *Alexandria Quartet* and is perhaps the greatest achievement of that disappointingly uneven work. On a less ambitious level, it was what Joyce had in mind when he wrote *Exiles.* In one of the preparatory notes for that play he wrote: "Robert is convinced of the non-existence, of the unreality of the spiritual facts which exist and are real for Richard; the action of the piece should however convince Robert of the existence and reality of Richard's mystical defense of his wife. *If this defense be a reality how can those facts on which it is based be then unreal?"* (Italics mine.) The sensibility of an earlier age—the Racine, say, of *Bajazet*—had uncovered such situations but had uncovered them with the sure knowledge that they were based on deliberately erroneous behavior and that, at some time, this behavior would be discovered and bring the perpetrator to grief or, in the interests of maintaining a tidier kind of reality, death. And beyond that there could not be much in the way of consequences.

Genet's reality is not that tidy and death is among the worst of housekeepers, since the dead cannot keep the reality they have been in any sort of accurate perspective. We shall see this during our discussion of *Pompes funèbres* and *les Paravents*. In these early books Genet is, probably unconsciously, laying groundwork upon which he will build according to the formulas of an architecture he has not yet defined. At this point he is merely probing, and the result of his probing is the tentative conviction that there are points of similarity between his way of life and the way of life of a society which would allow him short shrift and even narrower berth.

Such an attitude, because it suggests a curious kind of patience and absence of anger, can lead to misunderstanding. An example of the kind of misunderstanding I am alluding to can be found in the introduction, penned by an unnamed writer, to the first American edition of *Notre-Dame-des-Fleurs*. Here an effort is made to generalize this combat of equals by seeing it not merely as a reflection of different apprehensions of reality but also as a manifestation of a necessary tension within reality between two opposed but none the less complementary forces. The editor writes: "If in the organism we call society we are the white corpuscles, they [people like Genet] are the red, unalterably opposed. As it is between

29

the armies in our blood, so it is between the battlers in our community life. We must keep on fighting, because when the fight ends the whole body dies. It is no mean advantage we gain to suddenly see our opponents in the open" (*Gutter in the Sky,* Philadelphia, 1955).

Perhaps it is, but the giving of advantages is not within the scope of Genet's intentions. The tolerance and the balance between the opposed forces, which the editor finds so salutary, do not last long and may never have been intended. They are triggered into imbalance and, finally, open conflict. The goal is victory, not by any mutual declaration or even recognition of total war, but by a confusion which grows within Genet himself and which he candidly recognizes. Up to this point in his development the opposition has been between two different ways of arriving at the same conclusion: his and ours. Personal experience, however, brings him to the heart of a more fundamental conflict, which exists within each individual and seems to be the root of all other determinations. The original view of human motivations as nothing more than a way to get at a certain goal changes to be replaced by the conviction, supposedly based on experience, that what motivates all men is a basic combination of sexual instinct and power. All conflicting determinations of "good" and "evil" are nothing more than different qualities of topsoil placed over the same root truth: all human actions are similarly motivated, differently expressed; authenticity resides in determining which kind of topsoil allows the most honest vegetation to grow from the root motivation.

However neat the statement may seem, it was arrived at by a most uneven process with curious moments of bleak truth. In *Journal du voleur* (p. 34), Genet is open enough to admit that his desire to have this kind of comparison may be nothing more than a product of shame or, in the aftermath of shame, a desire to destroy all fundamental oppositions. Still, if the point of departure in his literary career was shame or even despair over the country being quit, the roughness of the sea and the rigors of the journey make the port of haven something quite different from a place of asylum or consolation; rather it is the vantage point from which a new attack is launched. The reader finds, having been touched by the evidence of despair to the point of feeling some personal qualms over his possible role in the circumstances that brought about the despair, that he has allowed himself to be brought into the core of a meditation whose ultimate purpose is to destroy him and his values. There is not conscious deception here but simply a fundamental change in point of view. The difficulty in accepting the change is that there is no guarantee that after it has occurred we are being presented with an accurate view of what happened, nor indeed is there any assurance that this later point of view will prevail. The perspective from the point of haven which is Genet's books is quite different from the perspective seen from the point of departure which was his life. Briefly, we have really no assurance that what we are being told in his later and most powerful works has anything at all to do with what happened and thus, if we are reasonable, we must stop to wonder how much truth we can ascribe to the conclusions drawn in those later works.

All this might be quite acceptable if we were carrying on a civilized conversation or merely seeking, in our reading of Genet, to find out something about the various ways in which human beings behave. But we are working with a clearly imaginative structure erected by a mind increasingly aware of its capacity not only to tell us something about itself, but also to tell us in a way designed to show us our moral impotence. It is not enough, then, merely to see Jean Genet as another in the long line descended from Narcissus—those who have fallen into the pools of their own self-imagined beauty. More often than not in Genet's works it is the reader who is being pushed to his watery death. Nor is it enough to say from the lofty heights of our discursive detachment that Genet is just another interesting soul struggling through to his kind of moral understanding—at least not unless we are willing to admit that his understanding will be the end of ours.

Since we cannot wantonly accept this kind of statement, we might ask ourselves why we are listening to his voice at all, especially since the consequences of un-impeded audition seem to be so grave. To say that the voice is strident, energetic, and increasingly present is too easy an answer, since it ignores both the impact of that voice and the serious attention paid to it by variously valuable minds. Rather we might listen to this voice in a manner similar to the way the narrator of *le Diable au corps* watched the mad maid ranting on the roof of her employers' house: as a symbol of a serious dislocation in the times, a precise representation of the out-of-jointedness by which we are led to an insight and under-standing that would otherwise surely be denied us. But in remembering the mad maid we might also remember that she comes to us both as a moving and meaningful figure because of the power of Radiguet's art. More than anything else it is the art of Genet that deserves atten-tion and, in looking more closely at his art, we may learn something both about the workings of his imagination and the power of art to make presentable if not per-suasive the most extraordinary human situations and inspirations.

The Definition of a Mission

Unlike James Joyce's Stephen Dedalus, Jean Genet does not set off on any perilous journey into art with the chivalric intention of finding the salvation of his race therein. If he had any literary cousin it would be Proust, though the enunciation of such a statement perhaps exhausts (albeit momentarily) all the truth it contains. What gives the comparison a reasonable basis is the similarity between the benefits Genet derives from his memories and those Proust discovered in his. The older writer had found in the spon-

33

taneous mechanism of the involuntary memory an ano-
dyne against the dissatisfactions of the particular moment
in which the mechanism was sprung and the longer and
more destructive dissatisfactions of a life which frequently seemed without sharp points. With Genet there is, at
least in the register to which we are exposed in *Pompes
funèbres,* a similar mixing-in of disparate emotions. The
journey back into the past, triggered by an experience
which gives the past vividness, is a journey back into a
moment of immediate and continued sadness; yet the re-
experience of the sadness is in itself a pleasant enough
event, as Genet explains when he writes (*Pompes funèbres,* p. 106): "To have lavishly produced these flowers
[his word-pictures of the past] calms me a bit from my
troubles. Though the lad has been dead for some time
now, the notes from which I am drawing the inspiration
for this book—which I dedicate to his glory—bring back
the sadness of those first days; still the memory of the
flowers is a dulcet one." What distinguishes Genet from
Joyce and Proust is that he shares neither the Irishman's
conviction that art can revivify the race nor the Frenchman's belief that in art the tides of dissolution can be
stemmed and immortality secured. Genet is more like
the child who discovers fire not only destroys but serves
a useful, even an appreciatory purpose. Though his initial intention seems to have been clearly autobiographical, in that works like *Notre-Dame-des-Fleurs* and *Miracle de la rose* recall precise events in his life, his awareness of the consequences produced by the act of writing
springs up immediately. The earlier remarks are quite
simply limited to noticing how, in writing of those whose
lives appear disreputable at best and criminal at worst,
one is capable of investing them not with a beauty they
did not objectively have but with a value they created
within the mind of him who writes.

Having made note of this, the writer is then able to invest his personages with a lyricism they did not possess in life. He does this with the clear intention of imposing them on his readers mantled with a value, even a beauty, they did not possess and the absence of which Genet is willing to admit (*Querelle de Brest,* p. 186). At first the justification of this kind of procedure stays this side of deliberate deceit and is based rather movingly on the writer's need to assert the love he sought from these people he is writing so confidentially about. The attitude is one that appeals to our sympathy but, as I have suggested, to a sympathy which depends for its expression on our generosity. We can be touched or not touched at will by this spectacle of a *voyou* seeking in the written word a love he never clearly found in the lived reality, thrusting toward us with stark expressions like: "But I needed to love" (*Pompes funèbres,* p. 30). But once the procedure of writing about subjects, with details usually confined to the Latin passages of Krafft-Ebing or the walls of *vespasiennes,* makes its shock value felt even on the writer, he himself comes into contact with an insolence that, in its dazzling effects, is something like a Roman candle. Though the initial desire to write may have been simple, its effects are multiple and move in several directions at the same time, introducing a kind of complexity into a previously simple act that transforms the act from chronicling into art or, more precisely, demonstrates added advantages that might be derived from an artful approach to the subject matter.

The insolence, originally unintended, involved in setting down a scabrous series of events ceases to be just another tired manifestation of the nasty little boy scribbling obscenities with a piece of chalk on the sidewalk of an upper-class district and becomes rather an expression of the writer's confidence in the reality (should one

35

read: the value?) of his life. To the extent that it is well done, the letters well formed, and the style more than passingly good, it begins to have a certain beauty, and the little boy who sat down to thumb his nose at you, when you stop to look at what he has done, does not run away but instead asks you to admire how well he does this kind of thing. A jaded passerby might shake his head sadly to note how early and how deeply corruption can make the young its own. And the passerby might be doing just the right thing if his headshaking had any effect on the little boy, if it called him back to whatever remnants of good sense he might still possess and thus urged him back to paths of little frequented virtue.

The invitation would have little appeal for Genet, however; or rather its enticements could not compete with the appeal Genet has found in the uses of insolence which, he suggests in *Querelle de Brest* (p. 307), "is our confidence in our wit, in our language." He goes on, in one of those moments of spontaneous honesty that dot his works, to suggest that it may also be a (necessary) veil over the pockets of cowardice within us, by which, I gather, he means to suggest that it is a way of simplifying the difficulties of thought, much as he once wanted to simplify himself. St. Aubyn (pp. 50–51), unlike our fanciful passerby, feels the gamble pays off: "By the gravity of the means, by the magnificence of the materials which a poet places in his works in order to draw himself nearer to man, Genet is able to measure just how far the poet is from men. The depths of his abjection forced him to this task. His abjection was his despair. . . . Genet believed for a long time that a poetic work proposed conflicts. Now he realizes that it annuls them." While such nullification is perhaps quite possible, one is led to wonder whether such a simple act of nullification really resolves anything. Sidney Kingsley's *Dead End,* also concerned with the conflict between differently privileged levels of society, sought to annul real problems, in the audience's mind at least, by appeals to sentiment. But such sentiment, like Genet's supposed acts of nullification, is rather easily and arbitrarily achieved and offers no guarantee that basic problematic situations have been properly handled.

But our insolent little boy, who has been growing up and out all this time, is little worried about the problems created by insolence and instead has become transfixed with the beauty he can bring to its expression. Transfixed, he can arrive at kinetic conclusions and write: "The beauty of a moral act depends on the beauty with which it is expressed. Simply to say it is beautiful means that it will be beautiful" (*Journal du voleur,* p. 23). The way to prove it is by vesting it with the beauties of literature. Since acts do not speak for themselves but depend for their value on what we have to say about them, he will speak nobly about the ignoble; if he speaks frequently and well enough he may manage to convince someone— someone as impressive as Jean-Paul Sartre.

At one point at least Genet himself is not really happy with the simplicity with which he states all this. He recognizes that there is, if nothing else, a temporal reality to acts and attitudes and that this temporal reality is only partially caught and fixed in the words used to describe it at a later date. To the extent that this is so, language is a deceiver; what it evokes must consequently be at least partially deceptive. But to the extent that language becomes a way of life (in other words, to the extent one becomes a writer), a sort of convergence of reality and words is achieved and any sort of dialectical passage from action into verbal evaluation of that action is rejected in the name of something else: a willed predisposition to view reality only as that reality can ulti-

37

mately find expression in the magical exercise of making literature. That his past life may have had quality X ceases to have importance if he can reflect that past life as quality Y. This is one value. It gives birth to another, which is the desire to proceed henceforth to see the world only insofar as it can find expression in what one will choose to say about it. Genet calls this magic and, as he describes it, it has all the characteristics of a sympathetic necromancy designed to set up a very special pact between him and nature. Were it only the act of a magician, or even a necromancer, the staid reader might be willing to let this kind of magic have its day; the results, however, are a good deal more extreme than Genet himself seems to realize, partly because he does not fully respect the terms of the pact, and partly because, by this time, his imagination has come into such full play and become so versatile an instrument that it has replaced any remnant of discourse in his life and found confirmations for its practices that give it a mark of quite dogmatic authority.

Genet may consider all this a deliverance from the insufficient equipment of his life into the prodigious equipment of art. Others have not. For Georges Bataille it is something more than a quiet disaster. He writes: "No interdiction gives him the sentiment any longer of a prohibition and, in the insensibility of his nerves which overcomes him, he manages to founder. There would be nothing left to him if he could no longer lie, if he could not bring, to the attention of others, values whose depths show them to be false. Horrified that he is no longer the dupe, he slips into this last resort: he attempts to dupe others in order, if he can manage it, to dupe himself" (*la Littérature et le mal,* Paris, 1957, p. 203). Bataille's evaluation is not quite honest, perhaps because it is an evaluation given us at a moment when we would profit better from description; it suggests disapproval and dupery without first establishing firmly that deception is really what is intended, or, more pertinently, that deception is the sole purpose behind this kind of thinking. Sartre makes a somewhat better statement when he writes (*Saint-Genet,* p. 278) that Genet sees in poetry an "antidote to his original condemnation which makes its appearance once a word permits the suspicion that language has a secret order and that there is between language and the hidden aspect of things a secret marriage."

Sartre gives us all the terms we need; he fails, I suspect, to interpret the terms as well as he might in order to make it unfailingly clear that Genet's increasing conviction that language holds the key to reality is a conviction so deeply felt as to subdue and eventually replace any lingering hesitations he may have about what others consider his cavalier treatment of facts. The facts of the past, as they might be reported in the idiom and ideology of journalism, are not real facts; the emotions that may have elicited these facts at a later moment are not the best expressions of reality either, because they do not represent the total picture. Reality cannot be limited to one isolated temporal moment; reality, especially if one agrees that it is best seen through an individual intelligence and sensibility, has depth and breadth and height which stretch over many moments. There is no terminal point save that supplied by the death of the individual who is thinking about the total reality of his existence.

This kind of conviction, which stresses the multifaceted nature of reality—its extensive qualities, its essential expression and organization within individuals—is something which lacks organizational assurance until Genet's later plays; it does not find adequate physical and visual expression until *les Paravents.* As a result it cannot, as a point of view, be found in any one of Genet's early works, but it does emerge as the most significant and readily available pattern of growth within the totality of those works. If no one novel gives the impression of reality as a vast, far-reaching, immensely convoluted and dense phenomenon, the body of the works gives, cumulatively, no other.

Some impression of this can be had from a brief look at *Notre-Dame-des-Fleurs,* which Genet wrote in 1942 while in Fresnes prison. It is a good as well as conventional starting place, because as a first book it gives evidence that supports our more comfortable commonplace beliefs about first books: its prose is of uneven value, characterizations are rough and sometimes not very convincing, the point of view, if not indeterminate, needs more courage and conviction. As Genet's initial work it is of value because it shows him already straining at the bit of conventional forms, irritated with them but not quite sure where he wants to go if he manages to break the bit. The plot can be easily summarized. Briefly, it is about the adventures and misadventures of Louis Culafroy, who escapes from provincial into pederastic living by becoming a male prostitute in Paris where, in the interests of some sort of consistency, he changes his name and identity to Divine. As we follow these events we are exposed simultaneously to the Parisian underworld, the manners and habits of the universe of pimps and pederasts, and the emotional disintegration of Divine as he loses lovers and keepers to the rising attraction of Adrien Baillou, the Notre-Dame of the title. This younger buck's moment in the sun is a brief one, for he is apprehended by the police, confesses to a murder for which he has not been arrested, and is convicted. This, along with Divine's death from tuberculosis and the belated recognition on the part of her/his pimp that he loves her/him, brings the book to a close.

The verbal confusion of the previous sentence is a measure of one of the book's most immediate powers, for Genet succeeds splendidly in convincing his readers that Divine's masculine identity has been totally absorbed by his desire to be a female. We have the sense, as we move back into Divine's past as Louis Culafroy, that that past is forever gone, that a new being has been created whose masculinity is only the clay, now totally transformed, from which he was originally shaped. That all this may be unsavory is a judgment which gradually loses meaning, the loss being measured by the degree of our credence in Divine as the being she wants to be. And because this portrait is so successful, the verisimilitude of the milieu which serves as a backdrop for the portrait is unquestionable. Why Genet convinces us is something which cannot casually be attributed to his dexterity and quality as an artist, for the method of presentation aims at something quite different, something which tells us the story line is not of utmost importance. Whatever importance and whatever sense we wish to find in the book must come from our apprehension of Genet's method.

Though the story line may be direct and straight, its presentation is not. The book does not open with Culafroy's arrival in Paris; it opens with Jean Genet in his prison cell, evoking the images and memories of those he had known and loved in the Parisian underworld in order that he may find consolation for his present dour situation in the sexual pleasures such fantasies will produce. The images he recalls are not those of the underworld he will construct during the rest of the book; rather they are as diversified as those which rambled

41

without apparent order through Molly Bloom's mind in the last pages of Joyce's *Ulysses*. But, unlike Molly's, which are of the past as something irrevocably gone, Genet's images will give birth to a world which, during the book, will seem to achieve an historical dimension.

We have an example of this rather early in the book. Genet has already evoked Divine from his past and has placed her at a table in a Parisian bistro where she awaits her first customer. Then he writes of a strikingly handsome young man called Roger whom he had once met and whose good looks made him so desirable that he became one of the most important furnishings of Genet's imagination, growing into full albeit invented life there, becoming Genet's lover and even producing, mysteriously, a son. His life in Genet's imagination has become more impressive than any life they might have really lived together. But Genet wants to continue this imaginary life he has given to Roger, and so he writes, not at all indifferent to the sexual cast of his vocabulary: "If I insist, he is going to sprout up, become erect and introduce himself so deeply into me as to leave me stigmatized. I can no longer hold off. I shall make him a character in my book, and I will know how to martyr him in my own good fashion: he will become Mignon-les-Petits-Pieds" (p. 26).

Since all the characters are introduced in more or less this way, either as figments of Genet's imagination or else as transformed by that imagination, a great consuming shadow of doubt is cast over the historicity of the work; but once the historicity has been consumed, there is more left than scorched earth. What is left is the use to which the semblance of history can be put in order to illustrate not the terms of the history itself but, more important, the reasons why that history is being created. There may at one time have been some reality of person and place to Divine and the Parisian milieu in which she moves; but that reality, if it is remembered at all, is remembered in order that it can be a point of consolation. It is with the point of consolation that we are living during the duration of the book. As that point moves and expands into many other points, the explosion it creates is not made up from the same munitions which went into the original story. Genet does not want to fool his reader about this; he tries, at times confusedly, to keep things straight, to let us know exactly what he is doing and how he is using these people for his own ends. The text is scattered with caveats of one kind or another directed at the reader, the most interesting of which is perhaps the following (p. 115): "Don't shout out that all this is improbable. What is going to follow is counterfeited and no one need accept it as negotiable currency. Truth isn't my domain. But 'you have to lie in order to tell the truth.' And you have sometimes to go even further than that. What truth do I want to talk about anyway? If it's really true that I am a prisoner who's playing (who's putting on for himself) scenes from the inner life, you can't expect much else but games."

We might be content not to expect more, had we not the impression that the games have purposeful players and consequential rules. The players are projections at once of Genet's imagination and of Genet himself. They are not meant to stand before us vested with the data of their lives so much as they are, each separately and all together, meant to bring us into contact with some element of Genet's existence. He writes (p. 106): "How shall we go about explaining that Divine is now thirty or more. And she must have the same age as I so that I can finally calm my need to talk about myself, simply, as I need to complain and to try to get the reader to like me." The characters, then, become representatives of various attitudes which express Genet's past involvement with diverse sentiments and situations. Invested with the dimension of objectivity they achieve when assigned to third parties, they may touch the reader as no straight autobiographical confession would. But the games, as he has just told us, are being played for himself, too, as a kind of compromised way of getting back to the events of his own life and reshaping them from what may have been unpleasant into something that, even if it doesn't change the status of the persons he may have offended, will give Genet a more comfortable way to interpret and then live with the evil he has done. A sequence in the book becomes, under these conditions, a transvaluation of a past situation, an exposure of it under a newer and kinder light, which may lead Genet to believe he has won the pardon of those he has offended.

Notre-Dame-des-Fleurs is clearly an experiment, carefully plotted and knowingly carried on in order to arrive at foreseen results: the presentation and exoneration of Jean Genet. It is, if you will, a cry designed to draw attention to *his* humanity by helping others to see in the more general presentation he arranges how it is that the have-nots go about finding outlets for their emotions, how it is they suffer, and how the tears they shed are real and no less bitter for being the result of the enjoyment of forbidden fruits. It is a deliberate experiment, for at this time Genet is convinced that poetry is the result of voluntarism; it is not subjugation to powerful tides of emotion, but is more obviously a planned attempt to use the beauties of language to put across a point.

Merely carrying out the experiment produces unanticipated results; setting down those emotional states to which he wishes to draw attention makes Genet aware of a power he has to transcribe them so that they are not without their emotive force. Evoking the personages he uses as test balloons for his own exploits uncovers what is perhaps a more essential and even a better reality than the one they had known—a reality that, because it takes into account what they have done and the impact of this on Genet's mind, is fuller, more weighted with total significance. The old guideposts are simply not as good as those found along the way, even though they had seemed at the beginning of the novel to indicate a clear way and to suggest a method which would make that way attractive for the reader without making him feel that the path was actually a new one. Mignon, Divine, Notre-Dame, and, most important, Jean Genet do not emerge from this book as they went into it because, in the act of helping them to emerge, more revealing soundings have been made in the depths of their reality. And the author has made a discovery of grave importance for his future work, a discovery which is tucked away in one of his comments on Divine's psyche (p. 123): "[Divine] did not yet know that every event in our life has importance only because of the resonance which it strikes in us, only because of the degree with which it pushes us closer to asceticism." *Notre-Dame-des-Fleurs* has given one of those pushes to Genet; intended to do one thing—present a "touching" portrait of Jean Genet, isolated in his prison cell, thinking back to those he had loved and the meaning of that love—it has done something else entirely. It has brought about a radical change in Jean Genet's way of looking at things and, especially, at himself; it has suggested a technique based on an increasing conviction that the core of reality is an infolding of many things, all of which must be considered together if that reality is to be known truly.

The kind of multi-leveled presentation chosen for *Notre-Dame-des-Fleurs,* though it may very well amount to a valid method of getting across a fundamental orientation in Genet's way of thinking, does not escape from the stigma of being arbitrary. It conveys his anguish, his wishes, his many tendernesses and brutalities, his basic though not necessarily overweening egotism. What it does not convey is an unmistakable air of being a fair and convincing portrait of reality, or even an authoritative statement of the accuracy of Genet's ideas on reality. He needs a better organized basic experience, an experience which will of itself offer the many levels he seems able to achieve here only through an expenditure of imaginative powers that is not altogether removed from the realm of hallucination. Though they have power and force, and though they explain much about him and open new paths for his understanding to explore, the images he calls forth in his prison cell never quite cease to be images.

Miracle de la rose, his second novel, offers him a better situation physically, artistically, and ideologically. Physically it is better because the locale of the action offers the sort of community he needs. The setting is the Centrale, whose diversified reality is only too clear; here we have a prison, which is a kind of unity, but here we have, too, the cells which are the essential composition of that prison. In each cell there is one or more intelligences, each of which possesses a separate existence; since the inmates of one cell may have friends in other cells, and since these friendships may have begun in another prison where the same sort of diversification existed, the possibility of multiplying levels of reality both in time and space is almost limitless. This is a real situation and not the kind of manufactured dream world of *Notre-Dame-des-Fleurs.* Genet in his cell is not the lonely young man fabricating images to keep his solitude from devouring him. He is a member of a community, involved in the life of that community, concerned with the fate of other members of that community. His membership, involvement, and concern, however, do not spring from any immediate vitality present in the community; they spring rather from the convergence of an experience from his past with an event of the present. A young criminal he had admired from afar in another prison is in the death house of this prison, awaiting execution. With this as the basic situation, the novel moves back and forth in time, between the other prison and this one, pregnant with the sounds and expectations of the forthcoming execution, to set up the bases that make Jean Genet especially sensitive to these present sounds and expectations.

Artistically, *Miracle de la rose* represents an advance because, in order to convey this situation where past and present meet in the fact of the approaching execution, it must move easily back and forth on several levels of time: the time in this prison, which has its days and hours, each of which is experienced in a different way by each of the inmates; but it has the time of the other prison, the reform school in which some of the present inmates had served time as youngsters, and that other time has its levels, too. As a result, the novel moves back and forth in two different categories of present and past: this immediate present and its most proximate past; the present time of the other earlier prison and its past. What has happened in the past is not handled with the pure technique of the flashback designed to explain things, to fill in gaps in understanding. What has happened in the past has an immediate relevance; it comes to life, as it were, within the terms of the present situation, giving meaning and direction to this situation and inspiration to those who participate in it. From his listening post in the Centrale, Genet is able to bring the total reality of his

47

existence as a criminal to life; vivified, it stretches before him, illumined by a newer and truer understanding and flourishing a great and imposing value. His life ceases to be that of a pariah, something to be recorded with a firm sense of how much it differs from accepted standards; instead his life achieves a fullness denied to others, a power others would not accept, and, with his awareness of that fullness and power, Jean Genet becomes better equipped as a stenographer of human experience. He has looked into reality and, claiming a desire to simplify himself and things, has found the courage and the skill to face its complexity and its multiplicity without flinching.

The courage and skill, conveyed by the art, find their energy in the ideology which has been growing within Genet as he looks over the sweep of his experience of men and events. While *Miracle de la rose* makes no strident complaints against society, it makes no abject apologies either. It becomes, then, a crucial turning point in the sense that the notion of alienation from society disappears to be replaced by a soft-spoken confidence which is seen in the direct presentation given to the circumstances of the book. It is brought to our eyes as human experience, lived by human beings; what we might consider essential differences—these events are criminal and these human beings despicable—Genet considers only a difference in emphasis and expression. Here the tolerance I have spoken of is at its apex; we have our world and he has his and *Miracle de la rose* is a presentation of that world designed, it is true, to convey some sense of Genet's nostalgia and emotional disappointment, but designed equally to give that world an import it has never before known. With *Miracle de la rose* personal hesitations over value are dispelled and the way is opened for a departure from autobiography into a somewhat less personal kind of art. In our discussion of *Pompes funèbres* and *Querelle de Brest* we shall see what the most far-reaching consequences of this breakthrough are.

Genet's *Journal du voleur,* though it postdates both *Pompes funèbres* and *Querelle de Brest,* represents a kind of mid-point in this movement toward a liberating versatility. Its autobiographical reflections amount to a stop to catch aesthetic breath before Genet undertakes the more audacious works wherein will be incarnated, not the processes of memory transformed and transfixed, but an all-out attack on us. Since the book records that moment (not a moment in time so much as a moment in thought) when Genet was beginning to come to grips with his talent, it is perhaps useful to begin our consideration of it now since it will help explain the changes detectable between *Notre-Dame-des-Fleurs* and *Miracle de la rose* and prepare the way for a better understanding of what happens with the publication of *Pompes funèbres* and *Querelle de Brest.*

In the opening sentences of the book we are given some significant indications of how much Genet's mind is increasingly dominated by his imagination and of how the latter is at once a traditional and quite revolutionary imagination. This can be seen in sharper perspective if it is realized that Genet's imagination is always active, as is the imagination of every man who seeks to make connections that do not establish themselves automatically. What begins to happen to Genet is that he discovers specific uses of the imagination and undertakes to employ them in order to arrive at a clearly defined particular purpose. He speaks in the opening pages of the *Journal du voleur* of the colored stripes characteristic of

49

the convict's uniform, then moves on immediately to tell us that there is thus (*donc*) a very intimate connection between flowers and convicts. There is, of course, nothing of the sort unless we wish to attribute to convicts a kind of sick humor they do not possess—the humor that would allow those for whom this particular shoe fits to think of certain vulgar identifications (e.g. pansy; the joke doesn't work so well in French) as nothing but poetic attributions designed to define their real value of attributed ontology. Yet the absence of such empirical data in no way stymies Genet. He proclaims—and this is the revolutionary aspect of his imagination—the existence of such "facts" and then assimilates them as quite indispensable parts of his artistic equipment and the statements it chisels out. What there is of the traditional in his imaginative operations is limited to the simple observation that the convict's uniform is colored. The usual bridge of metaphor or simile by which the movement from the really real into the poetically real is customarily established is simply, yet quite astoundingly ignored.

By the time one gets around to reading *Journal du voleur,* the reason for this is quite clear. As the goldsmith might plate metal of inferior quality, so Genet—this particular metaphor is his—will lacquer the shame of his life into a shining object through the use of variously alloyed language (*Journal du voleur,* p. 95). To the extent that his life is nothing but an accumulation of unrelated anecdotes, the alloy content will be heavy; but, by a somewhat more valuable token, to the extent that his presentation of these anecdotes manages to invest them with a unity derived from the beauty of the presentation, language becomes pure gold, the disguise becomes so finished that one would never suspect there is the inferior metal under it. If one is good enough not to scratch away at what the goldsmith has done—and why should one, as it only destroys the beauty—the past disappears, the shame is dismissed, only the chant by which the "once vile objects, beings and sentiments" (ibid., p. 115) have been rehabilitated abides. And it abides cloaked in a loveliness denied to us, principally, I gather, because we have no bard quite so devoted to our cause as Genet is to his.

How Genet manages to become a goldsmith rather than a simple historian or biographer is a somewhat more interesting process and tells us considerably more about his increasing awareness of the operations of his imagination as opposed to the way he has seen the world; some indication of the nature of this transformation can be apprehended in our little-boy-in-the-street image of several pages back. If the original recognition of the existence of beauty among those to whom society denies the applicability of such words sprang from a discovery of the care which a male prostitute brings to his love gestures, finding in them a poem wrought from the enduring symbol which is the beloved's body (*Notre-Dame-des-Fleurs,* p. 156), the desire to record such beauty is born from something slightly less intimately connected with voyeurism. Rather it stems from an inchoate recognition of the *vita brevis, ars longa* sentiment: in the evanescence of events there is a melancholy that coils through the mind, demanding that something be done to stem the process of dissolution. But initially, as Genet attempts to recall the lineaments of a boy he has loved, his cry is uttered in the tones of pain and disillusion brought on by a conviction that the imagination is no better equipped than any other instrument to preserve the reality, since all it can give us is an image which, with the accumulation of time, becomes increasingly blurred.

We get a moving description of just this process in

Miracle de la rose (p. 193) when Genet, trying to recall with precision the traits of that boy he has loved, writes: "Certain acts dazzle us, brightening up certain unclear reliefs, if our eye is skilled to grasp them quickly, for the beauty of the living thing cannot be grasped except in a brief flash. The effort to pursue it during its changes leads us inevitably to a moment when it ceases, unable to last out the span of an entire life. To attempt to analyze it, that is to attempt to pursue it in time with sight and imagination is to bring it back to ourselves always in a more diminished state since, beginning with that initial marvelous instant in which it was revealed to us, it becomes less and less vivid. I have lost the facial traits of that lad."

This kind of cry—like the one mentioned earlier in which Genet speaks of having loved—is bound to touch something within the reader, for it is an experience we have all had, as the voices and faces of those we love fade into the murkier waters of our memory, leaving us an augmented sadness over diminishing past experiences. And the sense of obligation which comes, in a later experience, to deepen the sense of wrong this evanescence brings, especially when coupled to the problem of maintaining reputation, is equally something which appeals to us. Genet's concern that the memory of one he has loved may be tarnished by insulting anecdotes or irreverent remarks reminds us of why we hurry to write memorials of those we have valued, hoping to preserve their honor and reputation from the Lytton Stracheys. All this, coming as it does from common wells of human preoccupation, is simple enough to understand and would be quite adequate to explain how Jean Genet is brought to the act of writing. Like Proust, he wishes to catch the past in the cage of form; like Louis Racine, he wishes to give the reputation of those he has loved a proper interpretation, stamped with the authority of his personal knowledge.

But, as I have been suggesting, the simplicity of the process is considerably removed from the complexity of the expression. To want to memorialize is one thing; to end up by memorializing something which may never have happened in the way the memorial suggests is a quite different and perhaps somewhat poisonous situation. What seems to explain it is the parallel development within Genet of a rather special view of the hardness of reality. Like Rousseau before the *pervenche,* or Proust tripping on the *pavés inégaux,* he has been in the process of discovering that real things have several faces and can induce a number of operations. The number of faces seems to depend quite clearly on the nature of the operation. In some cases the memory we have at 8:00 P.M. of something which happened at 8:00 A.M. gives a quite different color to what actually happened; so the memory of a children's prison, evoked in later circumstances, can raise questions of the relationship between what the prison was and what it has become in one's mind as the result of the operations of time and the growth of experience. Genet is aware of and concerned about this, though the degree of his concern has changed and is no longer involved with a possible dislocation dealt to the reader's sense of logic and order. It is more concerned with the impact of this sort of thing on his own capacity for maintaining the proper order, which may very well be very untidy, as we have seen in speaking of *Miracle de la rose*. In that same book he writes (p. 318): "I sometimes wonder if all this is real, so much does it seem so; and if the Centrale isn't a house of illusions." Here we have an example of the mixture of levels of apprehension in which Genet expresses himself from time to time. Of course the central prison is real and, as our earlier discussion pointed out, it is real in a way which is thicker and more diverse than reality is customarily considered to be. Genet's worry here is that he may have failed to convey that particular reality and given a bad semblance instead. The process in this instance is also something like the reputation of a university: one's memory of the class of '37 at Yale may be very strongly colored by the knowledge of how that class has fared since its graduation. If that class and others have performed well, one might conclude that Yale is a great university and, if an enthusiastic alumnus—and alumni magazines abound in examples—that there never was a class like '37.

The trickiness of reality does not, however, depend exclusively on the tricks memory plays on us. Those tricks are part and parcel of reality, and a rather large part and important parcel of the reality Jean Genet has known. Here the impact on him of the underworld in which he has lived is far-reaching. When one has lived in circles where the masculine and feminine personal pronouns are habitually interchanged (and for valid reason), where aliases become an indispensable kind of labeling, and where nicknames are efforts at more precise description of a criminal's real nature (Shifty Eyes, Fingers, etc.), the tricks are a bit more important than magician's games or anagrammatic diversions. They are at once variations on reality (the male prostitute referred to as "she"), or else efforts at perfecting what is incomplete in reality (the attribution of a more precise nomenclature to criminals). In *Notre-Dame-des-Fleurs,* where the male prostitutes gradually slipped into another sex and were designated by feminine personal pronouns, the verbal play sought to catch the ambiguities and variations within reality; but they sought to catch something else, too: that sense which lives and grows in Genet's mind of some higher, more binding justification for the playful usages. He writes in defense of these sexually ambivalent names (*Notre-Dame-des-Fleurs,* p. 158): "There is a relationship between them, an odor of incense and melting candlewax, which I sometimes have the impression of having gathered among either the artificial or the real flowers of the Virgin Mary's chapel." But the names, when they are applied to criminals, also represent an improvement on reality. One has the impression that a murderer is better named if he is called Shifty Eyes or Bluebeard, and that the pickpocket is more appropriately labeled if one refers to him as Fingers. Criminals, Genet tells us, have still another reason for liking these shifts (*Miracle de la rose,* p. 229): "They like to alter or change their names in order to make the person who bears the name unrecognizable. Louis may now be known as Loulou, but ten years ago he had been transformed into Little Louie who, in turn, became known as Tioui."

The title of Genet's only ballet, *'Adame Miroir,* is another example of this kind of process, in which verbal play seems to confirm a certain ambiguity in reality. Of the reasons for choosing the ballet's title, he writes (p. 40): "It struck me as facetious to write it down in this way, because I obtained a deformation of the word 'madame' which yielded 'adam.'" He could thus create the impression of both masculine and feminine identifications. But he could do more than this: by replacing the "m" with an apostrophe and creating the name Adam he could suggest that there was a connection between the two, a connection which could be seen in a mirror, for every male who looks at himself in the glass can find there the possible surprising sources for certain of his tendencies; or, that failing or being inappropriate, can see in the mirror what it is that has brought about his fall. Genet explains: "Adam was thus a slightly misty mirror, the stunted and deformed image of an object which has lost certain qualities."

Other examples of verbal play that have reference to sexuality can be seen in an expression like "c'est ici qu'on l'a tué," or in a title like *Pompes funèbres;* it can also be deliberately created by the use of seemingly inappropriate names like Vertu for the bosomy, voluptuous woman in *les Nègres,* or Lefranc for the dissembling prisoner in *Haute Surveillance.* What is carefully and often masterfully achieved as the result of such usages is the establishment of a kind of hesitation over the reality of these things, indeed of all things, and an immediately direct immersion in the ambiguities which are at the basis of the kind of authority Genet claims for his understanding of reality. The convergence of many realities which made the setting of *Miracle de la rose* so authoritative is not, Genet seems to say, so peculiar as a reader might think. To emphasize the diversity of all apparently simple things is to accentuate what can be seen in so many manifestations of life. With these examples drawn from the commonest coins of language, he is pointing to the same thing, not to say: isn't it amusing that such ordinary words can be turned to puns? but rather to say: these puns are no accident. It is not pure happenstance which attributes an obscene meaning to *Pompes funèbres;* nor is it chance that the name Adam is an integral part of the title madame.

Reality as a meaningful term is further complicated —and in a way quite different from that Calderón was given to mulling over—by the existence of dreams which, for their part, have been complicated and made more important by the knowledge we believe can be derived from them. If there was once any point to making distinctions between what is experienced and what is simply imagined, that point seems to have lost its thrust with the knowledge that the images of sleep are only more honest emanations from what is behind the several masks reality can wear. Life is not simply a dream, but dreams are perhaps the best indication of how we should go about depicting reality.

This is the value they serve in the canon of Genet's art. Faced with the multiple split which is reality, aware of the at least superficial contradiction between memory and experience, names and things named, values and the things to be valued, he has information which will remain in chaos until such time as he shall be able to organize it into some kind of imposing presentation. Dreams, because their language is that of symbol, give him the key how best to proceed. Since we cannot pluck from the usual norms of reality any methods which can present not that reality alone, but also what we have learned of it; and since we have no guarantee that reality may not, at the end of the day, be anything more than what we can now say either about what is happening at this moment or what has already happened, then perhaps the only way to present it is to follow the kind of presentation we receive in our dreams, where diverse objects, experiences, and persons converge into new and apprehensible images (*Miracle de la rose,* p. 322). The discovery seems to justify itself because of the symbol it contains. What Jean Genet has set out to discover is the means by which he can best transpose his insights into the bifurcations and fractures detectable in reality; what sleep represents is the bridge between the disparate events of human experience and the interpretations of those events the subconscious organizes in the images of our dreams. By seeking in literature the same kind of presentation, one may arrive at creating a kind of literature that, despite its shocks and even its horrors, will be more real than anything known up to this point.

The consequences of discovering such a device are, of course, both extraordinary and self-inspiring. The inspiration stems quite simply from having discovered a device others do not know about, a device that is going to rock the foundations of their vision of the world until the whole structure falls. Initially, the discovery merely seems to confirm Genet's right to give his "infernal meaning" to the products of our world. No longer will he read a novel on our terms; rather he will read it knowing what he knows (and here it is perhaps important to recall that the great therapeutic value of dreams is that they supposedly reveal the "ugly" things we don't want to know about), and using this equipment to spin out another interpretation which, ultimately, will force us into that world of the *au-delà* he is embroidering (ibid., pp. 241–42). Were he to remain a commentator he might serve a useful function; but, like Freud in the last years of his life, Genet is not content to remain a simple observer or even analyst. Instead he uses his device to create a new world, a new order of chivalry thought up and established by himself—and of which he is the sole member. That is his role; ours, quite as simply if not as authoritarianly pleasant, is to accept it as the most thorough interpretation of reality (*Pompes funèbres,* p. 45).

If, as I have suggested, the nature of reality demands that it be looked at syncretically rather than synthetically, and if we accept this kind of norm partially because of the information we get from Jean Genet, then we shall also be obliged to see whether the reality of Jean Genet is in itself syncretic. We are faced with a situation in which the process of development and growth is as clear as the motivation is murky. Like the dancer whose versatility has become so great that he no longer sees the world except in terms of dance steps to be derived from his experience of it (and it is interesting to note how often the dance serves as a basic image for Genet), Genet's growth as a shrewd and knowledgeable artist is not simply explained by the kinds of hows and whys isolated above. There is a certain determination in it, a forceful marshaling of his will (once it has been exposed to the polemical value of art) to use that art in order to make statements with, until *Pompes funèbres,* basically elusive intent.

It is elusive because, quite simply, Genet has not yet fought his way through to assurance in his art, nor has he, deprived of that assurance, quite the measure of insolence to bring the whole incredible enterprise off. In an early work he writes almost pathetically about his realization that his proclaimed love of prison is simply a reflection of a desire, grown from his homosexual practices, to believe that the inmates represent the highest level of attainable beauty (*Miracle de la rose,* pp. 269–70). This is beauty lusted after from afar and, on the level of events, the desire to get at it involves a certain kind of discipline: one doesn't win the love of a beautiful *mec* merely by wanting to; one must work toward it. Here again we see the extent to which the discipline by which one works toward success is a necessary precondition, whatever may be the ethical or moral evaluation placed on the desired object. Since the object is seen as beautiful (beauty and desire at more than one point being inextricably confused one with the other) something must be done to establish some sort of reconciliation between its beauty, usually condemned, and other modes of beauty which have society's approbation. The problem

59

of making the reconciliation will be complicated by the haunted sense that here is a real divergence and, to the extent that the divergence exists, the initial act of reconciliation will be little more than defiance. But the act of defiance, especially since it is accomplished through the act of writing, produces a new circumstance and new consequences. One learns two capitally important things by writing: that there is a power in art to make convincing if untrue statements and that these statements can be made beautiful, indeed must be made beautiful in order to be convincing. Where in an early work we are told of the consoling power Genet derived from his imagination, in *Journal du voleur* we have come almost, but not quite, full circle and are instead told that he can make heroes out of his people simply through the exploitation of his lyrical gifts (*Journal du voleur,* pp. 204; 285). This might simply seem like further, more strongly worded defiance, but it is a good deal more than that because, by this time, Genet has something to back up his claims: his knowledge of and theories about art and the relationship he can make between these and his life.

As he becomes aware of what he considers a parallel development of the criminal and the poet—parallel because each follows a process of penetrating through to the true reality behind the surface of things, parallel also because each is called upon to destroy the accepted meaning of the world in order to substitute another—he seems to find further verification of what he will henceforth do. This, however, is only a minimal part of the poet-criminal relationship. More important is the fact that each role is pursued in the name of a goal outside itself. The poet wishes to reorganize the world and to make his reorganization of it imposing by making his language seductive. The young *tapette* wishes to win the love of the *mec,* and it is this desire for that love which drives him to criminal acts. The medieval knight fought dragons to win the hand of his lady fair; the young criminal will enact audacious crimes in order to accomplish the same goal, though his sexual desires tend to be somewhat unilateral.

The parallel lines of the two developments veer and begin to converge with the striking realization that the most audacious, the most imposing of all acts may be the mantling of what is criminal in the cloak of what is poetic, the twisting of the world so vigorously as to create not simply a poetic reality, dependent in some measure on the recognizable *serpentins* tying it to "objective" reality, but to create an ultimate reality out of the discipline learned as a criminal and the power discovered in the uses of art. What this reality is is not at this point (we are still with the *Journal du voleur*) altogether clear; what its circumstances will be is only too clear: "I wish to fulfill myself in the rarest of destinies. . . . Oh grant that I be only all that is beauty! I will proceed quickly or slowly, I will dare all that must be dared, I will destroy all appearances, the tarpaulins will fall aside burned and I will appear there in the palm of your hand, quiet and pure like a glass statuette. And around me there will no longer be anything" (*Journal du voleur,* p. 219). The resonance no longer implies a simple effort to celebrate the past; it has moved on to Stephen Dedalus' challenge.

That challenge, in addition to being part of an effort to seek fresher points of view, deeper penetrations of reality, is related to Genet's goal of making a myth out of his life. The challenge, then, is important because, if it be true that literature is that device by which we come to accept new formulations, then the new formulation he will give to his life can only win belief through expression in literary form. This capacity of literature to give birth to a new emotion Genet calls *poetry* (*Journal du voleur,* p. 126). If elsewhere in his writings Genet has not been able to hold back one of the oldest poetic laments—that in which the poet mourns over the insufficiency of words to convey all aspects of his insights—the cry is only momentary. Genet, like Dedalus, is seeking something beyond the purely formal qualities of literature that are conveyed by its plastic and verbal beauties. He is seeking myth in the renewed sense of that weakened word—as a means of expressing imagistically that which cannot be adequately wrought discursively—and he is seeking to do this by relying on what has been the most potent conveyor of myth: its immersion in ceremony. The appeal of ceremony for Genet resides in his belief that through it "all kinds of creation are possible" (ibid., p. 178). Once such a decision has been made, he can begin to transform the past. To put it more accurately, the past must transform itself in order to contribute to the myth-making; what had seemed despicable can now be seen in this new light. The thieving, begging, and prostitution which were the occupations of his youth are no longer looked upon as the exterior manifestation of his appalling state; they are instead looked upon as the elements of an emerging discipline which has prepared him for the literary career he now embarks upon. Setting out from Ireland, Dedalus departed with a clear conviction that his past experiences had prepared him for the task he was proposing to himself; they had been the elements, flagstones along the path of his development, which had formed him into the being he was as he turned his eyes to the Continent. There is something of this in Genet; but there is more. He is not given to such reasonable and easy solutions and, rather than being happy with looking upon his disreputable past as the foundation of his new found literary instincts, he looks upon the development of the instincts as being, at last, a way of seeing what the real value in that past was. It was not, he discovers, simply a contributory value out of whose amplitude he can pluck the material for his books. Not at all. Rather the books will give him the occasion to see that earlier life more closely, to evaluate its meaning, and to generalize that meaning until it becomes the most authentic and honest in the world. Literature, it is true, liberates him; but what it liberates him from is us. In the process of being set free he finds himself drifting back inevitably to himself.

I sketched the movement—
I mean that nothing of it
could be seen from without;
but the intent of this gesture
had already made me more
masterly because I had described it from beginning to
end within me. I felt a light-
ness capable of pushing time
back.

—*Pompes funèbres*

'*Pompes funèbres*'

Intentions do not eliminate
problems, nor do proclamations, no matter how ringing,
of themselves change the face of reality or muffle haunting voices. To become that pure statuette of glass Genet
seeks to be, a number of weighty blocks must be got out
of the way and, since we long ago left the paths of
reasoned discourse, the only road still open is that of the
imagination. If the operations of the imagination can,
simply by the presentation they elaborate, bring about
certain resolutions, major personal and public problems

will be solved. Genet believes these resolutions can be brought about by those symbols which are at the heart of literary expression. Symbol, for Genet, is not simply a highly charged metaphor, but is rather a method of proposing accommodations between events and their meaning in which the event will be effaced by the power of the meaning. In this sense of symbol, the event has significance only to the extent that it is incorporated into the meaning. The result is that individual human actions are for the most part senseless until such time as they are seen as part of and therefore a reflection of a much wider principle. It is by the use of symbol that this relationship is established; quite obviously, the job of setting such relationships is an immense one. This is the vast task which is at the heart of *Pompes funèbres,* surely one of the most dazzling technical works produced in this century, all the more dazzling when one remembers that it predates the various *anti-romans* and, in the sheer audacity of its technique, makes them appear quite pale and wan. This is something of an accomplishment, when one realizes how singular its subject matter is.

The personal problem central to *Pompes funèbres* is not new; what is new is the rather crucial alteration in the methods used to present the problem. No longer is it to be visualized or represented as a dilemma needing to have its horns made one, but rather is to be presented as a creative work. It will achieve credibility and appeal by becoming a fictional reality, a persuasive force, and not merely a wooden embodiment of a certain register of exploratory ideas. The personal aspects of the problem and the anguish they unleash had already been given powerful presentation in *Miracle de la rose;* this unusual title is derived from a passage in the book where Genet, experiencing a most awful emptiness and frustration at not being able to associate himself with the murderer

65

The Imagination of Jean Genet

Harcamone (who is to be executed presently) makes enormous efforts to transform himself into a rose, a multifaceted symbol which can represent all things to all men. The effort fails, oddly, because the imagination's energies fail, but also because at the climactic moment of the enterprise, Genet moves into an erotic experience with his cellmate, Divers. The original effort is abandoned and another kind of climax is sought to replace what had originally been hoped for. In the aftermath of sexual fulfillment, guilt appears, and the convict Genet feels a terrible sense of treason at having been distracted at the moment of Harcamone's death.

It is a moving passage because in its elaboration Genet manages to involve the reader in the effort, to make him believe, for as long as the presentation lasts, that this attempt to associate himself with Harcamone's death is an important ceremony, not simply of erotic love but also of friendship. Some of the great human forces are marshaled in order to give appropriate attention to the death of a man whose importance is not only his unsurpassed excellence as a criminal but equally his association with Genet's past. In Harcamone, whom Genet had first heard about in the children's prison, there is a symbol of something which might be called the cycle of life; the child of Mettray, the children's prison, has grown into the arch criminal condemned to death row, where he seems to represent the fulfillment of all the dreams dreamed in Mettray (*Miracle de la rose,* pp. 189, 220). Because the reader can become involved in the prosodic sweep of these pages, stunned all the while no doubt, he must necessarily feel a rather startling letdown when the fugue suddenly goes flat, the ceremony is abandoned, and the mind which has made the transmigrating effort to associate itself with Harcamone's death yields to the aroused body which reacts favorably to the erotic assaults of the nearby Divers. Genet, I have pointed out already, shares some of the shock of this discovery, though his may be, unlike ours, shock born of noticing the contradiction between the lyricism of the mind's efforts and the obvious compulsive power of the body's suddenly excited desires. He tries to carry the whole thing off with bravura, to which he adds a touch of the audacity he is growing to love more consumingly, but he is not altogether convinced—not that what he has done with Divers is wrong (wrong, after all, is one of *our* words), but that it has been a distraction from the enormous effort to carry off this particular miracle.

He may write (*Miracle de la rose,* p. 357): "Divers and I were communing in the death of Harcamone," but he is not certain. A pustule of horror is there: horror over the failure of mental energies to produce the desired situation and not over the physical act born of the failure. Genet had already written, in *Notre-Dame-des-Fleurs* (p. 30), of the need to avoid any sense of horror by abandoning oneself to it fully: in total immersion is total conviction. In *Pompes funèbres* he will do precisely that; there the miracle first attempted in connection with Harcamone will be brought off with magnificient brio and a surer sense of technical mastery.

The failure to bring off the miracle in the earlier work had been annoying because the miracle had promised so much—the dissolution of time, the rediscovery of a kind of primal innocence, a glorious victory—but had instead been consumed by the needs flesh's fires create. In *Pompes funèbres* the fires are given the center of the stage and, while admittedly uncomplicating things by removing touchy dualisms, this also, and more subtly, changes the whole register of the problem. We are not here hunting after moral unions, but are rather in close pursuit of a justification of the kind of communion that

67

took place between Genet and Divers and where the death of Harcamone was supposed to have found its best ceremonial offering. If the basis of that communion is found, Genet will have discovered the principle of organization, a symbol, which was missing in *Miracle de la rose*.

Pompes funèbres begins in a quite conventional narrative manner: a young *resistant,* much admired, indeed loved by Genet, has been shot as a hostage in the last days of the liberation of Paris. Arrangements are being made for his funeral, which will be attended by Genet, the hero's mother, and the girl the hero loved and made pregnant. In the background there is the lover of the hero's mother, who, unfortunately, happens to be a member of the Waffen SS and may in some way have been connected with the apprehension and execution of the hero. The situation at this point is not terribly unlike that with Harcamone: the beloved is dead and some appropriate way must be found to give the proper weight to the rites surrounding his dispatch from the world. What happens is not the organization of any extraordinary funeral procession or dazzlingly impressive wake; what happens is the writing of this particular book, which will surely become the most striking votive offering this side of Pompeii.

It all begins when Genet goes to a cinema where he sees in a newsreel a portrayal of the street fighting between members of the maquis and the Gestapo as the struggle to liberate Paris unfolds. As he watches the frames pass on the screen, he notices the combat between a young French collaborator, a member of the Gestapo, and a maquisard; suddenly, without any specific willful triggering in his mind, Genet finds himself rooting for the SS man, who becomes in his mind, Erik Seiler, the lover of the hero's mother, and the collaborationist, who, in his mind, becomes Riton, a youngster whose defection is explained by his love for Erik. What Genet is rooting for is that these two together will kill another Frenchman, whom he visualizes as the dead hero. From this point on —and it is important to remark that there is no connection between the figures in the newsreel and the identifications Genet attributes to them—the straight narrative presentation dissolves and is replaced with a kind of cinematic parallelism. The preparations for the real ceremony continue; but as they continue there grows, within the framework their narration supplies, an enormous meditation on why it is that Genet has made the kind of transfer he has and, more pertinently, what this sort of transfer represents. As the meditation exfoliates almost stiflingly, the individual characters lose their reality— and what reality they posses is very little indeed, since the only importance they have is the use Genet's imagination can make of them in order to elaborate a rather special presentation of the meaning of human experience. It is, as Genet admits (*Pompes funèbres,* p. 37), a work of sorcery, and the sorcery consists mainly in supplying to a rather limited structure of fact (the real death of the hero and the real preparations for his funeral) a thoroughly imaginative narrative which is designed to explain one incident in that limited structure.

The incident is the sexual attraction Genet feels toward Erik, the *real* Erik, when he meets him at the home of the hero's mother. He feels a disturbance over this similar to that he had felt over the failure of his proposed miracle and, until the triggering of his imagination in the cinema, the disturbance continues. Once the triggering has taken place, all sense of agitation disappears under the pressure of the discoveries to be made in the book, discoveries which achieve their reality for the reader only through the unquestionable mastery with which Genet treats a very tricky technical question. He wishes to impress the reader—and, of course, himself, though at this point he is already moving into the kind of heady assurance which makes self-conviction of little importance—with the fact that his sexual attraction for the possible murderer of the hero is only one way of paying tribute to the hero. For Genet's memory of the hero has nothing to do specifically with his heroism; it is a memory of a physical love between two good-looking youths. What the memory suggests is that the tie that binds has nothing to do with abstract definitions of *virtù;* on the contrary, the tie is either the sexual attraction that grows between two people or else the essential sexual motivation found at the basis of every human action. What the hero represented for Genet was a good if infrequent bed companion, both because he was handsome and because he exemplified in his adherence to communism and the audacity he brought to his role of maquisard a kind of virile excellence. In so doing he presented Genet with a kind of ideal, but, since the ideal is a mixture of "civic" virtue and sexual attraction, there should be little wonder that the best memorial for him would be to pursue one's interest in this kind of excellence by associating oneself with those who are even better at it. And since Erik comes to represent the force that has stamped out the hero's life, Erik must necessarily be a more weighted expression of excellence. To love Erik is only to love a better embodiment of the kind of competence which was originally found with the hero.

The dead hero's glory, such as it was, passes because it was thought to be unique; its identification with and expression of what is considered civic virtue made it give the impression that it alone was enrolled in the registers of virtue and therefore had a special claim on beauty. Genet is making other discoveries, not the least of which is that even the most odious of crimes committed by the most odious of people can have its beauty, provided it is committed by a handsome being. Erik Seiler, immersed in the crimes of the SS, may seem to others the epitome of wickedness because he is engaged knowingly and voluntarily in despicable operations. Genet possesses no such reservations. Erik is handsome, as the murdered maquisard had been handsome; this beauty gives a special stamp to his "crimes" just as the dead hero's beauty had ennobled his "heroic acts." But the most significant aspect of Erik's beauty is moral rather than physical; it resides in the fact that the evil he does is done consciously. With this open avowal of his evil, his status, in Genet's mind, takes on more than one dimension.

There is, of course, an ethic working here, but since it is an ethic dependent for its statements and definitions on a dissolution of time and a merging of situations taken seemingly at will from different moments in personal or public history, it is extremely difficult to reduce it to even a discursive presentation. It needs precisely the kind of statement Genet has given it in order to impose itself upon the reader with any sort of force, but paradoxically it is only this kind of presentation—an ordered jumble one might call it—that gives power to the ethic. What Genet is suggesting is a kind of growth within the individual that (though it has echoes of similar developments mentioned by Freud) is very much (and perhaps happily so) sui generis. It is, however, a growth noticeable within the human race at any moment in history we care to look at. The ethic reads something like this:

It is every man's desire to be first man in Rome, to become *someone,* as Saïd says in *les Paravents.* To reach

this exalted position a number of hurdles must be nego-
tiated; but the very process of negotiating them is somewhat self-deflating since, in order to get to the top, one
must engage in acts which are going to start others off
in the same direction. In terms of *Pompes funèbres* the
ethical structure is worked out thus: the imaginary Erik
as a child had been the whore of the Berlin Hangman,
who is himself a kind of amalgam of many forces, most
often expressed, but at an obviously later moment in
time, as Hitler. Erik, then, had once been the victim of
the Hangman's power, but he had also been, as a result
of the uses the Hangman put him to, exposed to the kind
of activity he himself would have to engage in in order
one day to become the same kind of force as the Hangman. This opportunity is offered to him in the person of
Riton, who, having betrayed the Resistance of which he
was supposedly a part, has become Erik's lover in the
last pages of the book. As they stand on a rooftop in
Paris, awaiting an inevitable fall at the hands of the vic-
torious maquisards, they engage in a sexual act, a reproduction of Erik's relations with the Hangman. It is
a complete reproduction, too, for Erik, at the moment
of his glory, of his absorption into the ideal that has been
his, is also, by using Riton, setting up the same sort of
situation he himself had once been part of: he is inevitably
preparing the way for Riton to become one day the Hangman (*Pompes funèbres,* pp. 46–47).

In the interval between Erik's assumption of the first
man in Rome role and his replacement by Riton, there
is, of course, a moment of glory, the moment when he
can walk down the streets of Paris with the assurance
that: " 'I alone am Erik Seiler.' This certainty exalted
him. He was sure that no one in the street recognized
him, but he knew that the crowd was aware of the existence of the Erik Seiler he alone could be" (*Pompes*

funèbres, p. 123). However glorious the interval, it is doomed, for the ethic is circular. The moment of glory must necessarily be the first step toward inglory, toward replacement by the object. Having been necessary to the assertion of the glory, the object now becomes, as it passes from object to subject, the center of mastery and assumes the glory unto itself.

Since this is the way things are, the old hesitation—best exemplified by that moment of disturbance which followed the failure of the miracle—is calmed by the achievement of this new knowledge. Men are not bound together by the abstract qualities cerebration imposes on them; they are part of a kind of dynamic cycle which offers them an ideal, allows them to enjoy its most glorious hour as it most glorious exponents, and then replaces them with another, another, who, it cannot be repeated too often, has been necessary to that moment of glory. A reader might expect Genet to be depressed rather than cheered by what he has discovered, but this would be to miss the subtler implications of Genet's presentation.

Genet is working with two basic observations here: the first has to do with the triumph of evil in the world about him, which seems to suggest that all the bourgeoisie's morality does not preserve them from attack and defeat; the second has to do with his own place in this first situation (more complexly, with where he stands in the total situation described by the Hangman-Erik-Riton dynamic). Genet is convinced—and his conviction grows stronger as his investigations grow longer and touch on more issues—that he has empirical bases for his observations. As an example of the kind of dynamism he is describing in his analysis of the Hangman-Erik-Riton relationship, the choice of Hitler is one explained both by the assurance that Hitler, too, must one day pass away, and also by Genet's awareness that Hitler has a certain glamor that places him beyond the basic categories of evil or misbehavior. He is, Genet tells us (*Miracle de la rose,* p. 265) "in this century subject to poisons . . . like a princess of the Renaissance, a mute and deep Catherine de Medici." Genet's point is that Hitler's many evils were not enough to keep him from getting to the top. His ability to transform a nation supposedly devoted to all the bourgeois virtues into something appallingly different is, for Genet, proof that absolute categories do not describe real values and are not convincing. In the present, evil can have appeal, and if the appeal is strong enough casuistry will find some way of justifying it. Looked back upon as a phenomenon of the past, evil can be touched either with glory or fascination. One does not sense any immediate threat from Catherine de Medici or from Napoleon or even now from Hitler; thus one can admire Catherine as a strong woman, see Napoleon as a great vitalizer of the energies of a nation, and, if one is A. J. P. Taylor, look upon Hitler as part of the historical process and thus exonerated from the full weight of his crimes.

This kind of spectacle may at times strike Genet as a great joke, because of the hesitation it introduces about the respect with which one should listen to the voices of the good people who have borne with and supported so much evil. But it does more than this: it suggests that, hidden in this capacity for compromise, is something that, if found, will tell us more accurately what it is that joins us all together. Here it is important to point out that, unlike the Genet of *Notre-Dame-des-Fleurs,* the Genet of *Pompes funèbres* is a man convinced that there is a strong common cable among men. They are not divided into hostile camps, or even into those red and white corpuscles his American editor evoked to describe the phenomenon of Genet; nor are they met on some

Armageddon, fighting for the triumph of right principles over wrong. If Armageddon is their meeting place it is a rendezvous set to bring them into contact with accuracy rather than with the many falsified and manufactured truths with which they have lived.

A notion, then, is born; as it grows into maturity and becomes conviction, supported by observation of the surrounding world, it helps Genet define more fully the nature of that common cable. In *Notre-Dame-des-Fleurs* he had had inklings of a cousinship among men that had psychological depths not sufficiently explained by reference to vague phrases like the unity of the human race or the invocation of common if fallen parents. He had expressed this in a passage (pp. 142–43) rather typical of the way his mind operates and which leads him to what he thinks are thoroughly empirical conclusions:

> A warder opens the door and pushes the new-comer into the cell. Who is it who welcomes him: Mignon or myself? He brings his blankets, his mess tin, his canteen cup, his wooden spoon, and his personal history with him. As he begins to speak, I stop him. He continues talking, but I am no longer there.
>
> "What's your name?"
> "Jean."
>
> That's all that's needed. Like me and like the dead child for whom I am writing [Pilorge, to whom the book is dedicated] his name is Jean. What difference would it make if he were less handsome... I am playing with unhappiness. Jean here. Jean there. When I tell one of these Jeans that I love him, I sometimes wonder if I may not be addressing myself. I am no longer there because once again

75

I am trying to force myself into reliving those few times when he agreed to let me caress him. I dared to do everything; but to win him over, I agreed that he would have the male's superiority over me; his penis was solid as a man's should be, and his adolescent face was sweetness itself—so much so that when he came in my mouth he lost nothing of a certain virginal chastity. Now there is another Jean here, who is recounting his life's story. I am no longer alone, but that is just why I am more alone than ever. What I mean is that the solitude of the prison had, until now, given me the freedom to be with the hundred Jean Genet's glimpsed, in passing, on the faces of a hundred passers-by. In doing this I am very much like Mignon, who plucked what was peculiarly himself from those unthought gestures made by all the strangers he had rubbed up against. But this new Jean brings back —like a fan which, in closing, infolds gauze decoration—brings back some unknown quantity to me. And yet he is far from being antipathetic. He is even gullible enough for me to have sentiments of tenderness for him: small, black eyes; a burnished skin; his short-cropped hair standing up as though it has just been awakened...He has something of the aspect of a Greek street urchin you might see stooped at the foot of an invisible statue of Mercury, playing parchesi, but watching the god closely from a corner of his eye in order to steal his sandals.

This passage may seem to have little to do with *Pompes funèbres* and less to do with the observations I have just made about certain fundamental orientations of Genet's thinking about human experience. When looked at closely, however, it gives us, albeit in an early stage, certain of the phenomena upon which Genet bases his ultimate conclusions. Here we have the young criminal, incarcerated, cheering himself up with the memories of those he has loved. But here we see, too, a certain narcissism coloring those memories, its existence sustained by the coincidence of identical Christian names. We have seen this sort of thing before in Genet and seen what he does with it. Here, however, the idea that relationships can only be established on the bases of such clear nominal coincidences is destroyed by the establishment of a relationship between Jean Genet and Mignon, a relationship which is based on the fact that they both do the same thing in looking at others: seek for traces of themselves. The identity of names is just an added pretext for this kind of reflection; it is in no way the sine qua non for such reflections.

The narcissism is both strengthened and given a melancholy cast by the admission that it has been dulled by submission to others. Genet thinks back to Pilorge as someone he has loved and does so in narcissistic terms; but the narcissism is blunted by the pang of memory that tells him that he was the submissive person during their intercourse, he was the one dominated. As he looks at the newcomer, then, he looks at him with the same initial curiosity, for the newcomer's name immediately sets Genet off in search of what there is of Genet in this new arrival. But even as he does this his mind has been impregnated with the idea that identities are not complete or, more accurately, they do not create tranquillity, for if he and the newcomer are identical in name, they are also identical in the hostility and opposition they feel toward each other. They may love, they may be alike, but one of the terms of their alikeness is that one of them may wind up subordinated to the other. And so the passage ends with the image of the young, good-looking

77

Greek who seems subordinate to the god only for the time it will take him to figure out some way to steal the god's sandals.

Hidden not too deeply in this is a definition of that common cable that links human beings together. It is their absolute similarity, whose totality is in no way diminished by the conflicts and oppositions that crop up among them. These are only further proof that all men contain within themselves the same tendencies; the only point of individuation is: who will win the struggle once it is declared? In the excerpt above, it is Genet who is losing. The phenomenon needs that progressive tense, for not only has he lost to Pilorge, but he has the impression of being menaced, because of what he is, by a similar loss to the newcomer. The positive side of the phenomenon comes later, comes indeed with *Pompes funèbres,* by which time Genet has seen in his survival a kind of triumph which reduces minor questions of dominant or subordinate position in the sexual act to their proper perspective. His being still alive may not exculpate him from every degree of shame, but it does attest to the superiority given him by the mere process of breathing while others are six feet under the earth. All this is caught in the following passage from *Pompes funèbres* (p. 83):

> You feel a kind of shame in thinking, during a period of mourning, about voluptuous gestures. During my walks I chase their images away from me, and I have had to make violent efforts in order to write the erotic scenes which have preceded but of which my soul was nonetheless full. But once the discomfort of having profaned a cadaver is past, this game—which has a cadaver as its pretext— gives me a great freedom. It has brought a cry for

air into the midst of my suffering—not that I dare laugh, but I am assimilating Jean, I am digesting him.

The distribution of power could not be better adjusted, for not only has Genet fought his way through to a sense of his own superiority, he has also found a means of guaranteeing his escape from the apparently inevitable rhythms of the Hangman-Erik-Riton dynamic. What we have seen then in *Pompes funèbres* is a thoroughly imaginative structure which has as its basis what Genet considers irrefutable empirical evidence. The book is the incipient elaboration of a myth designed to convince us that, despite its thoroughly imaginative character, it is the best presentation of a certain reality. But it is also designed to give Jean Genet a place of such privilege that he, for possibly the first time in human history, will be able to escape from the inevitability of the cycle.

Like Lucretius writing a lengthy poem in order to show how similar his mental stasis was to that of the gods, thereby giving him at least a kind of immortality, Genet will show us how much he is preserved from the ravages of cyclic processes by his intuitive perception of what those processes are. He will be neither Mercury nor the crafty young man crouched at the pedestal of Mercury's statue; rather he will be a higher, more clairvoyant deity, watching the operations of both Mercury and the crafty young man through the spyglass of his literary gifts. By becoming the poet, the interpreter of the situations he substitutes for reality, he will preserve himself from the usual consequences of those situations. If it is all sorcery and magic, and more important, if it achieves its effect, then the most powerful man will be the magician who brings it off. He will then be able to stand back and eventually chortle over the way he has found his place in a sun whose rays are designed to blind and victimize us.

Everything about *Pompes funèbres* forces us inescapably to this kind of observation. The effacement of the historical reality which was Jean Genet and its absorption into imaginary figures will help him to claim as only a momentary thing the sentiment of impending doom that was always his when he was met with a stronger male. The introduction of the Hangman-Erik-Riton cycle will, because it is Jean Genet who discovers and presents it, place him outside its movement; and it will also get him past the thorny problem with which the book began: his attraction for Erik, the symbol of the forces which had brought about the death of the mourned hero. His subtle mixing of historical periods and physical places will enable him to generalize his observations so that they will escape the stigma of being merely of *his* mind and place. These are, each alone and all together, the strings by which Genet makes himself into a master puppeteer who is separated from his puppets but still able, by a jerk of one of the strings, to control their movements. There is a striking example of this in *Pompes funèbres* (p. 98) during an unpleasant scene in which Riton is trying to caress Erik. Unpleasant as it is, it is a valuable contrast to the scene quoted from *Notre-Dame-des-Fleurs* because, here, Genet is absent as a participant but present as an overseer:

> Very delicately Riton's fingers tried to distinguish the different parts of this mass which, abandoned to his hands, filled him with joy. All of Erik's potency was contained in this tranquil little pile which spread out despite his death. And all the power of the Germans was contained in those sacred, peaceful, and yet heavy depositories which, though now

somnolent, were capable of the most threatening awakenings, and which, always on the watch, were carried like precious cargo into frozen or tropic climes where they imposed themselves through a process of rape. With the skill of a laceworker, Riton's hand, passing across the black fabric, was able to disentangle the treasure from its storage place. I prejudged the splendor it would have in this action and so imprisoned it, a sleeping young girl, in my gross ogre's paw. I was protecting it. I was taking its weight and thinking: "There is treasure hidden there." Out of friendship I grew excited. I was worthy of it. My fingers squeezed it a little more, with even more tenderness.

The passage, after Genet's imposition of himself into it, continues for several pages, during which it becomes clear that his self-imposition is justified because the whole scene is a figment of his imagination created to illustrate, not the actions of real individuals, but the forces which are at work in all men. It passes from this moment of Genet's imaginative time back to another moment in that time when, in Spain, he had desired an episode similar to that he is creating for Erik and Riton, then moves into a disquisition on the meaning of Hitler for millions of German soldiers and the purpose those soldiers served for Hitler. He sent them to their death, Genet says, because "it was the only way in which he might possess all of them." He goes on to mention that he understands this wish because he, too, has frequently been tempted to possess the power to kill all the good-looking lads he hasn't been able to make love to. Prior to the meditation on Hitler, there is another revelatory passage in which Genet writes: "I have killed, pillaged, stolen, betrayed. What an accumulation of glory! But

81

let no murderer, thief, or traitor dare try to avail himself of my reasons. I have had too much trouble conquering them. They have no value save for me. Not just anyone would be able to profit from this justification. I do not like people who have no consciences" (p. 100).

It is a curious passage because it mixes the reality of Genet's crimes with some that, so far as we know, he has not committed and thus becomes a cause of perplexity. The perplexity is dispelled when we realize that it is here, in this book, that Genet has created those crimes, because it is here, in this book, that he has found the proper perspective for them and, in finding it, won his right to pre-eminence. The purpose of all this fluttering about from one moment in imaginative time to another is clear by now, and, with the repetition of the technique throughout the book, the purpose becomes even clearer, with the result that the most important thing about *Pompes funèbres* is not the audacious assertions it makes about human experience. The important thing is the way in which it tries to convince us of what the world is really about, what motivations are really most important, and, most vitally, why it is that Jean Genet deserves to be God.

He deserves to be God because, confronted with the complexities of existence, the thorniness of meanings, he does not experience the hesitations of other men. He does not hem and haw about the accuracy of his statements or about the question of there being some kind of conformity between his observations of things and the characteristics inherent in those things. In those areas where indecision makes us cautious about the sweep of our statements, Jean Genet takes the plunge, manifesting, as he dives into the pool of human experience, all the inventiveness of the child: bravura will get him past his initial fear of the space between the board and the pool; his imagination will supply a sense to his fear; an awareness of irony will supply him with a kind of distance which will actually bring him closer. And so he writes (p. 105): "This book is true and it's a joke. I will publish it in order that it may serve the cause of Jean's glory— but which Jean?"

The immediate consequences of this arbitrary process are so numerous as to defy listing. Language both falls apart and gives authority to his observations: a penis is compared to a sleeping young girl and then immediately afterwards is seen as a V–2, the most immediate and powerful manifestation of the Nazis' strength, indeed the source of all their motivation; the reality of past actions is completely transformed so that an act of degradation can become an act of love, simply because all acts now must wait upon Jean Genet's decision before they can be given their most pertinent meaning. Every obscurity in his own experience and in the experience of the race is illuminated by the inexhaustible searchlight of his imagination, which ranges beyond the surface appearance of things into their true essence. Born in the midst of mystery because of the anonymity of his parents, he comes to believe that all explanation must be supplied if there is to be explanation at all; it is not enough to rest with facts, because facts are missing or else incomplete. Something must give the facts better identity. Wherever there is indecision about their meaning, Jean Genet will copiously offer the insights and conclusions of his imagination. He does not pretend to be cavalier about this, since he is sure that the basis on which he establishes these prerogatives for his imagination are a good deal better than any other offered. For he has seen—and one cannot repeat it too often—visions other men have shied from; he has, because of his unchosen immersion in illegitimacy, vice, and crime, had a vantage point that others would not have the patience or the inquisitive courage to sustain. He has, like the heroine of Faulkner's *Light in August,* been places and seen things; but he has not just been traveling for the pleasures of the voyage. He has been traveling, he finds, in order to get somewhere. *Pompes funèbres,* which establishes what it is he wants to say about the true nature of the links that exist among men, has got him to the frontier. Arrived there he finds that his powers have worked well indeed. Bolstered by these powers he can turn to the task of writing *Querelle de Brest,* where he will lose any lingering traces of the marionette in order to become the master puppeteer, happily pulling the strings that make his creations dance the steps he chooses for them. With *Querelle de Brest* the lived personal experience of Jean Genet is completely effaced from his work; the meaning of that experience comes into its own by finding a world in which it is clearly recognized as the only authentic meaning we can assign to human behavior.

Querelle granted his star an
absolute confidence. That
star owed her existence to
the sailor's confidence in her
—she was, if you wish, the
breaking into his night of his
confidence in—well, in his
confidence; and, so that the
star might conserve her
greatness and her glory, by
which I mean her effectiveness, Querelle had to conserve his confidence in her.
—*Querelle de Brest*

'Querelle de Brest'

The brio Genet brings to the
writing of *Querelle de Brest* is an indication of the extent
to which he has calmed the inner antagonisms present
in the opening pages of *Pompes funèbres* in order, here,
to calm the antagonisms existing between him and us.
One of the opening phrases of the novel gives some indication of how audacious he has become and how much
pleasure he derives from his daring (the whole paragraph
is a stunning piece of imaginative logic): "We have let
ourselves go to a facile verbal poetry in which each

85

proposition is nothing but an argument in favor of the author's *complaisances*. We want to present the drama which unfolds here under the sign of a quite striking inner movement. Furthermore we want to point out that it is addressed to perverts. To the idea of the sea and of murder is added the idea of delight and *naturally* of love —rather of *unnatural* love." The inner movement would seem to be nothing but Genet's own bulging confidence, which allows him to withdraw as a participant in his works so that he may assume the more powerful, much more consequential role of Prime Mover. To withdraw in this way takes him out of the range of our pity—something he only rarely desired and could not have in his earlier works—and places him in the role of a very knowing, though not always discerning, adversary who will offer us constructs (the sea is to murder as love is to delight proportion) designed to win, not always honestly, our assent to his most startling propositions. In brief, we find *Querelle de Brest* to be the first of Genet's works which has a clear public dimension, for here the magic is no longer personal incantation; it has become ritual designed to involve the whole tribe.

Much of what we encounter in the novel is reminiscent of *Pompes funèbres;* this similarity does not seem to have escaped Genet who, in the preface to the clandestine edition, speaks of the book as something that is reforming within him where it is imposing its "turbulent and joyous guilt." What he means by the guilt which is productive of turbulence and joy we shall see presently, as we see what happens to Querelle; what the reformation means is that this novel will give him a chance to attempt an objectification of the Hangman-Erik-Riton dynamic discussed earlier. One hastens to add—with Genet one must run quickly in order not to be caught in the net of his destructive logic—that the purpose of the objectification has nothing to do with an effort on Genet's part to put a situation outside himself the better to understand and analyze it; it has quite simply to do with finding, outside the range of his own personal experience, the kinds of structures that will prove he is not alone in his dark night, that his own experience is only a sampling of the experience of all men, and that, through his art, he will go about, not convincing others of this, but seeking to seduce them into seeing themselves in the dark mirror he holds before them. If he succeeds in doing this he will, of course, escape from accusations that the dynamic was established merely to get him beyond the lapse of taste which was the unleashing force of *Pompes funèbres,* for he will have offered in Querelle an example, from which he as protagonist is absent, of the same sort of dynamic working within the experience of a fictional hero.

Since Genet's imagination is never fully under control —I will have more to say in my conclusion of this and the perplexity it creates for a critic—he manages to be as much revelatory as accusing, so that *Querelle de Brest,* though it lacks the almost exaggerated pyrotechnics of *Pompes funèbres,* none the less represents a further evolution of the ethical concerns first introduced in the earlier work. Here for the first time it becomes clear to the reader—as it never seems to become clear to Genet, who, strangely, is often very much of a mechanist—that there is a sex-power dialectic at work constantly in Genet's mind. This dialectic goes beyond the most fond imaginings of men like Freud and Adler in order to suggest that the search for power in sexual relations is not simply an indication of a desire to exercise empire over another by catching him in his shame, but is also, and less comprehensibly, an involvement with that other in order to attain a certain bizarre form of self-retribution.

The Imagination of Jean Genet

In his first works this dialectic had been within the reach of a reader's detective skills. In observing the replacement of Divine by Notre-Dame and the ultimate subjugation of Notre-Dame to more forceful thugs, the reader could readily see that the fascination with power was at the basis of the homosexual's attraction to possible lovers, much as the desire to exercise power was at the basis of the criminal's response to this love. In another register—that evoked by the quotation cited earlier where Genet watches with apprehension the arrival of a new cellmate—the reader could see the strong and at times moving emotional consequences insertion in this power elite had on the spirit of the young man most likely to suffer within the hierarchy. Divine's reaction, like Genet's, was struck on the keys of loss, defeat, and depression, but was never father to anger or revolt. In a way strangely evocative of Corneille's Pauline, they saw in the loss an indication of what had originally attracted them to the lover, whose eyes have now fallen on more exciting boys.

Much of this, especially in a book like *Miracle de la rose,* was predominantly descriptive, an exposition of the way things were and not, necessarily, an explanation of why they were that way or what, in discursive terms, their being that way meant. The result was a kind of empiricism either gone wild or else not assembled into order—an accumulation of anecdotal information about human behavior that was very much like a bank statement. You knew how much money had been spent and, observing the record of the expenditures, you could arrive at some knowledge of the spending habits of the individual; but you really didn't know enough, since you had only the details without either the pattern or the meaning of those details. The structure of *Pompes funèbres* sought to arrange the bank statement in another, more revealing, manner so that the presentation of the details would of itself be adequate. There would be no need to point out, blatantly and shrilly, what the moral was; simply by associating one's heroes with great forces of the world—Renaissance princesses, Hitler, the SS—one could set up a situation which all but the most obtuse of readers would quickly grasp.

Querelle de Brest seeks to establish the same sort of situation; by the deployment of action, by the juxtaposition of specific acts, by a knowing confusion of moments in time, it will seek to create a wedge whose angle will be the meeting of our understanding with Genet's method of presentation. The pun of the title unmistakably conveys the impression that this is the purpose of the book. It is to be more than an accounting of the adventures of the sailor, Querelle; it is also to be a quarrel, an argument which in the end will be resolved. And it might be; the juxtaposed incidents might once again carry the day if that ethic, which first appeared in *Pompes funèbres,* were not so insistent on creating constantly refurbished problems and hesitations within the reader's mind.

That ethic is at the very center of the novel's storyline. Its terms—the relationship between the shrewd exercise of sexual prowess and the achievement of power—are the strands of the thread which runs throughout the story and which, at the end, has become the common cable I have already alluded to. (Since those terms are sometimes more pronounced in the clandestine edition of the book than in the curiously expurgated edition published by Gallimard, I shall make references to both editions. The process is not haphazard, as it might seem, for in the Gallimard edition Genet has made changes and additions which show the extent to which the idea of the ethic has, with the passing of the years, taken firmer and more threatening shape in his mind. Yet, for all this to be clear

89

and the intention to be luminous, it is necessary to have fuller facts about Querelle's life than those supplied in the Gallimard edition.)

The navy is in town, bringing with it Querelle, a sailor who, in addition to his good looks, carries his life story with him. To it he adds a kind of curiosity about the meaning of his experiences and a desire to learn what his place in the world can ultimately be. He is led to this curiosity and this desire by a realization that he has in the past exerted a curious kind of influence over strangers and that this influence can still be detected in the attitude of his immediate superior, Lieutenant Seblon, whose attraction to Querelle, though muted and expressed frankly only in the pages of his diary, is strong to the point of obsession. Earlier in his life, at another port of call, Querelle had got involved out of curiosity with an aging, desperate homosexual, whom he had killed in the moments preliminary to homosexual union. What it was that prompted him, first, to allow himself to become involved with the homosexual and, then, to kill him is the center of a mystery lingering in that pocket of Querelle's mind devoted to contradictions. The most basic paradox is that, despite having killed the other man, he remembers with warmth and something approaching satisfaction the tenderness and admiration Joachim had shown him.

This remembered incident and the entries the coy Seblon puts in his diary are two thematic devices used throughout the novel. Early in the narrative Querelle murders another sailor, leaving at the scene of the crime clues that will involve someone else. Having committed the murder, he feels an odd compulsion to subject himself to an act of homosexual violation at the hands of Nono, the husband of the local madam. As a youth, the

Erik of *Pompes funèbres* had known a similar compulsion and, in giving himself over to the Berlin Hangman, had thought to requite the guilt he bore as a result of stealing a watch. Querelle later becomes involved with Mario, the local police chief; with Gil, a young man he will betray to the police in an act designed both to forestall his love for the young man and to give further evidence of his growing self-mastery; with Madame Lysiane, the brothel keeper; and with various and sundry other people, not the least significant of whom is his brother, Robert. He quarrels with him precisely on the subject of his homosexual activities. As a result of his involvement with these people he comes to understand the meaning of what was at play in his original murder; by passing through the series of events which are the substance of this book he comes to understand the meaning of those events and, having arrived at a resolution of the contradictions plaguing his mind in the opening pages of the book, he leaves Brest convinced that he has fought his way through to true dominion over the world of men and events.

In all these events there is a hint of what might mistakenly be called a sense of Calvinistic retribution, a belief that one act must be balanced by another. Initially, what moves Querelle to seek union with Nono is a compulsion to redeem his murder by allowing himself to be disgraced by another in an act of homosexual prostitution, where his role, like that of the man he has murdered, will be the passive one. In a similar vein Madame Lysiane, whose highly diversified brothel is a vivid indication of how deeply she understands and patronizes the stranger needs of humankind, has her moment of weakness when, afraid that she has offended her lover (Querelle's brother, Robert), she allows herself, by way of offering apologies, to be victimized. Seblon, the love-

91

sick lieutenant, allows himself to be accused of a crime he did not commit because the accusation and the penalty it will bring allow him some outlet for the guilt that has been growing out of the mixture of his timidity and his sense of the wrongness of his desires. He is doomed not simply because the stars were crossed, but more importantly because he has not entered as fully as he ought honestly to have done in the operations of the Hangman-Erik-Riton dynamic. He has not done so because he has sought to live in two worlds at once: the world of respectability and convention which frowns on his desires, and the real world which organizes itself ultimately around those very desires.

What we find with Seblon, however, is that any sense of Calvinism we might wish to bring to the interpretation of these acts is misapplied. It is the dynamic which is at work in all these instances and, where in *Pompes funèbres* it seemed to touch only those who were actively involved in it, here it reaches out to touch everyone for the simple if unsettling reason that what it describes is at the heart of all human desires and aspirations. Seblon has sought to escape from the dynamic by being careful of how he expresses himself in acts; he has, however, placed no such restraint on his thoughts, which linger erotically over his sexual attraction to Querelle and his more basic fascination with the whole mysterious world of homosexuality. Like the troubadors who preached a doctrine of thus-far-but-no-further in matters of sexuality (and his diary bears a remarkable resemblance to some of their poems), Seblon would have guilt result only from physical events, thereby downgrading the consequences of mental events. But, worse than this, he will seek in the discipline of naval life a replacement for his homosexual instincts, hoping that its artificial hierarchy will win him easily what would have to be fought for more shrewdly and at great pains in the outside world. Here we have the first expression of an idea that will grow stronger and become more fundamental in Genet's thinking in his later works, most especially in *les Paravents*. In this particular incarnation it is only crudely formed, but it has enough shape to convey the vivid impression that any escape from the ethic, and the dynamic which expresses that ethic, ultimately brings worse consequences. It is Seblon who is degraded in this book; others —Lysiane, Nono, Mario and even Gil—are defeated, but their defeat is met on honest terms and, to some extent, is not fully perceived by them.

If Querelle emerges as the unquestioned hero of this book, it is quite simply because he is the most natural, the most inquisitive of its characters, and the least decisively influenced by conventional modes of thinking. His curiosity has made him a cautious experimenter who recognizes that the logic of the body's desires has nothing to do with the more readily approved kinds of logic —the sort of logic discernible in my own dissatisfaction with Genet's ethic—but is a logic of its own, a purely physical logic, if you will, which when carefully explored and even more carefully yielded to is bound to put you in harmony with nature. He is then, the *anima naturaliter humana,* not the noble savage but the genuine savage, man as he really is. And since he recognizes this, he wins his ribbons honestly.

It may have been guilt which drove him initially to Nono, but the guilt was only the name for an appearance. In his relationship with Nono, as in his relationship with Mario and, later, with Madame Lysiane, he has discovered new forces and learned much; the sum of his knowledge is the authoritative assurance that guilt has no place in the register of values and experience in which he has been operating. He emerges guiltless because he has learned vivid truths about the true nature of man and has also exposed the diseased bases of some of man's more lingering and consoling mythologies. But he emerges guiltless also because the sources of his guilt have undergone a profound transformation; he no longer sees things with the same puzzlement which characterized him when we first encountered him sauntering jauntily but insecurely from his ship into the adventures of Brest. What he learns during those adventures is a lesson whose major points have to do with the extent to which love, as romantically or even Christianly defined, is a myth and the extent to which the existence of the myth is symptomatic of human weakness.

The kind of wavering human associations we discovered in the first two prose works and which sought to be called love was an association in which the beloved was constantly threatened with loss of his lover to a more handsome and usually younger latecomer. For the passive member of the relationship this created a constant precariousness, for no association was exempt from the rules of fragility and satiation which underpin all purely sensual activity. Because of this threat, so often experienced as to become a constant source of melancholy and disappointment, those who suffered from it found themselves forced back to their adolescent practices. These they could justify, because in them one avoided the pain that comes with the rupture of any appreciated union; but they could also furnish such resumed activities with better fantasies than those used in adolescence. Genet, himself a victim of this kind of repeated infidelity, tells us in *Notre-Dame-des-Fleurs* how it had forced him to raise masturbation to the level of a cult; and he defines the cult in this way (p. 59): "It is a solitary pleasure, solitude's gesture which allows you to be self-sufficient, able to possess others intimately, seeing that they serve your pleasure without in any way suspecting its existence; it is a pleasure which, even in anticipatory moments, gives your most insignificant gestures an air of supreme indifference to everyone else." Such fantasies offer an unequalled consolation, since they are filters clearing away all suggestion of the unpleasant and the transitory in sexual relations, allowing the fantasist to imagine himself in control of all aspects of the situation. He plays the role he chooses, dismissing all possibility of ever being miscast or replaced. But the remedy remains troubled. The very existence of the need for fantasy is the result of failure; it is compensation for the distempers and disorders of existence but is in no way a meaningful resolution of them.

There are a number of ways out. One could assert that the solitary practices are, in their way, a better kind of economy, producing pleasure yet preventing pain. But this is not much of a solution, as long as one has eyes to see other young men enjoying the attentions of brawnier and braver examples of male *virtù,* becoming centers of attraction, and thereby suggesting their superior cleverness over the individual who has fallen back on his youthful habits in order to avoid pain and despair. There is another solution, but in order that it not look simply like another violent and artificial dislocation of real forces, provoked again with the intention of compensating, it must be approached prudently. What one must do is prove that all sexual activity, whether it be carried on separately or with another, is ultimately a mark of loneliness, separation, and apartness. Men seek sexual companionship in order to pretend that their solitude can be overcome; but all this may be only another kind of fancifulness on their part and, if this can be proven, he who has proven it will then be able to sense a very genuine superiority to the rest of mankind. The new knowledge may not rid him of his own sense of solitude, but it will rid him of illusion, teach him the precise limitations to be found in sexual activity, and expose him eventually to the more profitable uses to be derived from sexual prowess and domination.

Pompes funèbres is a kind of test balloon for the postulation of this thesis and a most interesting one. In that book there was no character who held any suspicion of even the bare possibility of such a thesis. The participants in the events of the book were merely meant to offer case histories from which would emerge a pattern; the more discerning participant in the book was, of course, the author. He it was who had isolated the case histories, set them in revelatory juxtaposition, and begun to draw conclusions from them, the most powerful and consequential of which was the emergence of that pattern of behavior I have been identifying as the Hangman-Erik-Riton dynamic. Genet, having participated in the pattern and having suffered from it in his personal life, had in the final analysis managed to escape from it by working his way through to its definition. He may have been bruised and knocked about in life, but the final victory was his, because he had learned that at the root of every shift within the dynamic was the transfer of a basic capacitating energy: power.

There was a danger: the arrangement of *Pompes funèbres,* the intervention of the autobiographical and sometimes polemical "I," might lead a reader to look upon this particular argument as just another, albeit more sophisticated, evidence of fantasy. To avoid the danger the presentation needed to have another kind of expression in which the author, still unquestionably the master of ceremonies, would none the less have between him and the sceptical reader the object which was his book in which he did not clearly figure as a character.

Querelle de Brest, because it is purely a novel, gives him this opportunity; and Querelle himself gives him a personage more potentially authoritative than had been the intermittent "I" of *Pompes funèbres.*

The great value of Querelle is his perplexity; from it flows his curiosity. He has no idea of the existence of a dynamic in which he may possibly get caught; nor has he had the experience of being the passive participant who is more often abandoned than not. What he has, at the moment he offers himself to Nono, is the memory of the attraction he had represented for the murdered Armenian, Joachim, and the compulsion he has to "change his nature" in the aftermath of his latest murder. There is then some close relationship between his crime and the homosexual violence he will allow himself to endure. What the connection is he does not yet know; it is something intuitively seen and compulsively sought. Once experienced it becomes part of a fund of information that is ever growing. At a later moment in the book, Querelle discovers the police chief has heard of his experience with Nono and finds in discussion of that experience with Querelle a source of sexual excitation. Made aware of that arousal, invited to audacity by the police chief, Querelle fellates him.

It might seem on the basis of these two kinds of experience, each of which is repeated with some frequency, that Querelle has become the universal victim, the whore both of Nono and of Mario, the police chief. What prevents the victimization is the liveliness of Querelle's mind; even as he draws pleasure from these experiences, he is learning more and more about their nature and has stored away in other corners of his life other patterns of events which offer a reservoir of information he can consult to find out what he is becoming. There is, first of all, the adoring worship he receives, always at a distance, from the lieutenant; secondly, the fact of the murders he has to his credit, one that of a man who wished to make love to him; there is, finally, the attraction he represents for Gil and which can lead to the same sort of activity he is experiencing with the policeman but in the accomplishment of which he would play Mario to Gil's Querelle. In the initial phases of this act, when Querelle discovers his power simply in the process of thinking over whether he shall carry through with it or not, there comes to pass an illuminating convergence of all he has been learning. At the start he thinks he will have anal intercourse but hesitates for reasons which are not yet enunciated. Immediately afterwards he encourages Gil to fellate him but interrupts the act before it can be brought to climax. The reason for this is unmistakably clear: such an act would be a manifestation of love, and might indeed kindle the nascent love to a flame Querelle would find it hard to extinguish; but extinguishing it is precisely what he is in the process of doing, for Gil is the young man he has already betrayed to the police. The attraction to the simulacrum of love, Querelle discovers, is very great, but not nearly as great as the attraction to the reality of power.

This event, then, becomes a key to open a door through which his perplexity will depart to be replaced by understanding. He learns that Nono assaults the bodies of young men only when he feels these young men may become the lovers of his wife; his intercourse with them is meant to be Nono's revenge, enacted before he has been cuckolded. Having discovered this, Querelle can then, reluctantly, have sexual relations with the wife simply in order to enact his revenge on Nono. The police chief's attraction to him had led to Querelle's seduction because of Querelle's fascination with the policeman's power, with his avowed commitment to honest fulfillment

of his responsibilities even if that honesty were to bring
about the arrest of his sexual partners. But during his
sexual relations with Mario, Querelle learns that the
sexual relations are essential to dispelling Mario's belief
that his constabulary work may not really elevate him
above the rest of men; and he learns, too, that during the
act Mario is afraid that Querelle may mutilate him. From
all this there emerges an unquestionable pattern which
demonstrates that, rather than being a victim, Querelle
is at the center of the world. Nono needs him and, all
Nono's justifications to the contrary notwithstanding, his
need puts Querelle in the dominant position, since in his
sexual acts with Nono, Querelle discovers a great truth:
the very position they assume as they have intercourse
is a symbol of the true distribution of needs and emotions
in the world of men (pp. 220–21):

> Nono was exerting himself as though in an impor-
> tant and weighty enterprise. He squeezed Querelle
> with the same apparent passion that a female animal
> uses in holding the corpse of her dead young—in
> an attitude which leads us to understand what love
> is: an awareness of the separation of the individual,
> an awareness of being divided and having your own
> self contemplating you.

As the keystone of this vault of assurance he is building,
Querelle learns that Mario has given himself to Nono,
as Querelle had. And he has given himself in order to
have the same experience as Querelle; the police chief,
who ought to be the everlastingly unintimidated exemplar
of male assurance in society, has had to pattern his sexual
adventures after those of Querelle. The sum of these
activities, accompanied by his penetration of the motivating forces behind them, liberates Querelle from his
befuddlement into a dazzling clarity which assures him

of his superior position—a position which is superior because it places him outside the hierarchy, spares him the worst consequences of being caught up in the dynamic, and empowers him to use the information he has derived from observation of the dynamic in order to rule the world.

His immense satisfaction with himself—and by the end of the book it has achieved such enormous dimensions that one doesn't know whether to be impressed or appalled—springs from his sense of dexterity, his realization that the world has become his oyster because he alone (with the possible exception of Madame Lysiane) understands the world, he alone has discovered the proper use of actions in order to guarantee personal success. One might tend to dismiss all this as balderdash (and ultimately many will), but this kind of justifiable caprice would lead us to overlook another important sophistication Genet here introduces into his basic argument. In *Querelle de Brest* he breaks away for the first time from the underworld in order to introduce, speculatively and not with complete assurance, the suggestion that the events of Querelle's sojourn in Brest are just more brazenly expressed counterparts to ours. Or, more precisely, that what Nono, Mario, Seblon, and Querelle want and what we want is very much the same thing: an outlet for our need for power, the kind of outlet which will develop our sense of assurance, make us feel we have found our rightful place in the sun. That that sun may eventually usurp the place of the real sun is only an indication of how rich are the benefits to be derived from power; it should in no way intimidate us.

The suggestion, as I have said, is uncertain; in this book Genet reaches only the outer fringe of the underworld: the lieutenant, the madam of the brothel and her pimping husband, the policeman Mario—these are individuals who do not quite belong to our world but, if one must assign them some place, it would be unfair to put them inescapably within the universe of the committed criminal. If crime does not bind them all together, desire and dissatisfaction do. Like Querelle, they are not yet what they want to be, and they can only get at what they want to be by following in Querelle's footsteps. The measure of their success is, then, the degree to which they embrace Querelle's honesty; that degree assigns them a place in a hierarchy which begins to organize itself. He who fares worst is, of course, the lieutenant, and he fares badly because he has not been honest; still, in his decline and fall there is at least a self-consciousness which may bring him some satisfaction. True, he has not achieved his desire, but he can go off with the police feeling whatever cheer the lesser forms of martyrdom bring. No such consolation is offered to Mario, however; and the reason for this explains much that is going on beneath the surface of the novel.

Mario is, of course, the exemplar of our society; he is assigned the weighty function of protecting it from the kind of assault Querelle threatens and, worse, performs in his periodic murders. In any of Genet's earlier works, Mario would have come across as a kind of lesser god, master of the ceremonies to whose mysteries the young criminal aspires. But Genet's imagination has been reorganizing his own earlier beliefs, fears, and hesitations, and in *Querelle de Brest* the policeman comes off a very bad second indeed to the more dazzling, more authentic, and more forceful Querelle. Why? Principally because, defender of the public weal that he may be, Mario is, if not a criminal in disguise, at least basically a member of the same kind of club. What he seeks from his métier is the kind of power-sex ethic we have been discovering in the presentational structure of this book, but the qual-

101

ity of his possession of the ethic is influenced by the fact that he obtains his sexual satisfaction through his possession of power, whereas Querelle achieves his sense of power through his careful exploitation of his sexual potential and attraction for people like Mario. In brief, Mario's function—this word *function* will become of very crucial importance in Genet's theatre—depends on Querelle's existence as a criminal, and the sexual pleasure he seeks to derive from the exploitation of his function depends on Querelle's willingness to cooperate. It is this Querelle recognizes as, in the process of bringing Mario to orgasm, he hears him screaming out exaggerated claims about the important function he serves in society. Mario has duped himself into believing that Querelle's willingness to bring him to sexual climax is an indication of his superiority over Querelle and the likes of him. But he gives himself away; his cries bring Querelle to the realization that it is *he,* Querelle de Brest, who is the indispensable agent of Mario's pleasures. With this discovery, the privileged position of the police chief disintegrates and is carried away with the other debris of convention, for Querelle has learned that fellation is not a debasement for the person who performs it. It is his moment of triumph, since the passive partner could not have his pleasure were it not for the consent of the active partner. Fellation—and this is an incisive insight on Jean-Paul Sartre's part—can be the homosexual's most pertinent act of revenge on the world. The situation which results from this exposé implies that what Querelle seeks from Mario is very much an analogue to what Genet is seeking from his reader.

Along with most of the other people in this book, Mario lacks the combined assurance and detachment into which Querelle grows; or, in a more complicated register, the assurance he does possess, and which is given him by his function, is an assurance that is ultimately not enough to blind Querelle to the deeper realities. Mario may not know how precarious his assurance is; but Querelle does and so, too, does the reader, though he may not be quite so overjoyed about it as is Querelle. This introduction of detachment is a strange kind of surprise and, as I have indicated, has curious consequences, one of which is the privilege it confers on those who possess it. They seem to win their right to it by a frank admission of the connections that exist between the thirst for power and the need of sexual fulfillment. And so the most real people are Querelle and, in the closing pages of the book, Madame Lysiane. They are real—with all the rewards that brings them—because they do not seek to whitewash the truer interests of humanity. They have had the courage to look at the world coldly and objectively; indeed, they manage ultimately to look at themselves in the same way. And seeing that they are no different from others, and that others share their own desires, they project themselves onto a lofty promontory from which the view may not be strikingly beautiful but on which they experience the heady, dizzying, power-begetting sensation of knowing that, alone among mortals, they have reached this particular summit.

The way up the mountain is, of course, one many would not be interested in following. Not simply because the way to the heights passes first through some rather seamy depths (the depths of ourselves or of what we are being told about ourselves), but because we are being asked to accept discursive conclusions on the basis of a quite nondiscursive kind of presentation, the kind of presentation suggested by the passage already cited above: "To the idea of the sea and of murder is added the idea of delight and *natural* love—rather of *unnatural* love." The man of reason, in his most generous moments, can hardly be expected to or even want to understand this kind of statement; the best he can do is observe the movement within Genet's mind which makes such statements possible, as well as the kind of empirical data Genet includes within the circle of his book to verify his conclusions. Aesthetically, the man of reason can note the parallel violent yoking together: if the sea is associated with murder, then there is no reason why delight cannot be associated with unnatural love. Such aesthetic assent, however, is connected primarily with a recognition of stylistic usage and not truth.

This development of images is not the exfoliating sort one has grown accustomed to expect in Western poetry, where a basic metaphor—Rimbaud's *bateau ivre,* for example—moves out of imagery into symbol by a slow, expanding process. With Genet images do not develop into symbols but rather into explanations which result from a kind of leapfrogging. One of these hopping movements is observable in the text cited above; another has already been mentioned in connection with the equation he establishes between convict uniforms and flowers in the opening pages of *Journal du voleur.* It seems an arbitrary process, but the arbitrary is saved from complete anarchy or playfulness by two things. First of all, there is the simple if startling fact that leapfrogging strikes Genet as a quite seemly way of getting at truths; secondly, there is for him the reality of this kind of procedure. It is not something he alone indulges in, but something he has observed elsewhere in life and which plays a quite important functional role in *Querelle de Brest.*

Querelle's gnawing hunger for self-abasement after the murder depends upon this kind of leaping connection. This is an easier kind of dilemma, however, which could be explained by the simple presence of various kinds of compulsions within one human being. Other connections —those which to the man of reason seem to disfigure reality—fit more tightly into the kind of procedure I am describing. One of the young criminals in the book persists in seeing one of his comrades as a kind of mirrored image of that comrade's sister whom he loves. Madame Lysiane is convinced that a young accomplice of Querelle is in reality the child produced by the love which exists between Querelle and his brother, a love whose reality exists only in the mind of Madame Lysiane, but which none the less drives her to verifying that there is really a difference between the two brothers: the dimensions of their sexual organs. Querelle at the end of the book would like to immerse in crime all those he has possessed, and who have possessed him, so that they might love only *à travers lui*. Madame Lysiane, in order to feel sure of herself after an argument, is compelled to step into her high heels. Others might call these sorts of observations the illusions of life, all the while recognizing the crucial importance of such illusions; but, for Genet, they are life's core realities, its hardest truths, its most revelatory facts. The illusions come when we seek to disguise them and replace their essential disorder with our violently imposed order. That Madame Lysiane calls her brothel a *maison d'illusions* is a sign of the extent to which the more authentic realities are her special possession. She becomes a great Ur-figure, a kind of Mother Earth whose tenacity in the face of willful contradictions is the substance of life, for this kind of insight is indeed what holds life together; she is the muse, if you will, who in her couplings with Querelle is the symbol of Jean Genet, *criminel,* of Jean Genet, *écrivain.* That she is somewhat inarticulate in her first incarnation here in *Querelle de Brest* is significant perhaps only of how bumbling and uncertain are all first couplings. When the myth that she is appears in *le Balcon* under another name, it will have become more sure of its own terms and the mission it is preaching. And it will have become thus assured because the imagination of its creator will by the time of this deft and dazzling play have no hesitations over its powers.

At the end of *Querelle de Brest*, Lysiane has learned a bitter lesson: there can be no compromise with one's uncluttered vision of reality. In the direction of her brothel she had most customarily kept her eyes unblinded by her own emotions—until she had become involved with Querelle and his brother. From the brother she has learned the dangers of insertion into the ethic, for he has made her suffer, has debased her, and then turned her aside. From Querelle she has learned that her earlier instincts were her better: one must remain outside the dynamic in order to profit most generously from its existence. As a result she watches his departure with melancholy: "Madame Lysiane learned painfully but thoroughly that it was thanks to Querelle that she, like Mario and Nono, had emerged from the solitude in which his departure would now plunge them once again. He had appeared in their midst with the speedy promptness and the elegance of a joker" (clandestine ed., p. 249). Frustration results; she is not quite sure how to face the future and win back her former assurance. In the clandestine edition we last see her defeated; in the rearranged Gallimard edition we last see her angry, turning toward fantasy in order to wreak her vengeance on those who have hurt her. We leave her thus, as a character in this book, to find her in another, more sophisticated and wiser incarnation in *le Balcon*. And, as we leave her, undecided, angry, and annoyed, we have in mind the contrast of Querelle's departure (p. 317):

Querelle had tamed the forces of the night. He had managed to familiarize himself with all the shadowy expressions, to populate those shady areas with the most dangerous monsters he bore within himself. Then, with exhalations of breath from his nostrils, he had conquered them. Now the night, though she was not yet entirely his, was tamed. He had grown accustomed to living in the repugnant company of his crimes, keeping a ledger of them in small format—a ledger of the massacres which to himself alone he called "the bouquet of flowers grown midst the cobblestones." This ledger contained the layout of the places where those crimes had taken place. The drawings were primitive. Whenever he did not know how to draw an object, Querelle named it, and sometimes the spelling was faulty. He had not had any education.

> . . . even to knock off an
> Infidel one has to engage in
> such theatrical labor that one
> cannot be both actor and
> director.
>
> —*les Paravents*

Genet and the Theatre

The paragraphs prefatory to the picaresque adventures of Querelle had suggested, indeed had asserted, with all the affirmative spirit found in declarations of war, that what the reader was to encounter was a *drama* whose presentation was justified by the existence, within the author, of a striking tendency to make rather unusual discoveries and even more startling connections between apparently dissimilar phenomena. In the existence of this kind of internal-external tension, there is something that, if not essentially dra-

108

matic, will surely achieve its most convincing or imposing presentation when translated into the rhetoric of the stage. The limits of narrative prose presentation—the most striking being probably its association with traditional logical expositions, prose being the vehicle for reasoned-out explanations—must gradually make themselves felt and suggest the need for the utilization of new forms. So long as Genet remained locked within this particular cage, identified as it usually is with a certain manner of exposition, he would be restricted to struggling with sentences and paragraphs in order to present something which is fundamentally dramatic in a form where the drama might or might not make itself felt despite the broad hints contained in a punned title. But he would also be using an inappropriate form when a better one was easily within reach. What he needed—and the need is expressed in his first narrative work—was a form that would allow him what he calls "the logic of the stage" (*Notre-Dame-des-Fleurs,* p. 6), where, by the simple presentation of juxtaposed forces, he could give them the reality he thinks they have in life.

We have already noted several of these juxtapositions; indeed, we have seen how very much the juxtaposition of opposites is a commonplace to Genet, because he believes it to be the most characteristic note of the way men look at, approach, and live out their experience. But the habits of narrative and especially narrative reading (which allow the reader to stop and argue with the author) are bound to compromise the power of the simple prosaic presentation of such juxtapositions, no matter how much ardor may be brought to it. The reader whose eyes spot a sentence which declares that Querelle felt himself a black among whites (p. 230), but only because of a delicately applied make-up, may readily feel that the realm of nonsense is without boundaries; but the spectator who goes into a theatre where Negroes wear white masks in order to become more deeply involved in a dialectic with other Negroes will have before his eyes a reality with which (or with whose consequences) he must either live or else come to terms. He may not like the basic idea, may even condemn it; but the fact is that he has a quite physical image presented to him during a measurable moment in time, in a place of some ceremony. However reluctant the spectator may be to dismiss his hostility, all these things combine to make him come to grips with what is meant by this kind of dramatic usage. Quite the same imposing quality can be conferred on other actions that, in the limits of narrative, might strike us as silly or easily forgettable. That Madame Lysiane puts on shoes after an indelicate argument, the better to assure herself of her superiority, may also seem silly; but if Madame Lysiane were to appear on the stage—as do the judge, bishop, and general of *le Balcon*—in buskins, towering over all the other actors as well as the audience, she would create an impressive physical presence and, probably, given a basic amount of visual impressionability among the spectators, make her or the author's point.

This kind of graphic exploitation of the strange kind of reality that is the theatre—we sit still in order to observe the actions of others that become, to the extent we are moved by those actions or merely attentive to them, *our* action—is a commonplace. Still, starting with Plato's original objections, it has become one of the persistent enigmas haunting the Western imagination's discursive tendencies. And it is an enigma which produces potential conflicts, if only because a theatre-goer can, if he chooses, resist what he sees and hears. Some commentators on the Broadway theatre resort to this explanation in seeking to find reasons why the vaporous triumphs so readily

in the commercial theatre: it makes no demand, changes
no point of view, insinuates no unpleasantness, and therefore spares the spectator all anger and opposition. Richard Rodgers and Samuel Taylor's *No Strings* may deal
with miscegenation, but somehow the problems of miscegenation seem eminently solvable if the young Negro
woman who is involved is garbed in a wardrobe that
costs tens of thousands of dollars. The challenging play
offers no comparable ease, primarily because it makes
indifference and inattention difficult if not impossible. A
theatre-goer might resist its stimulation but, in doing so,
he becomes like the man who, detesting Martinis, orders
one so as not to drink it and thereby show that he is a
man endowed with independent judgment.

Since theatre-going is a kind of social discourse it
would seem to demand the politeness of audience attention. But since impoliteness can exist on both sides of the
footlights, the audience cannot be expected to exercise
unilateral good manners. It is here that Plato's objections
find their source. The register of his complaints is that of
a man who has been insulted in his intelligence; any
Broadway theatre-goer who has been exposed to some
of the commercial theatre's more strident vulgarities
(Menotti's *The Saint of Bleecker Street,* for example)
would tend to agree with Plato, though possibly for different reasons. What we are confronted with in this case,
however, are objections based on the insufficient challenge of the work, not objections based on the power of
the work to unsettle. It is in this area of choice between
keeping the theatre static and making it dynamic that
the enigma exists most powerfully, for once the theatre
is unbridled it is liable to go anywhere. What is novel in
Genet is his awareness of the value to be derived from
deliberate exploitation of such unbridled tendencies. In
his early plays we notice his conviction that the confu-

sion of levels of reality on the stage is only a mirroring of the truest aspects of his reality. That the stage allows one to strew and scatter indiscriminately thoroughly disjointed, disparate, and contradictory images is no cause for lamenting; rather one should rejoice that there is a form still capable of reflecting certain aspects of the chaos which oftentimes characterizes personal and common experiences.

The image-creating potential of the theatre is really only one aspect of a vastly more important function it can perform: ritual. From the very start of his career as a playwright, it is this ritual quality which fascinates and emboldens Jean Genet. In *Haute Surveillance* the public dimension of this search for ritual is quite severely restricted, because *Haute Surveillance,* like the earlier narrative works, is very much an inner dialogue, yet another prelude to the development of assurance. Here again Genet is not confident of his right to carry on dialogue outside the underworld, and so he limits the extension of his play to meditations on the meaning of crime for criminals. The dramatic conflict here never leaves the stage or, more precisely, never leaves the actors. It is still theatre we attend, not theatre in which we are supposed to participate. That it is ritual is quite clear, but the ritual is limited to the professional side of the footlights. The argument is among the actors, and we can leave the theatre refreshed or depressed but still able to feel that we have been somewhat removed from the proceedings; we have been spectators and not participants.

Genet, of course, is in no way removed from the proceedings. In *Haute Surveillance* we again have argument over the significance of individual actions; again we have the kind of movement in which the work of literary art, now turned toward drama, is used to argue through to explanations of why one is what one is. Yeux-Verts, in the action of the play, comes to understand what he is, why he is this thing. Equipped with this understanding, able to reflect its limited light against the lesser lights of his cellmates, he reaches out toward a limited apotheosis. But he will learn this because of the play, and in the play he will teach the others *on the stage* why it is he is superior to them. To Lefranc, who has tried to assume his role, Yeux-Verts makes the following comment: "And I danced . . . I took the steps that started easing me to the guillotine. Now I'm calm" (p. 132). The dance, of course, is the action of the play; the ritual is the external manifestation of what up to now has been, in the mind of Yeux-Verts, inchoate and inarticulate; the understanding is the product of the dance become ritual and, indeed, the ritual has taken place only because understanding was being sought. The basis of the understanding is the fact of the dance, so that the dance is not merely the movement expressed in the play, it is also a representation of a moment of liberation in life. This seems to come in unexpected moments when the tracked and oppressed spirit realizes that those who pursue and bear down on it are unjust and wrong. With this realization there comes a sense of deliverance and joy, the sort of thing Querelle experienced at the moment he learned that his subjugation to the police chief had really been a triumph. In the most recent New York production of *Haute Surveillance,* the moment in which Yeux-Verts dances emerged as a moment in which he is trying to explain to his cellmates what the past experience of discovering one's real value and place in the world was; the production caught this well for, as the actor's movements intensified, the two other actors became involved in the dance in the most appropriate way—by providing an accompaniment for it.

Behind all this is Genet, the *early* Genet, expressing

the same kind of preoccupations found in *Notre-Dame-des-Fleurs* and *Miracle de la rose,* preoccupations designed to give form to his nostalgic desire to assert some claim on eternity for the criminals he has loved and admired. It is important to note, however, that in the process of embodying the nostalgia the movement from interior apprehensions to exterior expression of certain truths is already taking puissant shape. The conclusion Yeux-Verts comes to is not the sentimental summation one might have expected: *I have, though a voyou, been loved, admired and envied.* Instead it is a strong, aggressive assertion: *I have learned to live with the horror that is within me and it is because of this courage that you* (the "you" here being not us but other, lesser criminals) *envy me and desire to be what I am.* Here the theatre has a certain therapeutic function, expressed in another of Yeux-Verts' speeches (pp. 161–62):

> Lefranc: I want to be let alone. I want everyone to let me alone! I wanted to become what you were . . .
>
> Yeux-Verts: What we are in spite of ourselves. And what I wanted to destroy by dancing.

The hesitation, the twinge of dissatisfaction in the last line might become a locus of perplexity for the spectator were it not, too, dissolved by the end of the play. By the time the curtain falls the theatre has moved out of its limited therapeutic role into the more important role of explaining things to us. Genet may have begun his play cautiously, saying "we are playing tragically, but we are playing none the less"—but he ends it with one of those strange, pregnant resonances he uses so diabolically in order to seduce his audience. The guard says (p. 142): "You still don't know what a guard is. In order to learn (he points to Yeux-Verts) you've got to be in his boots."

He thus suggests that this play and its statement are preliminary to something that will come later. We may not
be able to understand Yeux-Verts because we are not
in his position, nor in the position of the guard; but in
the later plays, when the guard moves off the stage in
order the better to persuade us, we shall be brought into
this situation and taught to realize that it is ours, too,
though we may be possessed neither of Yeux-Verts' honesty nor of his courage.

We will be brought to this point because of the change
that takes place in Genet. Between the intellectual mood
of *Haute Surveillance* and the later plays, Genet strips
himself of anything that suggests either the apologist or
the pariah. Practice has led him to believe in his perfection and our imperfections; the arguments of *Haute
Surveillance* convince no one quite so profoundly as they
convince Genet himself. As a result his sense of personal
authority will become the source of his increasing audacity. One has the impression of something awakening in
him one day to say: *how persuasive it all is, how very
believable.* Having said this, he can begin to apply his
energies to the examination of the relationship between
his accomplishments and the greater human questions
and make the sudden leaps of which I have already
spoken, not the least of which is Genet's conviction that
God is nothing more than the courtroom of his imagination. From the bench of this courtroom Jean Genet will
make judgments on the merit or demerit of all actions
(*Journal du voleur,* p. 261). What leads him to the
theatre, then, is an inevitable progress within his imagination; arrived there, his judicial eye surveying the stage
and the auditorium, he will define an apparently new
and yet quite ancient theatrical canon.

Henceforth he will use the stage to break down the
possible separation that exists between it and the specta-

tor. The spectator will no longer be called upon to watch the play; he will be asked to become involved with it. The bad notions of theatre he has picked up will be progressively destroyed; no longer will he be allowed to watch what is happening, but rather he will be seduced, very gradually and without immediate pleasure, into realizing how closely he is involved with what is being presented for his entertainment, into knowing that the unpleasant actions brought before his eyes are brought there so that he may see himself better. The theatre is to become a symbol, a vibrant symbol, and from its vitality the spectator will derive a presentation of startling, shocking dimensions, the most startling of which will be his awareness, when the ritual is over and the lights dimmed, that he has been looking in a mirror. The therapy Yeux-Verts sought in his dance, the therapy Genet sought in writing of that dance will now be extended to the general public in what is surely the most unbenevolent act of generosity this side of Freud. The actors will be only the agents of a vast theatrical metaphor of quite unmetaphorical real situations. The purpose of that metaphor will be to strip away the false natures we have assumed and bring us back to an understanding of our true nature. The tone is no longer simply incantatory; it has become tough and aggressive. Beneath the aggression there is a mixture of anger and the snickering laughter of the practical jokester.

The most systematic presentation of Genet's ideas on the theatre can be found in the letter which follows the text of *les Bonnes* in the Isère edition (pp. 142–48). It is a valuable text because, though it does not take into consideration the latest developments in his sense of the theatre, it gives a remarkably clear presentation of what drew him to the theatre in the first place. In a rather typical passage he writes (p. 114): "I tried to obtain a rupture which, while allowing for a declamatory tone, would bring the theatre to the theatre. I hoped in this way to obtain the abolition of the characters—who ordinarily hold up only because of lingering psychological conventions—to the advantage of signs which initially would be as far removed as possible from what they should signify, but none the less connected to those later significances in order thereby to forge the single link between the author and the spectator. In short, what I wanted was to bring about a situation where the characters would no longer be anything but a metaphor for what they were supposed to represent." This desire is, of course, quite in conformity with his definition of symbol as a device which allows the bearer of meaning to efface himself before the emerging meaning, so that he loses individuality in order to become only significance. So with the theatre: it will demand that the characters, initially appearing on the stage as what they are, will in the process of playing their roles cease to be actors and become recognizable forces, real forces imposing their presence in the spectator's imagination. Genet's anger is a mixture of personal rage over the infelicities of his life and artistic pique over the insufficient use to which the theatre has been put. His joke is that he will pretend to play along with the conventions only in order to make the conventions cease to be their normal selves and become what he wishes them to be.

At this point a reader or, more respectably, our trusty man of reason, might legitimately ask why, despairing in so Olympian a manner of our ability to understand ourselves and thus to understand him and his world, Genet bothers to let us in on the scabrous secrets he has discovered. Surely a mantle of the most profound and brilliant scepticism would better garb this particular pose; surely detachment rather than polemic would be the most noble of gestures for this man who dotes so on gestures and believes so firmly that there can be no communication between him and us. Like so many other aspects of Genet, this question of communication is a robe of many colors, the more violent of which are kept infolded until his latest works. In *les Nègres,* for example, there is no question that something is being communicated to us, even if it be nothing more than a muddy message designed, as Marc Pierret has suggested, to let us know that, unlike the central figures in this incantatory play, we can have only a nostalgia for a world in which communication takes place and has meaning. The realm of true communication has been usurped by the Genets and the blacks of the world, not because they have won any sort of pitched battle, but principally because they, unlike us, understand the terms of the battle.

That we must be informed of this kind of thing in order to understand what it is we are missing out on is more than evident; that this kind of transfer of attitude is none the less communication remains quite another problem altogether. Georges Bataille would resolve it by pointing out that Genet, because he argues, is really quite incapable of communicating or even knowing what communication is. And, Bataille says, his loss of the ability to communicate goes beyond argument; it is brought about because Genet's limitless addiction to evil deprives him of any vocabulary which could be considered common coin and therefore negotiable. If, as Bataille suggests further, there is some connection between dialogue and communication, between analysis and statement, then the preaching of Genet is hardly a two-way street. It leaves us as it necessarily must have found us, willing victims who agree to be shouted at for unannounced

118

measures of time. For Bataille—and other readers will agree or disagree with *him* on the basis of their experience and their interest in disinterested generosity—this not only is not communication, it is not literature either, despite the frenzy with which Genet proclaims his own *poétique* and the strange sacral character he claims for this *poétique*.

This frontal attack, which begins to assume force, drive, and thrust only after Genet has become a figure of some public importance and notoriety, is also a change for Genet. The voice of the plays is not the voice of the early works; it changes as Genet's imagination changes, and where there might have been a note of supplication in the early prose, a note that is even more pronounced in the wretched poems he has written, that note is gradually silenced by the noise created by the trumpets of Genet's assurance. But no matter what notes may have been sounded at what moment, the movement toward the final strident voice has always been monotonously in the same direction, away from us and into the comforts of an imagined world. In *Notre-Dame-des-Fleurs* we may have been left a certain liberty to imagine what we might like; but the cadence there was hesitant and ironic (p. 56): "I leave you to imagine the dialogue. Choose whatever may charm you." In words like this we are still left some authority, an authority that, despite the irony Genet brings to speaking about it, remains a force in his life, though it has some very queer consequences. In *Journal du voleur,* for example, he writes (p. 72): "In order that the rupture with your world would be less brutal I used to wear trousers under my skirt."

Mockery is frequently born of reluctant respect or modified fear; at its worst it is silly, at its best, bellicose. But the moment of combat in Genet's mockery is rather short-lived, not because he moves into silliness (though

119

some might decide that ultimately this is precisely what he does), but because he finds a podium which allows him to hoist himself to an even higher position than the one possessed by the things he mocks. This is a curious kind of Operation Bootstrap, principally because it seems to follow the same kind of dynamic we have observed in the growth of his imagination into the authoritative source for his statements about reality, indeed as the sole corroborating principle verifying the presentation of a highly private universe. But in the movement from despairing of his audience to deriding it, Genet is propelled by something beyond his energetic imagination. He is propelled also by his recognition of certain qualities characteristic of modern art.

His sudden fascination—the vocabulary he expresses it in is full of the only nonsexual wonder he seems capable of—with the work of the sculptor Alberto Giacometti gives us testimony of this recognition. Genet's reaction to Giacometti's work goes well beyond the not too uncommon impact of an artifact on an individual; what he finds in these rough-hewn sculptures is something of greater consequence than the simpler aesthetic norms. He finds in them a new kind of ontology, for in order to have their impact they must presuppose an inherent power to bring the viewer away from the limiting data of his known world in order to insert him in a new world where all experience will be novel if not refreshing, informative if not satisfying. The problem of communication must necessarily, in this kind of world, be removed from the register sought by Georges Bataille. Since the world is new to us, since the object is an imposing mystery, we must necessarily be on the receiving end of whatever messages are being delivered.

This sort of operation is new neither with Giacometti nor with Genet; certainly something akin to it was in the mind of Jarry when he limned the strident cadences of *Ubu-Roi* to become the father of a proliferating progeny. That it is not new has, of course, nothing to do with its importance in understanding Genet and the impact of his work. Once he realizes that the work of art is not simply the locus for an aesthetic experience (measurable in terms of other aesthetic experiences) but may very well be transformed into a thoroughly new kind of experience, he has discovered something quite essential to the success of the mission which is becoming ever more clear in his mind—a means to destroy the viewer's place in history in order to bring him significantly in contact with something far outside the data absorbed from that place in history (*l'Atelier*, p. 34). This is the first part of his discovery, and it is easily within our grasp. We have only to look at Reg Butler's sculpture of the Unknown Political Prisoner, or Henri Matisse's faceless personages to be brought to a level of perception formerly unknown to us but immediately available and appropriate. It gives us, as it were, the perspective we needed in order to understand what before was obscure to the point of nonexistence. The second part of his discovery is a good deal more tricky. What Genet seems to have seen is that there are elements of experience which, because they are generally ignored by *us,* can be made to have the same kind of impact as the artifacts of Giacometti. In other words, there are phenomena of experience which can be presented in such a way as to bring about the same kind of nude moment in which the moved viewer is simultaneously stripped of his usual information and assurance to become a victim to the presentation of the phenomenon.

This is what was happening in *Querelle de Brest,* where the apparent sources of power were uncovered in all their artificiality and nonreality. Nono and Mario, thinking themselves the aggressive, superior males, learned in the moment of Querelle's departure that it was actually he who governed the world. While *Querelle de Brest* represented an advance of a kind over *Pompes funèbres,* in that it managed to place the problem outside of Genet's autobiographical experience, it had one serious limitation. Its examination of the true forces in the world could very readily have been taken as an examination of forces visible only in the underworld, among the dispossessed of society. The problem of generalizing the situation so that it can be applied to all—the decent and the indecent—is the one Genet must now work with.

The convergence of his two observations when confronted with Giacometti's sculpture—that they have an inescapable impact and that his own personal experience can be organized so as to have the same sort of universally applicable impact—gives him the beginnings of a solution. An early manifestation of that convergence can be seen in the striking radio conference Genet never got to broadcast, *l'Enfant criminel.* He says at the outset of this minor declaration of social war: "To the mystery that you are, I must oppose and unmask the mystery of the children's prison" (p. 153). The common, and even the uncommon run of men might have expected, in a talk concerned with juvenile delinquency, to have heard sociological patter bolstered by an appeal to us to change our patterns of behavior. Instead we are offered a confident statement of love and all-out admiration for these young criminals in whom is found an almost instinctive rejection of our false society. I am not now concerned with the social value of Genet's statement but rather with its aesthetic value. Here we are in a register of shock, but it is shock encountered at that critical moment, already alluded to, when the little boy scribbling obscenities on the pavement suddenly defies us instead of scurrying off under the scorn of our frowns. He defies us knowing fully what he is doing, happily aware that the impact of his remarks will go beyond shock and become perhaps a disturbed revelation—the kind of revelation we sometimes feel when confronted with a painting by Bosch or, in a more contemporary and perhaps analogous vein, the music of Edgard Varèse, whose sirens and horns and typewriters are designed to remind us that these rather than the melodies of Mozart are *our* truest music.

Genet himself seems more enthralled with the aesthetic dimensions he can give to his analysis of the juvenile criminal than with any objective analysis of the possible range of motives behind such delinquent activities. It is, after all, quite possible that some youthful delinquents are the result solely of broken homes, social unsettlement, and the other situations so frequently cited by contemporary behavioral scientists. And, if they are, it isn't going to do them a great lot of good to be told that they are really manifestations of a novel structure discovered by meta-social criticism. What Genet is interested in is the artifactual information he reads into (or better, out of) this segment of experience. He talks of these criminals, of whose blessed congregation he is a member in very good standing indeed, as the "resistant matter without which there would be no artists" (*l'Enfant criminel,* p. 167). Once this bridge between the "matter" of his imagination and the clay with which men like Giacometti work has been established, the challenge of a new kind of artistic endeavor can be offered. He writes (p. 170):

> [The young criminal] is about to offer you a bit of majesty which he is able to obtain from a more solemn session where he will appear in secret while

you continue, under his eyes, to play your childish games. For a time, familiarity may lead you to pinch his cheek, chuck him under the chin—that is, if you've no fear of being accused, not of paternal indulgence, but of the most abominable sentiments.

Our little boy scribbling on the sidewalk has decided not to run away from our disapproval; he stays there and looks insolently at us. And as our disapproval turns to compassion and we reach out to show that we understand his problems and want to help him, he raises his thumb to his nose and threatens to call the police lest we molest him. Here we have the terms of Genet's theatre; its purpose, expressed with equal resonance: "I want to insult the insulters." If this is not communication, its goal is none the less clear.

That there is a very conscious desire to deceive underpinning this communication or goal indicates only that the deception is an essential quality of the communication being sought. And the purpose of this kind of communication is precisely to deceive in order the better, the more profoundly to shock. On a primitive level this desire is part of the sort of involvement Genet tries to create by accusing us of having grown so interested in his work as to be unable any longer to deny it its particular kind of validity (*le Funambule,* p. 87). This kind of accusation is closely connected to the nature of the benefits he seeks from the involvement. Having won us, however grudgingly, to his side, exploiting whatever vile devices he has at his disposal (our interest in and fascination with the scatological and pornographic), he can accomplish not only a record of his experiences and their possible range of meaning, but he can also enlarge his experiences, seeking in them even more extensive and all-embracing meanings. We get something more than

124

a hint of this in *Journal du voleur* when he writes (p. 87):
"None the less I would never reject this most monstrous
of my sons. I want to fill the world with his abominable
progeny." We are, of course, still living through moments
of challenge and thus incertitude in these citations.
Through the sounds of defiance, though they grow ever
more strident and assured, there can be heard a counterpoint of guilt—perhaps it is only an echo from an imposed structure of values, *our* values to be sure, which
has not yet been toppled. But, to the extent that defiance
and the hints of guilt it evokes can be transformed into a
grudge, eloquently and elegantly expressed, the defiance
will disappear and the guilt will be transferred from him
to us.

That there is reason for a grudge is clearly seen in
les Bonnes, a more sophisticated if not a more dramatically imposing play than *Haute Surveillance.* Here the
levels of deception are designed simply to reproduce the
kinds of confusion we coddle within ourselves in order,
by our confusion, to show our scorn and indifference for
those classes or functions in society with which we have
no sympathy. All this, our indifference and the reaction
of those to whom we are indifferent, however magnani-
mously, is summed up in the basic dramatic structure of
the drama where two maids play at the relationship that
exists between them and their mistress—in her absence,
of course. Claire, who is pretending to be the mistress,
says to her maid-sister (p. 72): "Claire or Solange you
annoy me—yes, I always get you mixed up, Claire or
Solange—but you annoy me and drive me to anger.
Because it's you I blame for all our misfortunes." The
sophistication here, while it represents a significant advance on Genet's part toward overweening confidence,
is principally technical. We are in a rather somber fun-
house looking at people who are gazing into distorting

125

mirrors and experiencing a shock which is compromised out of its full severity by the recognition of the distortion, of the bad knowledge grown from the suspicion that the distortion may in some way be meant to involve us.

When sophistication both of idea and form is reached, it is attained because Genet, with two plays to his credit, has become a vastly more practiced artist and dramatist, increasingly possessed of a sure and quite natural dramatic instinct. The experience of having written *les Bonnes* and fought over the manner of its presentation with various producers seems to have allowed him to make a most important connection between *his* desire to deceive his audience and his awareness that deception has always played an important and complex role both in the better works of the Western dramatic imagination and, more importantly, in the method used to present these plays so as to profit from conscious deception.

Much of this is implied, when not raucously stated, in a curious little text called *le Funambule,* a kind of invocation-evocation of a clown and his function in society. For Genet the most basic aspect of that function is the link the clown establishes between his body and the idea he seeks to express by using it (p. 192). To the extent that he uses it in order to create an identity possibly different from his own, and to the extent that he imposes the idea on his audience, he has succeeded in impersonating an idea the audience otherwise would not have known. Genet calls the establishment of this kind of relationship dance; one has only to think of the kind of ideological commitment Martha Graham announces through her dances to understand how perceptive and pertinent his idea is.

There is, of course, a difference. Miss Graham's choreography presupposes a conception fully developed before the curtain rises, so that she offers us a point of view from the very start and a clearly artistic presentation. What she is doing in *Clytemnestra* and *Phaedra* is expressing certain forces in terms of dance because dance can place them within an incisive perspective. In plays like *Haute Surveillance* and *le Balcon,* Genet is creating the point of view because of a moment of dance that has taken place before. One dances in his theatre to express this earlier moment of dance—which is the moment of revelation, within experience, of a man's liberation from his own limitations or the limitations imposed upon him by his ambience. One dances in Miss Graham's theatre in order to express an interpretation of an already closely established relationship. On the basis of this it is obvious that Miss Graham's notion of dance is a more directly aesthetic one than that of Genet, for whom dance represents the instinctive rhythm of life and not its imprisonment within formal movement. Dance is the moment of release and, as such, it is a preliminary to his theatre, where its use will become part of the larger rhythm of ritual or ceremony.

Genet's interest in the clown goes beyond this kind of basic observation. Despite certain sexual extensions he mentions, his basic concern turns on the devices that go into the embodiment of the idea, the preliminaries, if you will, which are essential to the presentation and which explain so much about the muddier realities Genet is excavating below the fallow land of our conventions. The several means by which the clown embodies his ideas represent a mixture of the more fundamental realities and the more extreme artifices. If he wishes to elicit a sense of danger from the audience that watches him perform on a tightrope, he must be possessed of a perfect body and the completely assured control which would give either the necessary drama to his fall, were it to occur, or the appropriate éclat to his expected success. But even as the well-developed body and the assured technique are necessary, so, too, is the excessive make-up with its deliberate distortions of human features. Why? Possibly for two opposed reasons. First, the make-up can serve as the necessary distance factor between the spectators and the possibility of danger; at once a kind of protective coating which, because it suggests a fool, might also conceivably reduce the impact of any eventual catastrophe. If the clown falls and is killed, we will not have the idea that his is really a human presence; if a Negro is lynched we can console ourselves, if we are Southerners, with the knowledge that he is a stalled moment in the evolutionary process or, if we are Northerners, with the fact that it is the first lynching in ten years. The make-up is, then, a necessary sugar-coating over the basically dangerous nature of the performance. But when put to more pyrotechnic uses—as it will be in *le Balcon* and *les Nègres*—the make-up, secondly, can represent the line (whose finesse is never too easily determined) between our conscious and subconscious motivations, and so it can serve as the symbol of what separates us either from a firmer grasp of the more authentic elements of our experience or else from those sectors of human experience we pretend to abominate.

Though this may shock us—at best, because we are innocent; at worst, because we are in truth disturbed— and lead us to believe it represents something novel in the theatrical spectrum, it has a rather long and fairly distinguished history, so distinguished that it evokes for someone like Francis Fergusson the essence of the theatre. What may initially seem novel in Genet does so principally because, alien to his technique or else accustomed to its expression in other more familiar plays, we may not see beyond the surface of Genet's later theatre to its substance, with the result that we may be startled to think that there may be rapports between it and, say, a play like the *Oedipus*.

Yet the method of presentation in Sophocles' play, like the exploitation of deception, is structurally quite similar, albeit Genet's later variations aim at something far beyond simple questions of structure. In the Greek tragedy we are confronted with a protagonist of notable and recognized excellence, whose qualities seem to make him exemplary and to persuade us into the kind of admiration from which will grow our later sympathy. We are deceived, as indeed the hero is deceived, in order that we may be the more deeply involved at the moment of frightening revelation. To the extent that the method of presentation works, we will be somewhat personally involved in the downfall of the hero and, by a process of rather vague metonymy, will experience a certain downfall ourselves. We have identified our cause with Oedipus', have seen in him a fine expression of something we label—with an increasing absence of malaise as the play spins out its noble magic—our ideals, only to see all these things come tumbling down before our eyes, toppled by the force of fate, or what this age might call the recognition of deeper, more disturbing truths within us.

That we should be shocked by the use of a similar process in Genet's theatre is perhaps only a reflection of what has happened to our theatre, an expression of its impotence. The theatre—what academic mind ceases to lament it?—has become entertainment and, stripped of its power, is looked upon as little more than a diversion. That word, diversion, holds within it a trove of information, since it suggests precisely why it is the playwright of serious intention or even pretension (the thinking playwright, Eric Bentley calls him) must be distraught with the theatre of diversion. Instead of communicating with his audience he is asked to divert them, to distract them from what they might really be capable of thinking and what he might really need and be able to say. But the theatre as communication is equally poverty stricken, for communication demands a certain amount of common presumptions and common *propos* (one speaks more easily today, and more vaguely, of a consensus) that probably has not existed since the time of Shakespeare or Racine.

When the Greeks went to the theatre they knew what they were being told about or, more precisely, they had a frame in which to insert any new images. As a result they brought a sense of readiness with them, a sense of preparedness that was of incalculable value to the dramatist. He wrote for a known audience and could count on the audience's familiarity not only with the personages of his work but also with their significance. Euripides might shock, but he shocked because he as well as his audience knew the body of received ideas and could evaluate how far his interpretation strayed from established norms.

The contemporary playwright of ideas has been less fortunate, as the reaction to Archibald MacLeish's *JB* showed. Those who could look upon it without a firm memory of the Book of Job seemed to have come away with a somewhat more coherent experience than those who knew the Biblical Job and were unhappy with his transformation into a prosperous American businessman. But without a knowledge of Job one was prone to interpret the play in one's own way, and so it became a commonplace of cocktail party chatter in Manhattan to hear it being characterized alternately as a play of hope and a play of despair. It depended very much on whom you had chosen as a companion for your life—Zuss or Nickles.

Other solutions have been in their own way halfway

houses whose architecture is of varying merit. Brecht confuses and survives because he writes for an age which is willing to pluck from the nettle of confusion the flower of understanding (whose or what understanding remains another, frequently a personal question). Pirandello, with a delicate and persuasive imagination we can only admire, is none the less a persistent and somewhat monotonous propagandist for the theatre, and of his propaganda there was and still is need. He convinces his audience of the value of his imagination, but he establishes no dialogue with the spectator. If anything his plays are a meditational preparation, a school for dramatic understanding that may prepare the way for others.

What is most distinguished about Pirandello's plays is what is most distinguished about Ibsen and Strindberg: their honesty, their commitment to finding the courage necessary to face up to the stark and unrelieved vision of things their imagination offers them. It is precisely in this business of commitment that Pirandello seems stronger than Brecht, whose outlook, however harsh and analytic, is underpinned by optimism. Things are bad, very bad indeed, and Mother Courage knows it. But she carries on; and though, at the end of the play, she may not have got very far, she is still there, a bit battered and depopulated, but there none the less, holding on and looking confidently ahead. There would be nothing wrong with this if it were seen from another angle, the kind of angle Shakespeare uses in his plays, where there can be no misapprehension of the fact that those who bear the ideals of a society can be destroyed by that society or, more accurately perhaps, within that society and within the scheme of their own ideals. The great temptation of the modern theatre, even when it wishes itself serious, is to find some source, no matter how deep and dry, of consolation. The common man in Robert Bolt's *A Man for All Seasons* is there apparently to remind the audience that stalwart beings like Thomas More come to their unhappy end because the ordinary run of humanity are willing to close their eyes and allow evil to pass through their lives, hoping that silence and concentration on other things will keep them from the contagion. It is not a bad device; structurally it unsettles the audience and thus is efficient. But in the end, the common man is not made to feel abject. More treats him well, if ironically, and becomes a kind of benevolent Big Brother assuring us all that if our indifference is an evil, men of his stature can manage to arrive at dignity despite it and keep on loving us all the time.

Does Jean Genet promise a better, more honest situation? If nothing else he has the courage (or perhaps only the determination) to avoid the lesser consolations of the cheaper kinds of cheer. Intimately connected with this is his ability to see in certain theatrical conventions examples of the kind of useful cheerfulness he wishes to rid the theatre and humanity of. We have a most pertinent example of this in *les Nègres*. Genet wished his play to be presented as a minstrel show, thereby establishing one of those on-stage situations bound to appeal to a spectator's sense of familiarity. But in choosing this human décor he wanted to derive profit from that familiarity. A ministrel show is usually a pleasant experience; one feels safe at it because one knows that the exaggerated use of blackface has put the actors on the level of society's pariahs, and society's pariahs are not going to do anything dangerous or even insubordinate. Whatever insolence they demonstrate is not going to raise them out of their comparative abjection, and so the insolence can be readily borne. And, anyway, it is all pretense, because the Negroes really aren't Negroes at all, but only white men in disguise. We shall see later what Genet does with this sort of basic early comfort, how he uses it to turn his audience to grief, not the least bitter of which is the audience's realization that they or their forebears have fed him with the situation he uses as a point of departure. There is shrewdness here and cleverness; but these are not necessarily virtues, nor are they automatically forces capable of sustaining a full evening in the contemporary theatre, where spectators represent a vast range of divergent beliefs. It is here that Genet's contribution offers its biggest boon to the theatre.

If he does not spring—with the clarity literary historians like and, not finding, create—from Pirandello, he does represent a way of getting around the problem of creating ritual among those whose beliefs are divergent, simply because he preserves what the Greeks had —a sense of theatre as ceremony—and abandons what we can no longer possess, a common outlook. Not for him is the desire to speak with his audience about consciously shared beliefs or tendencies. He will show us the semblance of such beliefs in order, by showing them to us in this indelicate overcoating, to bring us closer to his idea of reality. It is here that he advances beyond Pirandello, who, for the most part, is limited to presenting his view of the multiple levels and depths of reality by expressing this multiplicity in terms of the old and worn-down conflict between art and reality. Genet needs no such antediluvian argument, since he has moved from reality into art as the result of a process which has convinced him that art allows the only way of expressing the complexity of reality. His theatre rediscovers ritual and its power, but the faithful, expecting a ceremony of the guaranteed innocence to which they have become habituated, find more often than not that they have been invited to assist at a Black Mass and, worse luck, that the blasphemy has been organized because it is, at the end of the day, what they wanted to assist at anyway. If the dramatist contaminates their innocence, Jean Genet reminds them, it is only because, true servant and faithful dramaturge, he knows that the innocence is feigned.

'Haute surveillance' and 'les Bonnes'

The kind of clinical interest a curious reader might have brought to Genet's prose works is dissipated by the dramatic thrust of *Haute Surveillance* and replaced by a kind of aesthetic sympathy. The playgoer becomes more directly involved in the suspense aspect of the drama than he ever became in the earlier writings. There is nothing especially remarkable about this since it is very much the trademark of even less adept playwrights. What is remarkable is the directness with which Genet accepts this form and, though he works clumsily with it at first, exploits it in order to establish a new kind of relationship with his audience. As I am suggesting, this kind of relationship is not yet what it will become in its boldest and noisiest moments. What *Haute Surveillance* manages to do is to involve the audience in the action on the stage, principally by arousing curiosity. Still, the establishment of the curiosity is a significant achievement, since it reduces the possibly pornographic quality of the earlier relationship. There is an arresting stage setting in which the whiteness of the light glares down as though to remind us disturbingly that the three participants are involved with basic, unavoidable questions which burn into them with luminous intensity. For Genet, however, the light has a different dimension. He writes (*Journal du voleur,* p. 12): "Jail is in the sun. It's under a cruel light that everything takes place, and I can't keep myself from choosing this as a sign of lucidity." Though a spectator would not know at the time that the light was to be seen as signifying something beyond a prison custom, he cannot avoid being impressed by the cruelty of this light, which shines constantly like a bad beacon into the lives of the cellmates. Another device, one of the oldest in dramatic literature, allows explanatory information to unravel slowly and thus enlists and holds the interest of the audience.

Haute Surveillance is not so much a whodunit as a why-did-he-do-it with the question of what it is he did hanging in variously significant imbalances. One's attention is arrested, a higher level of one's dramatic intelligence and appreciation is appealed to, and a kind of rhythm of transfer of information is established among those on the stage and between them and the audience. The result, then, is technically a conventional play, not very different from the plays of Eugene O'Neill or Jean Anouilh and, in the same way, not very different from

136

the plays of Samuel Beckett. What is to be revealed may lift veils from scenes, arguments, and discussions that are not within the experience of the spectator; but the revelation will be made through the dialogue among the participants and thus allow the spectator to involve himself or not in the reality or importance of what the actors say. And yet there is something more, something like a hesitating thrust toward a more direct involvement of the audience in the play. The setting in its starkness is meant to shock; the diction, highly stylized through the use of deliberate verbal gesture and speeches addressed directly to the audience, moves in a direction which will be even more notable in the later plays. The acting is marked by moments of great violence which contrast starkly with other moments, when everything comes to a halt in order to allow Yeux-Verts either to move back in time or else to establish that mysterious sacral element of his experience which sets him off under a halo of begrudged respect.

The basic intrigue, despite its dramatic interest, represents nothing essentially new in the canon of Genet's preoccupations. Indeed, many of the more recurring and therefore more fatigued clichés of his imaginings are here, accompanied by the persistent weakness he never overcomes—the gradual exhaustion of his imaginative fertility until it becomes repetitive argument. All the young criminals we meet in the play (and their youth is a thematic note, though Yeux-Verts, at 22, is a grand old man of this college of crime) are handsome, the only distinction in their beauty being the question of its relative intensiveness. They are all involved in seeking positions in a dangerously disordered hierarchy, where the security of the mighty is very perilous indeed, and where young men are always involved in efforts, either physical or "moral," to displace the higher and mightier. What happens in the play may best be summarized through the characters and their actions.

The central figure is Yeux-Verts (Green Eyes), a convicted murderer, 22 years old, big and beautiful (what else?), whose feet are chained because he is about to be either executed or shipped off to French Guiana. This is the result of his having killed a young girl he had seduced in what he claims was something of an *acte gratuit:* he had not been motivated to this particular kind of crime, but merely formed for it by the general misfortune in which he lived. Balancing the misfortune and the motivation, he comes to the conclusion that his crime had been an especially distinguished one because it had none of the pettier motivations of theft or mere sexual satisfaction. Mirroring Yeux-Verts' judgments is Maurice, 17, small and pretty. He was vividly interpreted in the 1962 New York production as a cat-like, effeminate youth who alternately flitted and slinked across the stage, conveying through his actions an unsettling sense that his fragility was not without its threats. In him we find again the presence of the unmistakable hero worship from which Genet suffered so often and which comprises some of the most touching and annoying passages of his initial works. It is the sort of situation which existed between Divine and Mignon in *Notre-Dames-des-Fleurs,* where Divine had no means of protest when replaced in Mignon's affections by Notre-Dame. In *Haute Surveillance,* however, the paths of hero worship can be shorter for, unlike the situation encountered in *Notre-Dame-des-Fleurs,* the victim can pass from disappointment over his loss into disgust over the erstwhile victor's own decline. The disgust, in its turn, can produce a kind of letdown as the victim watches his prestige falling away with that of his lover and must once again enter the scramble, so vividly presented in *Miracle de la rose,* to

re-establish himself at some firmer notch in the hierarchy of the underworld.

As *Haute Surveillance* begins, the paths of Maurice's
hero worship are reaching their end, because of his discovery of the growing power of Boule-de-Neige, a Negro
inmate who appears in the play only as a powerful outside force. As the play closes, Maurice, having seemed
to abandon Yeux-Verts with the discovery that Yeux-
Verts is in league with Boule-de-Neige, is killed by Jules
Lefranc, the other convict, whose persistent apocalyptic
pronouncements have been the sources of Maurice's information and dissatisfactions. The crisis of faith Maurice experiences is in the register of loss. He has gambled
the sense of his existence on his conviction that Yeux-
Verts is the best of men; the realization that Yeux-Verts
is leagued to Boule-de-Neige represents, for Maurice,
the destruction of Yeux-Verts' independence, since that
independence had earned him the accolade "best of
men."

Lefranc, 23, also big and beautiful, is the fulcrum of
the teeterboard relationship between Maurice and Yeux-
Verts. He is on the verge of being released from prison
where, in addition to repaying society for the crimes
done against its honor, he has served as a kind of corresponding secretary to the illiterate Yeux-Verts, in-
diting letters to Yeux-Verts' wife. In the opening scenes
of the play these letters become the source of tension
between him and Yeux-Verts, because Yeux-Verts is
convinced that Lefranc has used the letters in order to
wean the wife from her death-marked husband. To
justify himself and reassure Yeux-Verts, Lefranc is committed to killing the wife. The eventual consequences of
the promises are not so much of interest as the promise
itself; it is primarily an emanation of Lefranc's desire
not to sever himself from Yeux-Verts' friendship until

he is better able to determine Yeux-Verts' continuing value. So might a wavering Christian act before deciding on renunciation of his beliefs.

At this point Yeux-Verts goes off to have a visitor's hour with his wife; he returns to the cell with a changed mind. Understandably enough, this strikes Lefranc as being too much to take, and he accuses Yeux-Verts of being a fraud, capable only of maintaining his supposedly exalted position as the result of a sexual subservience to Boule-de-Neige. Dialectics ensue between the two men in which Yeux-Verts attempts to establish the extraordinary nature of his unmotivated crime, and dialectics have a rather somber day, since the power of Yeux-Verts' arguments pushes Lefranc to the murder of Maurice—a crime which is immediately stripped of its power by the realization that Lefranc has not acted without motivation but rather has sought his own glory in the murder of Maurice.

There are three distinct situations here or, better, three separate expressions of the same basic but evolving situation. In the first we find Maurice defending the interests of Yeux-Verts against the taunts of Lefranc, who has decided on a kind of interest-motivated alliance with the apparently more powerful Boule-de-Neige; during this first movement Lefranc's decision seems to derive added power from Yeux-Verts' attitude to his wife's supposed infidelity. The second situation develops during Yeux-Verts' absence (he is off on that visit to his wife), when Maurice tries to convince Lefranc that Yeux-Verts is indeed the best of men; his opinion is bolstered by that of the guard (young and good looking, no age given), who announces cryptically that Yeux-Verts is unquestionably the *mec* of *mecs*.

In the third situation the tables are turned both on Maurice and Lefranc, as the result of a kind of double play that establishes a common deception which neither of them has expected or intended—the revelation of the reconciliation between Yeux-Verts and his wife and of his alliance with Boule-de-Neige. This well-disguised union of two criminals, housed in different parts of the same prison, becomes the center of the alienation and deception of Lefranc and Maurice, though for different reasons. With a kind of bourgeois commitment to the importance of consistency and logic as well as the reality of appearances (surely his name must have some ironic significance), Lefranc has opted for the person who seems to be the more powerful, and he has been wrong. Maurice, unable to resist the persuasive impact of Lefranc's information, has sought to justify the gradual weakening of Yeux-Verts' pre-eminence by appeals to sentiment; but he, too, is wrong, because the real action of the play and thus the determining influence on Yeux-Verts' position is that secret alliance between him and Boule-de-Neige. In the end it is Yeux-Verts who triumphs, not merely because Maurice is murdered and Lefranc responsible for the murder, but more importantly because this sudden reduction of the other two men is the result of his coolness under pressure, his mastery of his criminal vocation. He alone survives; he alone has been the reality ✓ of the play. Maurice's hero worship is meaningless, and Lefranc's crime is robbed of its value because it has been committed for a specific purpose—to prove that he is capable of the same kind of crime as Yeux-Verts— and not as the result of something essential and characteristic deep in his being.

In all this we have the same preoccupations we have noted elsewhere in Genet: his commitment to the belief that the real criminal is a superior being, his conviction that "pure" crime results from a state of being imposed on the criminal by the place society accords him, and his rather special ideas of the value of treason and the traitor so long as the traitor and his treason manifest a special kind of control over reality and its less adept citizens. We see this through Yeux-Verts and through his planned deviousness in masking the liaison between himself and Boule-de-Neige. By not revealing these connections early in the play he deliberately deludes Maurice and Lefranc, but he deludes them in order that victory over them will be complete and exclusively his. *His* existence is thus consistent, and it is consistently triumphant; but it is thus only because the world dances to the tunes he pipes. Who pays for the piping is another, as yet unraised, question.

In his discussion of Genet's fascination with the criminal as a representative of a kind of superior being who wins his claim to superiority by the purity of his commitment, Jean-Paul Sartre suggests that this is only a manifestation of Genet's intention to revenge himself on society for the revenge society has taken on him. The terms of Sartre's discussion set themselves up in this way. Society, even as it punishes criminals, sees them as an incarnation of its own negative powers—its tendency toward evil, its desire, hidden and perhaps even subconscious, to live dangerously and disgracefully. In his career the criminal satisfies these subconscious needs, and newspapers and films are diligent in bringing criminal activities to the attention of the widest possible audience in vividly detailed terms. Genet wishes to reciprocate the gesture, and so he creates his criminals with heroic dimensions, establishing them as an ideal. As he contemplates the ideal, he not only glorifies what he would like to be but also gets his revenge on the society which has originally put him in such a situation.

In the early narrative works there can be no doubt that Genet's virile criminals are his heroes, described

lovingly and admiringly so that each of their powerful
traits will create a sense of gravity and beauty. With
Pompes funèbres there had been a movement away from
this admiration from afar and toward something which
struck Genet as more real, and because real, a firmer
and more enduring terrain on which to sow the seeds of
his protest. In the growth of his preoccupation with what
I have identified as the Hangman-Erik-Riton dynamic,
Haute Surveillance is vaguely at the same point of development as *Querelle de Brest*. Yeux-Verts has bypassed the inevitable replacement inherent in the dynamic, as his manipulation of Lefranc and Maurice
shows. His excellence, threatened as the excellence of
the criminals Genet has personally known and loved
has always been threatened, is unimpaired at the end of
the play. Thus, like Genet himself in *Pompes funèbres*
and Querelle, he is an improvement on what Genet
wants to say and the manner in which he chooses to say
it. Perhaps the dynamic had seemed inevitable in *Notre-
Dames-des-Fleurs* and *Miracle de la rose,* an intrinsic
part of life which could never be escaped from; as such
it was susceptible to the kind of analysis Sartre brings to
it. But the dynamic seems inevitable in those first two
books only to a mind that has discovered it in the later
books. Genet had not yet worked his way through to it,
nor had he worked his way past it to a position where
some men manage, in imagination if not in fact, to escape from it. As he does work toward this possibility
of transcendence, he slips out of Sartre's grasp, for he
is deeply convinced that there *is* such a surpassing excellence and that *he* is the embodiment of it. Buoyed by
such a conviction, he can seek a better based and therefore stronger form for his revenge. *Haute Surveillance*
is not quite that base, primarily because it is still limited
in its analysis to the world of the criminal, and, so long

as the dynamic and the transcendence of the dynamic are recorded in this register, the decent seem safe. The barriers of the prison wall are still there as protection against intrusion of the dynamic on their beliefs. Other plays will be needed to break those walls down and build new ones.

Beyond these recurring and developing preoccupations, *Haute Surveillance* represents something of greater significance to Genet's maturity as an artist and the persuasive rights and privileges it wins from his audience. What we have in embryo here is what we will remark on, with some astonishment, in his later plays: a commentary on the semblance of our reality, or, to put it more clearly, a frank reversion to the use of the theatre for purposes of challenging and shocking. This goal will become pronounced as Genet's imagination becomes more masterful in its control of what he wants to say. Normally in the theatre we are called to watch a representation of reality, a representation which is rendered complex by the fact that it is action in the present tense, but a present tense made possible only through semblance. The events we watch on the stage seem real, but we know they are not. With *Haute Surveillance* things seem to be real only to become false; but, because they seem real, they produce consequences which are real, and those consequences point to the extent to which we (or certain of the characters in the play who seem to embody some portion of our attitudes) misapprehend reality. Our traditional notions of reality are based on preconvictions and prejudices that are more than St. Paul's glass through which we see darkly. They are a high and thick wall over which we see wrongly, or a cavern deeper than Plato's, from which we look out on obscure images with our myopic eyes. In this play we think we see the central character rightly through the

144

eyes of Lefranc and Maurice. We think, as we follow
their discussions, we are being presented with the terms
by which we can judge whether Yeux-Verts is really
strong or really weak. But we are deluded because the
sources of our information—Lefranc and Maurice—are
deluded, and though we do not pay quite the steep price
they must pay for their misapprehensions, we do pay a
price. We can no longer accept the conventions of the
theatre as we have become wont to do (and that is perhaps a good thing); and we can no longer, because this
particular moment of theatre raises the question, accept
our conventional ways of following and assessing real
situations—and this is perhaps a much less good thing,
since it involves an estimate of what Genet thinks of
reality. On this we shall have to defer definition and
look for a moment at *les Bonnes,* which, because it exists
in two remarkably different versions—one predates
Haute Surveillance and the second was produced five
years later (1954)—indicates the turbulence (the less
generous might say confusion) in Genet's own approach
to the new scepticism he is formulating for his theatre.

As it was in *Haute Surveil-
lance,* the dramatis personae of *les Bonnes* is limited.
Here again only three personalities appear on the stage:
Claire, one of the maids who, in the absence of her mistress both amuses and cheers herself by impersonating
her; her sister, Solange, who assists rather muddle-
mindedly at this particular form of play-acting, deliberately obscuring what might be her point of view on the
whole proceedings until, finally, she becomes involuntarily and reluctantly involved in the extreme action
which brings the play to a close; lastly, there is Madame
herself, distraught because, as a result of Claire's betrayal in sending the police some letters they should

not have seen, her lover has been put momentarily in jail. The role of Madame is one of the few constants to be noticed in the two versions; in each her presence provides an essential interlude in the action by which that action is both measured and achieves sense. Her importance is weighed in the indifference with which she notices the existence of her maids, little suspecting they are capable of any action more dramatic than the accomplishment of the routines for which she has hired them, confident that their situation is necessarily better than hers, sure that it is generosity which prompts her to remind them (p. 54): "You are really lucky, you and Claire, to be alone in the world. The lowliness of your situation spares you all kinds of misfortunes." These are her attitudes and thoughts, and they ring with a confidence that, in addition to being enormous, is misplaced, for Madame surely has no intimation of how thoroughly inappropriate this confidence is when tallied against the precariousness of her situation in a world whose sense is defined by Jean Genet and his spokeswomen. What value she assigns to her maids is limited to the restricted world of her own egotism; to the extent that they flatter her or second her desires, she pays careful attention to them and even gives their judgments an unaccustomed authority. This, of course, is primarily convenient; by listening to them, at the right moment, for example, she can assure herself that she must wear bright, modish clothes in order the better to mourn her imprisoned lover. But little does she suspect that behind these supporting and encouraging expressions of opinion there rests both hatred of her and a plot against her security and assurance.

Inflexible, almost indeed a caricature of the selfish employer, Madame provides a necessary fixed point within the rhythm of the play, since that rhythm would not exist were it not for her inflexibility which, in the eyes of the audience, justifies to some extent the instinctive and powerful hostility the maids express toward her. When the curtain rises, we find Claire and Solange in her bedroom, where they are acting out a scene in which Claire plays the part of Madame. These particular games are not novel but have become an essential part of the pattern of substitutional revenge the sisters have woven as a menacing tapestry forever invisible to Madame. Like Penelope, they undo the fabric of their actions with inefficient care before Madame's return, so that what she is allowed to suspect is not the real nature of their inefficiency but only the indications it offers of careless housekeeping on their part. Nor does she suspect that their games are nothing more than preludes to a real action—her destruction—which they have not yet had either the courage or the opportunity to bring off.

Solange, the elder sister (in the second Paris production much was made of the age difference between the two maids), never comes into anything resembling clear focus in the first version. The difficulty goes beyond the indication that she is also given to impersonating Madame in her and her sister's games, and enters into the larger problem of determining which of the two is stronger, the clearer minded, the more determined. Part of the trouble—and, one suspects, it is deliberately created—is that her role in the fun and games is murky; whether she is playing herself or Claire is not clear (again we note Genet's attraction to puns: Claire-clair), since Claire-Madame alternately insists on calling Solange either Claire or Solange, settling at least once for the double name, Claire-Solange. The dramatic movement of their own play—its progress toward a conclusion to which they make references—is interrupted by Madame's return, in the remote aftermath of an evanescent Sapphic moment between the two sisters, and the more immediate aftermath of a phone call from Monsieur announcing his temporary release from jail. The confidence with which they have been carrying on their travesty peters out, with a sense of growing danger in the situation now before them, a danger which reduces to total unimportance the tension between them. Confronted with the possibility of discovery, they can effect an armistice in their own quarreling, which had been designed to determine which of the two was the more fixed in her opposition to that level of society embodied in Madame and Monsieur. With the return of Madame and the release of Monsieur, Claire's treachery in turning Monsieur over to the authorities may be discovered, as indeed the treachery in impersonating Madame may also be detected. The proposed solution to the problem—a decision to kill Madame by putting a poison into her nightly infusion—does not work for the simple reason that Madame, excited by the impending rendezvous with her lover, refuses to take it. She leaves for her rendezvous and the original movement of the play—Claire and Solange's play acting—resumes.

There is at first a moment of common panic in which Claire speaks of Madame's growing consciousness of something awry in her rapport with her maids, and Solange desires to flee. In the midst of this conversation Claire suddenly slips back into her impersonation of Madame, hurling insults at Solange and all that her position as a domestic represents. The trick works and Solange, who a moment before had been anxious to flee, resumes her role as the knowing and revengeful maid who, contemplating the death of her mistress, begins an incantation to her condition not simply as a maid but as the maid who, through the courage of her action and the single-mindedness of her dedication, will release all the maids of the world from their servitude. But her courage fails her almost as soon as her rhetoric has reached its climax. Seeming to detect that her sister's fortitude has not quite the measure of her verbal richness, Claire forces Solange to give her the poison intended for Madame. Here it is Claire who triumphs, imposing her will on the reluctant Solange who, even at the end of the play, cannot rise to the heroism she has prophesied for herself. As the curtain falls she stands on the stage "her hands crossed as though handcuffed."

What we have here is probably the conclusion referred to in the earlier part of the play, the conclusion which was interrupted by Madame's return and which, in its earlier moments of frustration, was little more than a mirror reflecting their thwarted efforts to kill Madame. What it all means is in no sense clear, principally because whatever individuation Genet has sought to establish between the roles of Claire and Solange does not come off distinctly, but also because, at the time of the composition of the play, Genet may have lacked the courage to say overtly what he meant. A certain substratum of repeated concerns is easily detectible: the involuntary subservience of the maids to a callous employer, a theme already introduced in *Pompes funèbres;* the various values of betrayal; the range of action that necessarily takes place in obscurity because one part of society, accustomed to its self-imposed blinkers, cannot see the real capacity for action possessed by another part of society; and finally—and here is the area in which Genet's proclamatory courage seems to fail—the extent to which the haves of society are thoroughly dependent for their illusive prestige on the tolerance of the have-nots.

Yet most of it is inchoate and dramatically confused; the rhythms are blunted, and the meaning never comes to anything resembling full or significant life, because

149

we are never really aware of how much the poisoning of Claire is real action or illusion, how much it is intended to be an achievement, or how much it is meant to be a commentary on the frustrating limitations represented by the invisible handcuffs which imply Solange's awareness of some level of guilt from which she cannot escape. And surely these problems in understanding would not have been reduced had Genet's idea of having the maids played by transvested young men been adopted. Had another idea of his, first expressed in *Notre-Dame-des-Fleurs,* been put to use, it might very well have produced the sort of studied ambivalence Genet cherishes. In that earlier book he had looked forward to a theatrical work in which the transvestitism of the actors would be constantly announced to the public by large proscenium placards.

Apparently Genet was no more certain than his audience about these things, or at least about their clarity or even perhaps their integrity—a concern more likely to inspire him to revise than any interest in the immediately lucid. In the second version, presented in 1954 (the first presentation had been supervised by Louis Jouvet) at the Théâtre de la Huchette, Genet sought to delineate certain brushstrokes more cleanly. In the earlier version Claire had seemed to emerge as the center of action and indeed of courage, albeit the action and the fortitude brought about her own self-willed destruction. In the later version she is much less strong, much less a center, though, by sinking into indecisiveness, she in no way loses her special claim on ambiguity. She acts here without confidence; more precisely, the only actions to which she can bring any assurance are those she performs within the circle of the impersonation she effects. When she has the role to play she plays it rather well, principally, I suppose, because in playing the role she finds a release from her professional domesticity. Solange, whose desires in the first play had only the reality of verbal expression, emerges as a stronger person. Amid the mixture of illusion and reality Claire offers her, she remains untouched, still her authentic self, conscious of the nature and consequence of her position. Because she understands Claire she is able to make use of her, so that at the very end of the play—its penultimate moments will be explained presently—she experiences joy rather than guilt. There are no handcuffs here because she has preserved the innocence of fidelity to her situation, while Claire has sought to escape from hers either by impersonations or else by bravura.

By her fidelity to all the consequences of her position (some of which are unfortunate, others of which are preludes to triumph), Solange has liberated all the maids of the world and is thus entitled to the rather perplexing apotheosis which is hers at the end of the play. It is an apotheosis in which Claire is both a participant and an absent force. At a late moment in the play, she seems to have lost all claim on such lingering glory and seems also to have lost her life to Solange's stronger hands, which have strangled her. But, even as we think her dead, she appears again, startling her sister and, no longer dominated by her earlier fears and hesitations, urging her to administer the poison intended for Madame. This unexpected appearance seems bad stagecraft, for it is inconsistent with the emphasis this later version places on Solange's single-mindedness of purpose. We do not expect Claire to emerge with such convictions at the moment of near-conclusion, because we have been led to believe that she is unworthy of the very abjection Solange embraces with such energy and enthusiasm. What seems to explain the switch is a curious phrase which appears in both versions, a phrase in which Claire tells Solange

151

that together they comprise that "eternal couple of the saint and the criminal." This is part of a larger dialectic, elaborated principally by Claire, that sets off a process where Solange's imagination (which, Claire says, "has invented the theme") is seen to lack a certain final strength necessary to carry its own insights to fruition. The final impulse for success must come from Claire who, in recognizing herself as the traitor Solange insists she is, will know her abjection fully enough and with hatred sufficient to urge Solange's decisive participation in her own suicide. Given the final payment for such self-awareness, it is little wonder that she has earlier referred to the whole process as a dangerous game.

That lucidity of which she has spoken seems finally to have led her through a self-examination that has exposed the several motivating influences underpinning her character. For her to be a maid was to be vile, and it is surely for this reason that, in her moments of playing at being Madame, she tended to address Solange as "Claire," finding in such a means of address the best way to express her own personal revulsion. To be Claire and to be a maid is to know abjection as the unwanted condition the bourgeoisie consider it. But to seek to escape from it, especially by accepting *their* modes as values to be pursued and harnessed, is to court something worse than acceptance by them or even, other things being unequal or impossible, death. It is to court the rancour and revenge of the Solanges of this world who, like Yeux-Verts, have the ultimate control over what happens because they have not corroded the chain of true action with the false veneer of categories. Still, Claire's weakness becomes, by an uneven metamorphosis, her strength; it is the source of the final perspective she achieves and communicates to her sister. Precisely because she feels the attraction to a change of state, she seems to legitimate the superior opinions the bourgeoisie have of themselves. Only by a final act of rejection, an act by which she will both assert what it is that gives them a supposed right to their sense of superiority (the envy of their inferiors) and reject it in an act of violence, only then can she point a way to the tidier hierarchical structure that will emerge when the maids of the world have signed and proclaimed their particular declaration of independence.

There is a better containment of statement in this second version and certainly a clearer expressive register, for from the opening moments of the 1954 version the power of Solange's intransigent point of view, as the most appropriate means of masterminding these particular revels, is evident, and the audience has consequently a clear center upon which to fix its attention. The new version has its weaknesses: the more explicit lesbianism and the accumulation of apparently irrelevant anecdotes make it unnecessarily diffuse. But it has its strengths: the more intelligent deployment of necessary ambiguities between the two sisters, expressed in the carefully planned shifting of personal pronouns from *me* to *us,* and the exclusion of Solange from psychological involvement with Monsieur. From these strengths there springs a tighter, though not necessarily more comprehensible, kind of communication. The similarities and contrasts between the two sisters are more pronounced, and their polar roles in maintaining an axis about which the world of Jean Genet can spin become more explicit. The rhythm here is also clearer and, in that special economy which is Genet's imagination, more harmonious. This allows him in the final scene—the apotheosis of Solange, made possible, we have seen, only with the unexpected co-operation of Claire—an incipient ritual quality in which we can detect the pegs on which he will hang even more sophisticated robes, more carefully elaborated ambiguities in his later plays. What may explain the several poverties of *les Bonnes* is something which was necessary to Genet's growth out of what were becoming monotonous types, both in his ideas and in the characters used to express these ideas. While *les Bonnes* does not completely get him away from a rather typical register of ideas, it does bring him out of a devouring subjectivism and closer to the use of other situations, fresh kinds of characters, and a consequently more convincing presentation of his own point of view. It also affords him the opportunity of working with dramatic forms which have some value other than being vehicles for autobiographical expressions. The play, then, is something of a hinge between what preceded it and the three plays which have come after it. If in the two versions we have seen a basic idea—the union, the necessary union of the saint and the criminal—fight its way out of confusion into self-contained clarity, we shall in later plays watch the union dissolve, the saint become the criminal and the criminal the saint.

What Genet has done, finally, in *les Bonnes* is break out of the world of the unseemly more effectively than he had been able to do in *Querelle de Brest*. There the reduction of the milieu of criminals did not seem much of an accomplishment ultimately, because of Querelle's murders and the activities of his associates. The atmosphere of *les Bonnes,* despite the vengeful tactics of the two maids, is that of the conventional bourgeois drama; and that is precisely the atmosphere Genet needs, for the employer-domestic relationship gives him, in the bourgeois world, a situation which is immediately susceptible to his preoccupations. It is a commonplace that maids do dislike their employers; from this commonplace it is not too exaggerated to move on to say that maids also imitate their employers and dream one day of being in their position. In the total body of Genet's work *les Bonnes* is important because it is a kind of breakthrough releasing Genet, his imagination, and his ideas from the restricted world of crime and homosexuality, while simultaneously allowing him to carry his ideas and his imagination into more spacious chambers whose grandeur and ornaments will be their only difference from the confined spaces he is abandoning. Though the hinge on the door which is broken through is not without rust and the inevitable creaking sounds, the hinge and the creaking are necessary if those new chambers are to be entered. Without the hinge the peculiar powers and several beauties of *le Balcon* and *les Nègres* might not have been possible. With it there comes into being a major transformation in Genet's self-assurance: the shy, petulant, aggrieved child has become much more conscious than was Topsy of how it is one grows.

> Every object in your world
> has a different meaning for
> me than it has for you. I
> bring everything within my
> system, where things have an
> infernal significance.
>
> —*Miracle de la rose*

'*le Balcon*'

Madame Lysiane, the bedeviled madam of the local brothel in *Querelle de Brest,* had spoken with some insecurity of her place of business as a *maison d'illusions,* a sort of haven for the other bedeviled members of the race. In her more secure moments, before her entry into metaphysical and dangerously imaginative speculations about the nature of Querelle and his brother, Robert, and of the difference between them, she had had dim but none the less illuminating glimmers of a way to control the world, of a way of getting close to the kind of hard apprehension of the world's firmer realities that would place her in a position of detached mastery; indeed, the mastery would seem to depend precisely on such detachment. That distance is involved in winning the detachment does not in any way mean disapproval; disapproval is one of our attitudes, easily assumed to protect our modes of action. Detachment is a method of looking at the world in order the better to understand it and, in a limited sense, the better to sympathize with it. Madame Lysiane, though she comes very near the possession of such detachment —primarily because she accepts the strange categories of knowledge picked up in the direction of her fleshly enterprise, without making any effort at moralizing comment —never really attains it. She allows herself to be victimized by devices she should know more about and, at the end of the book, is reduced to sentimental tears and vengeful fantasies in which she would like to burn her brothel down—why should others have illusions when hers have been destroyed?

Madame Irma (more *dure* than *douce*), the tight-lipped, efficient madam of the *maison d'illusions* which is the *mise-en-scène* of *le Balcon,* avoids these dangers, and the stances by which she arrives at her mastery or, better, the stances she is allowed as the result of her mastery, form the substance of the piece. The balcony from which she looks down at her "visitors" and the closed-circuit television that allows her to look in on the actions taking place in the various chambers are the devices by which she expresses her mastery. The world is quite literally at her feet: a curtain pulled back or a switch turned on become as so many windows opened, not merely on what is going on in this particular home, but more importantly (and deviously) on what is going on in the world. For Irma's dominion is not limited merely to the chambers which make her house of illusions.

157

Her dominion is a kind of generalizing omnipotence over the whole of reality, drawing its powers from the sources of insight and statement she finds in the practices she observes.

That the genteel might find such statements the stuff and nonsense that only a Freudian world could articulate has little to do with the workings of this play; nor would any protestation dim the cautiously structured intimations of the play, which, rolling like a powerful stone that gathers festering moss, seeks to articulate a presentation of the true mobiles of reality from which none can escape. As in *Haute Surveillance,* the basic data of the statement are assembled through the presentation of character. But here, unlike *Haute Surveillance* —where, after all, the ambience was limited and the generalized force of the intimations muted—we are faced with a greatly enlarged dramatis personae whose interrelationships, though not always clear, are symbols of the kind of interlaced connections essential to the statement Genet wants to make. However essential the connections may seem to a respectful reader, they have rarely been preserved in a staged version of the play. Both Peter Brook's Paris production and José Quintero's New York production made cuts in the play which reduced noticeably its integral sense. It was not simply a question, in either production, of shortening speeches or reducing dialogue, but rather a question of extracting whole forces whose absence damaged the tight and self-contained universe Genet wished to create in the theatre.

Coming after a silence of several years, one might have expected a roughness in the form of *le Balcon,* insecurity in the voice, and perhaps tedium, stemming from a further iteration of already familiar views. It is important to point out immediately that the voice speaking here is eminently secure; if, as has been reported, Genet

158

had serious, almost mortal hesitations over where to go after *les Bonnes,* they have been dissolved by the sense of a new-found direction. All may have seemed to have been said with the presentation of *les Bonnes;* and there may have been, in his mind, a fear of his own growing tendency to warm over increasingly less savory dishes. These doubts are dispelled with the appearance of *le Balcon;* with them is gone any sense Genet may ever have had that his ideas could not get beyond the limitations of his life. The voice heard here is neither that of the apologist nor of the aggressive debater. We are not to be argued with; we are to be challenged, subtly and cumulatively, until the accusation passes well beyond the level of allegation to become fact. At the end of the play we are no longer the accused but have become the guilty, though admittedly for Genet the word "guilt" would very possibly have definitions quite as startling as the terms of this play.

In rats' alley, the dead men lost their bones; in Madame Irma's house of illusions the dispossessed enter into their kingdom. Regrettably enough, that kingdom is the domain of our most prized accomplishments, our most cherished institutions, which shall be laid waste before our eyes with a cheer and inevitability that are at best unsettling, at worst dismaying. And it shall be laid waste by the example of three individuals, whose public and private worlds are either without importance for us or else are the causes of our most fervently expressed shock. They come from the lowly—the world of the clerk, the mechanic, and the unskilled white collar worker—to enact in Madame Irma's therapeutic center the fantasies that are their escape from the tedium of their days. Where shock first registers is in the matter of their choice, for these single-mindedly imaginative men do not come to Madame Irma's to act out the more

159

fanciful or populous images of Sade; they come instead to put on the mantles, respectively, of bishop, judge, and general. Where shock registers its second wave is in the audience's realization that the value of these various fantasies is specifically in their fantasy nature. There is no aspiration within the motivation of these people to *be* bishop, judge, or general; the limit of their ambitions knows its range, and the cutting-off point of that range is the thin line between pretense and reality. They seek✓ merely the reality of their illusions; that is, they wish, in order to derive true sexual fulfillment from their performances, to be at all times aware of the illusory nature✓ of what they are doing, and this places them quite apart from the pipe-dreaming habitués of Harry Hope's saloon in *The Iceman Cometh.*

Harry Hope's people wanted nothing so much as to be left alone; their endless conversations were designed to convince them of the need to live as they did. In their public dimension they were designed to present the audience with Eugene O'Neill's conviction that such people should be left in their dream worlds and that the spectator's tolerance of the need for such a world would be his most appropriate attitude. Genet has no such concern with creating sympathy for his three men. They are what they are, indications that the sex-power drive has many expressions, not the least of which are those expressions thought to be eminently respectable because their function as replacements for more instinctive drives has never been fully examined. The components of that examination, the clerk, mechanic and white collar worker, are not brought before us as evocations of a world different from ours. They are our essence; their needs are ours, and their play acting is a manifestation of ours, though we carry ours on in broad daylight while they must seek the obscurity of the bordello.

160

They come before us, unknowingly and stealthily, furtive so long as they must wear the garb of their lowliness, but increasingly confident as they put on their different robes, secure in the assurance that none of the personnel in this particular house will come to remind them of anything bizarre in these out of the ordinary needs Madame Irma's well-paid generosity so diligently serves. In discussing other dramatists it would be commonplace to point out that the nature of the theatre makes the desire the three men express for invisibility a complete delusion. But with Genet there is a manifest rejoicing in this particular kind of commonplace deception. The fact that the actors are paid to pretend and, in the pretense he has written for them, are called upon to feign ignorance of the audience's presence even in the moments when their cries are addressed most pertinently to that audience—these are situations which make the theatre almost a symbol, for Genet, of the sort of thing he is in the process of attacking. As the actors pretend, so do all decent people, with the result that the actor's call for invisibility is no more bad faith on their part than our pretense that our values have true objective quality.

Even as the three men enact their chosen roles, they are careful never to move involuntarily into any belief that the chosen function is their real function. Thus the meter reader, whose glory rises strong within him as he puts on the tacky garb of a bishop, is careful to protest that he does not wish to stumble into being a bishop, for such miscalculation would create too much distance between him and true episcopal dignity. He says (p. 6): "I wish to be bishop in solitude, for appearance alone." At a later moment in the play, he who would play the general repeats the same phrase: "I wish to be a general in solitude. Not for myself but for the image of myself, and that image for its image and so on." He who impersonates the judge is also highly sensitive to the planned character of his enactments and is consequently alarmed by any variation, any unsettling ripple on the surface of his carefully plotted illusion. This concern with images, and with images of images, is one of the more confused and possibly unintentional metaphors we encounter in Genet. When linked with solitude, it seems to have the effect of guaranteeing the unopposed autonomy of the imagination in creating whatever it wants, for the deeper one moves into images the less danger there will be of reality's coming back to question the veracity of the images. The metaphor, as we shall see presently, gets even more confused when it becomes involved with mirrors. In either case, it is a strangely vulnerable point in Genet's usually sophisticated deception, for it seems to leave him as much exposed as the three characters he is dealing with here.

Structurally, the alarms felt by each of the impersonators are necessary to the play; if they did not exist, the audience would have its moment of voyeurism, Genet would have his moment of complaisance, and the range of statement *le Balcon* is designed to make would never spread before our eyes, insinuate its noises in our ears. The source of the alarm is only indirectly the unaccustomed drop of inefficiency in the generally well-oiled machinery of Madame Irma's establishment. The more direct source is a revolution which is disturbing the city, surrounding the house of illusions with terror, and disorganizing the usually steel-strong nerves of the madam and her employees. What the revolution means, I shall deal with presently; what it does to the usually calm surface of the tableaux we watch is of more direct concern. The theatre allows Genet the kind of dialectical structure he never clearly found in his narrative works. Indeed,

this may very well have been one of the reasons originally attracting him to it; but to preserve the dialectical
character of the genre he must have warring principles,
a touch of disorder within the action of the play. In
Haute Surveillance that disorder centered on the apparently waning pre-eminence of Yeux-Verts; in *les
Bonnes* it was centered in the hostility between the maids
and masters which, as we have seen, was only a mirror
of the hostility between Solange, a woman fully aware of
the qualities of her being, and Claire, a center of dissatisfaction seeking to move into another, more attractive
circle.

In *le Balcon* the disorder will center on the revolution;
but like a complicated machine built of interacting
wheels, its turns and spins will be so numerous as to
challenge comprehension. Because of the disorders it
brings to customarily well-rehearsed entertainments, it
jars the audience out of any desire to reach into the
storehouse of its labels in order to isolate these practices
and instead makes disturbing connections between the
entertainments and the realities from which they take
their point of departure. He who impersonates the judge
is the most articulate exemplar of this kind of diversification.

His major concern is to preserve the normal quality
of his diversion. But since the diversion is upset, its
ordinary flow ruffled, he will, by his increasingly hysteri-
cal efforts to preserve the routine, make important comments for the author on what the meaning of judges
really is. By sharing the concern of the impersonated
general and bishop with the preservation of illusions, he
does more than maintain the kind of cheerful monotony
he likes; he also comments, though quite unknowingly,
on the obvious parallel between him and all judges. His

desire to maintain illusion in his performance does not create an unbridgeable chasm between him and real judges; rather it brings him closer to the essence of all judicial exercise. His illusion specifically is not to have the responsibility he assigns to real judges; by a not too distant metonymy, the judges' illusion is to have a guarantee of the righteousness of their function. What Madame Irma's diligence is to the judge-impersonator, society's assurances are to the real judge.

Here are the details of the scene: As the lights brighten the judge-impersonator is stretched on the floor licking the foot of a well-rounded young female thief, costumed more to emphasize the curves of her charms than those of her crimes. In the background there stands an executioner, whip in hand. Both by his costume and his gestures he creates at various moments in the scene the impression of a homosexual attachment of some kind between him, as executioner, and the judge. This, of course, places them and the thief in the Hangman-Erik-Riton dynamic, but with several changes. Here the dynamic moves up one notch to where the highest level of desirable achievement becomes not the executioner's function but the judge's. Here, too, the participants in the dynamic change, raising the question of who is the most important: the judge who passes judgment, the executioner who carries the judgment out and thus gives it meaning, or the thief who makes the whole business of judging and executing possible.

One has the impression that the brightening light is a kind of slow thrust into a certain kind of reality, for as it becomes more intense the judge's initial activity is subsumed into his more usual function: the hierarchy is reversed as he moves into the role of judging the girl's crime, his authority immediately and visibly supported

by the executioner's whip. The girl's guilt, and her admission of it, is necessary to the performance of his function, and, under the disruptions brought on by the noises
of the encircling revolution, things do not come off well.
The girl moves too easily between what she really is and
the role she is supposed to be playing, and it is her fright
and the distemper it produces that allow us to learn how
precarious is the analogous situation of society. For,
were any similar disturbance to come and upset the
wheels of our justice, we would learn that it is a system
which has no authority on its side except that we arbitrarily give it; and we would learn also that, without
the existence of criminals—those people whose existence
is the contrary of ours—we would not be able to afford
ourselves this pleasure of judging them and feeling the
resultant superiority of our situation. Though he is dis-
tressed by this knowledge, the judge-impersonator is dis-
criminatingly aware that his possession of it is an indispensable part of the pleasure he seeks in the house of
illusions, and so, by implication at least, he is somewhat
better than the jurist whose function he assumes virtually.
The final panel of the tableau becomes a resonant verbal
and a brilliant visual presentation of the truer situation
(the intimate bond existing between the thief, the judge,
and the executioner) as it becomes the climactic moment
of the judge-impersonator's pleasure. He stands, towering
on his buskins, the source of his erotic pleasures (the
thief) at his feet, the expression of his erotic desires (the
executioner) in his arms. Such exquisite rectitude evidently demands exalted language and, to the executioner,
he incants (p. 14): "Mirror that glorifies me! Image that
I can touch, I love you." The light fades; the whore, who
reconciles him with the world, resumes her original position and, as the light disappears and the artificial coating

165

of several thousand years of Western effort is removed, the whore's voice, shrill and chill, rises, crying out the truth: "Lick, lick. . . ."

Since we do not escape quite so easily from the qualifying words of our psychological vocabulary—abnormal, perverse, aberrant—such a scene and such a voice are not altogether nor immediately convincing, though they do define well the terms of the accusation and state clearly if not attractively the kind of definition being assigned to our prouder attitudes. To attack the functions of church, judiciary, and army by making them the centers of rather extraordinary sexual performances is, however, a chancy kind of risk, since the world of the bordello, especially a bordello so heavily tinged with exhibitionism as Madame Irma's, remains, however sound the label, an aberrant world whose seaminess is not easily dissimilated by the attractive packaging of a *maison d'illusions*. That Jean Genet believes the contrary is something we can, admittedly, learn by assisting at these three tableaux; but Jean Genet is not content with this particular kind of ideological democracy, where we would all listen tolerantly to the other's beliefs. Not for him are the usual positivistic compromises; his longings are metaphysical, simply because he knows he is right. Before the end of the evening he must either persuade or bludgeon us into seeing just how right he is. And, worse luck, he has almost the art to carry the enterprise off.

How he does this defies the blunted equipment of the more usual kinds of logical examination and analysis. His immediate problem, once the initial shock of the opening tableaux has been dealt, is to use subtle devices to bring us to a dual stance (if such a thing be physically possible). He must, first, place the bordello in some register of understanding available to us and, second, he must cast some sort of credible bridge between the bordello and our world. And he must do both these things with a rapidity designed to dizzy us just enough to keep us from protesting with the meaningless vocabularies of our ratiocinative processes; yet he must allow us enough self-control to grasp the principal precepts of his argument and enough independence to feel, at the end of the evening, that we have come to self-recognition and that the rape to which we have been subjected is something we wanted after all.

With our memory stored with impressions of the first three tableaux, we are quite prone to think that the bordello is little more than an escape from the harsher realities with which we daily live. And, to a point, Genet would have us believe this, giving us encouragement and even corroborative information to cheer us on. It is not the three impersonators alone who serve this purpose of seeming to justify our unease and condemnations; there is also Carmen, an idle whore whose waning star has deprived her of the peculiar pleasures of impersonating a sacred person and turned her into Madame Irma's bookkeeper and confidant. If she has not Madame Irma's tolerance for the habitués of the maison, it is simply because, in her own way and with her own variations, she has similar needs. Carmen, like Madame Irma, has had a previous incarnation in Genet's other work, though, unlike Irma, she has managed to keep the same name from one book to the other. In *Querelle de Brest* she was the whore who, when not impersonating Saint Teresa, expressed her fears to Madame Lysiane that some of the habitués might be homosexual. Lysiane, whose sense of the consoling value of appearances was markedly greater than Irma's, dismissed these fears by demonstrating an interesting if not convincing syllogism: Men who have relations with women are heterosexual. The men who frequented her house had relations with women. Ergo and Q.E.D., though it does leave aside the whole question of whether the kinds of relationships they have with the women are heterosexual. The value of looking at the former appearance of these people is to see an earlier stage of Genet's imagination where Carmen was more deeply possessed of assurance and critical inquiry than was Lysiane. In asking her question she was getting close to Lysiane's single weakness: Lysiane's refusal to carry her hard-headed sense of reality as far as she should. When the two women reappear in *le Balcon* not only has Lysiane's name been changed but her role has been altered, too, so that it indicates a switch with the part Carmen had played in *Querelle de Brest*. It is not Lysiane who has grown wiser and learned to change; rather it is Jean Genet's imagination which has finally got the confusions held over from *Querelle de Brest* straightened out. Unkinked, they can be used to show other principles which Genet now holds more firmly. One of the results, in addition to the new emphasis given to Lysiane become Irma, is that in this later incarnation Carmen is a whore who has come into the brothel in order to get away from the world and to reject its pretensions. But even the most objective spectator is persuaded to believe that this kind of rejection is really a flight from the unpleasant, the imposing, and the inescapable in the world. Carmen says (p. 42): "Your laws and orders and the passions are my reality!" That there is a startlingly wide range of subterranean human needs fulfilled by the various services offered by Madame Irma's house of illusions is something which causes Carmen no especial concern. She agrees that it takes a little bit of everything to make the world—her dreams of a solid bourgeois background from which she has fallen; the desires of those who frequent the brothel—but in her particular recipe for tolerance there is one dash of bitters: a certain hostility toward the police.

The springs tautening this opposition are tightly coiled; their principal strain seems to be a fear that the police represent some threat to the security of this world into which Carmen has escaped and in which, before her fall from splendid and specialized bawdry into account books, she had known her own gaudier hours. Their threat is not simply the more usual menace of sudden crackdowns on the bordello's operations, but rather finds a more complex expression in the personality of the police chief who, because of frequent allusions to him, is a significant presence within the circle of the play even before he appears, swaggering and confident, in Madame Irma's salon. Why Georges so disturbs Carmen is pretty much why he disturbs us. He wants to take the brothel more seriously and, by seeking in it something more than therapy (Carmen's approach) or release (ours), he becomes the material with which Genet will build a needed bridge between the bordello and our world.

Though sexually powerless, Georges is none the less possessed of the puissance derived from his function in society; indeed his policeman's billy is very obviously a replacement for the inefficient equipment he possesses in other areas of activity: it gives him a certain overweening dominion over the inmates of the brothel, allowing him to use the more prosaic constabulary privileges as a thin coating over his real needs. Though he seeks to give the impression of the wily, graft-touched policeman, the wiliness and the graft are only so many distractions from his quite thorough conviction that the desires of those who come to the brothel are a kind of charismatic energy from which flow the only true realities. What bothers him, in brief, is that no one has yet come to the brothel seeking to impersonate a chief of police and, until such time as this transcendent activity comes into being, his function in society will not have been stamped with that brand of realism sexual illusions manufacture. In certain primitive societies the boy does not become a man until he has successfully passed through elaborate puberty rites; in Georges' society, a man does not break into reality until his function has been consecrated as a proper object for sexual fulfillment. Other men (Don Juan, for example, at least before he became one of our more tired myths) might seek whatever kind of confirmation they needed in their own prowess; Georges, however, is committed to seeking his kind of confirmation in the performance of his function, but the function itself makes no sense unless its appeal becomes sufficiently strong to be a sexual outlet. Until that function achieves this appeal, this particular policeman's lot is indeed an unhappy one.

Georges' problem, in addition to serving as a vehicle for the expression of one of the more pervasive of Genet's ideas, is also an important device for the development of the play, since from its needs will be born the action of the play. We have up to this point been faced with a purely presentational sort of statement and, as I have suggested, the mere fact of presentation does not convince. It becomes the playwright's job now to find some way of developing his presentation, of taking the various facts, needs, and attitudes with which we have been confronted and make them go somewhere before our eyes, preferably through them and into our souls, there to fester. The revolution whose sounds have, throughout these earlier scenes, been penetrating the walls of the bordello and upsetting the spirits of its inmates and visitors, will serve this purpose, for it will come as a kind of test of the several attitudes we have witnessed and, as it measures them and finds them wanting, it will also measure us. Though its particulars are never reasonably nor fully designed, it will represent a threat to the functions we have elaborated and seen in rather perverse expressions in the house of illusions. As these various functions react to this menace we shall assist at the disintegration of the functions, their gradual impotence before the power of the threat.

The intercalations Genet introduces into the play with the revolution are profligate to the point of confusion and are not readily dealt with in commentary, nor, as I have already pointed out, are they much helped when the play is truncated. The precise nature and goals of the revolution never become altogether disengaged, though its function as a symbol does achieve its kind of precise definition before the end of the evening. The revolution is the whole register of change and turbulence, and it is not altogether necessary that the change be for the better or even for the worse. It is the existence of change which provides meaning, by providing a backdrop against which individuals will react quite differently, expressing dismay that their cherished ideals are about to fall, seeking a fulfillment of their ambitions if the revolution is successful, or simply registering fear that change will deprive them of the known and offer in its place an unknown whose consequences cannot be prejudged.

What is important is the effort Georges makes to dominate the revolution and thus win mastery. His plan is not without a certain imaginative cleverness, since he proposes to use Madame Irma's clients as a kind of façade to be placed before the citizenry in order to dupe them. Their private needs, expressed in their respective impersonations of bishop, judge, and general, will achieve an unwanted public expression in order that they may

171

serve as docile, subordinate instruments of Georges' grand design. The scheme does not come off with either the brilliance or the results Georges anticipates, and for several reasons.

On the most basic level, failure results from Georges' egotism; he is too sure of himself, in a fake enough way, to understand what confronts him; and his delusions of grandeur—evidently patterned on those of Franco, as evidenced in the mountain tomb he has had sculpted to receive his dictatorial ashes—become a drop of contagious corruption in the general cleverness of his scheme. On a higher, potentially even more dangerous level, Georges' ambitions are still tied to his several needs: his continuing dependence on the guarantees of an outside supporting force, suggested by his insistence that for him there must be a fixed locus of authority and that the Queen, rather than being an object of verbal play, must be someone. His hope, never fully expressed, is that his role in controlling and ultimately directing the revolution may goad someone into seeking in the house of illusions the chance to impersonate him. On a purely instrumental level, his instruments try to rebel: the bishop-impersonator and his two counterparts, once invested with exercisable functions, want nothing so much as to exercise them, especially after they have noted how easily the public has been duped by their impersonations.

Here Georges manages to win a victory—however pyrrhic and temporary it may be. He wins it by a double invocation. In the first place he recognizes that there is a community of motivation among them and says (p. 47): "I do as they do, I penetrate right into the reality that the game offers, and since I have the upper hand, it's I who score." But he manages to make them cringe before his invocation of the essential role he, as policeman, plays in supporting the exercise of their function. His appeal here is not simply to some abstract principle of history, but is also directed to the most recent revolutionary events in their lives. He has given them their place in the revolutionary sun of his creation, and he has no intention of allowing *conferred* places to usurp his. The irony of Georges' energy comes into play here and spins its way slowly into something which might very loosely be called tragedy since, had he taken the same advice he gave to his subordinates, he might have spared himself his own final impotence. Yet, though he counsels and convinces the others that they had better go back to their original apprehensions about the nature of their needs and not seek to mix illusions and realities (thus calling them back to definitions they have themselves made earlier in the play), he does not give himself the same advice. And, in a final boomeranging gesture, he has placed Irma on the throne, convinced no doubt that he will be the power behind that throne. All his wishes save one have achieved fulfillment; there remains only the consecration of his function by its inclusion in the range of activities conducted in the house of illusions.

His apotheosis is his undoing, for a young man presents himself at the door of the brothel wanting to create an illusion of himself as a police chief. Here is Georges' moment of splendor; but splendor, unfortunately, has many faces, and the exaltation he experiences as he looks in on the newest tableau sours, as well it might, with the unexpected denouement of the tableau: the young man, evidently because of his disillusion over the failure of the rebellion, castrates himself. This act is one of multiple import. Admittedly, it acknowledges the failure of *his* revolution, but it also expresses what he would like to see happen to the police, for if their power were compromised, his side might have had more of a chance. He cannot, in his dejection, see the victory he is achieving by forcing Georges' function into the brothel and therefore bringing about a more meaningful eclipse of power, since entry into the brothel's sideshows means a commitment to respecting the limits imposed by the function and a resultant loss of free play in human enterprise. Nor can he understand that his gesture, designed to dislocate reality through violence, is actually indispensable to the perfection of the tableau: impotent, he becomes a complete replica of Georges.

Bravura is the best energy Georges can find as a response to this messy apotheosis; but bravura, though it assures him that his own sexual organs are still intact (albeit as impotent as ever), cannot keep him from being absorbed into the mythological pantheon already garnished with the images of the representatives of religion, the judiciary, and the military. He has his heart's desire and, in obtaining it, he has lost the power he momentarily possessed. He seeks to cheer himself by claiming that now he can experience the more refined sentiments not usually associated with the police. But even he is not convinced and, though Irma offers him words of pity and even of love, he none the less withdraws from the mainstream of the brothel into his mausoleum, there to be fixed in the image he has created for himself. He had, at an earlier moment, suggested that "they got me," then rejected the possibility. But his withdrawal from the world of action and planning into the world of the brothel, where his function must necessarily become passive, is a defeat. They have in the end got him, and they have got him by making his role as police chief part of the "nomenclature."

Who got him has by this time become clear: an uneven mixture of his own muddled illusions and the better grasp of the more pervasive realities by others, to which can be added his own deceptive hope that somehow the

fate met by others whose functions are secondary will
be spared him. If he is not a direct victim of Irma, his
fall is a result of his failure to see in her the kind of
attitude which might have saved him, by taking him out
of the world of secondary authority and placing him in
the more direct, the more original range of activity pimping would offer. For there can be no question of it: it is
Irma who triumphs in this play; she alone wears the
stamp of heroism and knows, in wearing it, that it brings
sadness and fatigue. Against the tides of our disgust,
Carmen's momentary rebellion, Chantal's defection,
Georges' indifference and the encircling social turmoil,
she has swum strongly and quite expertly. The only il- ✓
lusion she has allowed herself is the realization of the
important place illusion plays in life and, since this is
not illusion but primal reality, only she is in sufficiently
knowledgeable communication with the world to control
it. She has her moments of weakness—her relations with
Georges, her lesbian attraction to Carmen, her extreme
lyricism when speaking of her house of illusions—but her
weaknesses are the defects of her strengths; they have
none of the illusory basis her entourage bring to their
dreams. It is quite possible, too, that her weaknesses are
direct manifestations of her strength, mere apparent
compromises she makes with her grasp of reality in order
to continue her unchallenged control of that reality. In
preserving some visible signs of the same kinds of instincts as the others, she keeps them from discovering
too much about the lessons she has learned and according to which she lives.

She knows the world turns on sexuality, and she knows
that power, when not directly a means of sexual fulfillment, is only a means of sexual replacement; secure in
this knowledge, she can indulge a passing fancy. What
shocks others—especially what shocks us—only confirms

her grasp of reality, with the result that her clients become as so many supporting premises for her omni-explicatory thesis: In a world where sexuality rules not just the rooster but also the roost, the more authentic reality will be found among those who give the most authentic expression to their desires. True judges are the product of sham; judge-impersonators seek only to accomplish the explicitly sexual aspect of the function they impersonate. Her house, then, becomes "the most knowing, the most honest of all houses of illusion," and she bids the audience goodnight with these words: "You must now go home, where everything—you can be quite sure—will be even falser than here. . . . You must go now. You'll leave by the right, through the alley. . . . It's morning already." In the New York production, especially at the 10:30 P.M. performances, which came to an end well after midnight, the words were like an icy hand reaching into the audience to turn their complicity in being there at all either to guilt or the self-recognition I have spoken of. It made little difference that the de-glamorized Irma who appeared at that final moment dropped hints that the conflict which had been at the heart of the evening's presentation—the struggle between the brothel and the revolution—may have been only another illusion, may have been only a kind of group performance drawing its participants from all the smaller performances going on in her house. Whether the revolution was real, whether the executioner was killed, whether Roger was castrated—all these are events intended to have meaning rather than to convey purely physical facts. They have achieved their purpose, which was, immediately, to upset the clientele and place Georges' longings in a perspective; but they have also achieved their less immediate effect, which was to upset the audience and turn them to thoughts of guilt.

Once he has escaped from his own sense of exclusion from a world he grows to detest with eloquence, guilt becomes a rather meaningless word for Genet. This is so principally because that world, formerly so out of reach, now comes to applaud his plays and celebrate in him the bard of the end he brings to its romances and functions. Since guilt has, then, become a word increasingly without value, it is surely self-recognition Genet is seeking to arouse within the audience through the impact of *le Balcon*. But self-recognition, especially if it be associated with activities and tendencies we have been told since childhood are not or should not be ours, amounts fairly much to the same thing as guilt. Irma's implied accusation at the end of the play has the truth of immediacy. The audience has sat there throughout the evening, secure perhaps in its ability to judge these matters, able to excuse its fascination with the things it is supposed either to detest or disapprove by appealing to any one of a range of modern mythological norms, only to find that its presence and the decision-making behind the presence (the purchase of the tickets, the trip to the theatre) are being turned against it in order to demonstrate just how much its real, though repressed and subconscious, interests are, if anything, worse than what it has been watching. For what goes on on the stage is, after all, an honest expression of possibly dishonest needs; but it is better than the substitutional kind of experience the audience is trying to have.

This direct, between-the-eyes accusation is the most striking single device in the play; yet, before its impact can be made—and note that it does not become verbally articulate until the very last lines (lines Genet added to the play at a later moment)—it must be underpinned by a whole series of devices, whose dramatic exercise is only a mask over the structure of accusation that is being erected throughout the play. So a theme in a fugal composition works its way through the various counterpoints to a final tonic chord which, once expressed, seems always to have existed and always to have been inevitable. Here we have something of the same kind of development: an initial presentation made in the opening tableaux, variations on the sources and implications of that presentation, new harmonies or dissonances introduced into the presentation by the fact of the revolution, a final expression of the presentation which reaches across the footlights in order to include us in its purview. The composer of it all, and the conductor, too, is Irma, of whom Carmen says (p. 34): "You've been able to surround your loveliness with a sumptuous theatre, a gala, the splendors of which envelop you and hide you from the world. Your whoredom required such pomp." In the concentrated statement of these two sentences we have a fullness Carmen does not suspect, since her phrases, like our feelings, are keyed to a kind of accusation. She is charging Irma with escapism, little realizing that Irma has escaped from our illusions into the reality these illusions seek to hide. Irma's brothel, as we learn in the last lines of *le Balcon,* is a promontory from which she sees clearly into us by observing clearly what is going on in her house of illusions. This is not done with complete dishonesty since, in at least one instance, the audience is reminded of its voyeurism when the judge-impersonator asks his performing whore (p. 11): "Are all the doors firmly shut? Can anyone see us, or hear us?" So long as there is an Irma who, from her balcony or through her television screen, can watch what is going on, no door is really shut nor are ears ever efficiently stoppered. It is not simply the technological devices that provide such mastery; it is the simple recognition of what we are. Throughout the evening the audience has been invited to assist at and, finally, to accept Irma's vision, to recognize what she recognizes and to find the proof for the whole activity in the interest, fascination, and absorption with which it has followed the development and conclusion of the play. That this is ultimately proselytism is unquestionable; that it is done with skill is also unquestionable; that it is art is another question altogether, a question better answered in a final note to this essay.

Preliminary to any such aesthetic valuations of the play there must be a frank avowal of the skill Genet uses to present his beliefs, showing a clear grasp of the promising power of distance as an important theatrical factor. The various surdities of *Haute Surveillance* and *les Bonnes* are missing here, because there is less visible concern with argument and more immediate recognition of the theatre's inherent power to create a self-contained world, or simply a metaphor, whose originality, in the course of the evening, can become credible if not altogether acceptable. Had Genet contented himself, as he does more often than not in his first books, with a kind of frontal attack, redeemed as it may be at moments by a certain lingering note of pathos, he would have ended up repeating himself. But his voice is not what dominates here; rather does his imagination come fully into its own by seeming not to be couched exclusively in the terms of propaganda. If what he says here has been said elsewhere in his work, we must admit that it is here said in a more objective way. The autobiographical soundings are absent, and with their departure a certain kind of communication becomes possible, simply because the register of *le Balcon* is at a mid-point between us and the author. Earlier he had used his imaginative powers to create replacements or substitutes for emotions he did not feel at the moment of the original experience; thus the miracle of the rose, evoked at the climax of the book of the same title, was an effort to fill in a void left by the insufficiency of emotions and perhaps even the failure of will in his own life. The setting of *le Balcon* is something else entirely. Here the imagination finds objects to embody, in a quite dynamic though not always confident way, situations created by that imagination. This, of course, does not mean that the situations and the expressive objects—costumes, gestures, and verbal play—do not, in the end, come back to the same preoccupations; what it does mean, and here is its importance, is that Genet's imagination ceases to be a clinical phenomenon in order to become an articulate and thus possibly a persuasive force. Its dynamism stems from the skill with which Genet, having offered us an object, moves us relentlessly from contemplation of that object into involvement with it, for we learn that ultimately what we have been contemplating is the gospel of ourselves—according to Jean Genet, of course.

Since we're on the stage,
where everything is relative,
all I need do is walk back-
wards in order to create the
theatrical illusion of your
moving away from me.
                    —*les Nègres*

'les Nègres'

In addition to being an evi-
dently autonomous work, *le Balcon* serves as a technical
preparation for *les Nègres*. The earlier play set about
making its statement by first creating an object, sus-
pended, as I have said, at some mid-point, a vague convergence of the author's experience and ours. We have
seen what happened to that object, how it became, after
having won our assent to its terms as something independent of us, a missile designed to penetrate into our
consciousness in order to awaken self-recognition and

181

whatever guilt such recognition elicits. *Le Balcon,* then, is less personal and more direct than its predecessors, and while this serves principally to involve the audience as those other plays did not (except, of course, as potentially impressive dramatic exercises), it has important secondary consequences. Its success, the evident impression it makes on an audience as the result of the manner in which it goes about involving that audience in its workings, gives further force to Genet's audacity and that force in turn gives *les Nègres* an insolent register where the tones of accusation are at no moment muted. This is primarily the result of a realization on Genet's part that the subject he has selected is one which allows him to accuse with more brio and conviction than do the special interests of his personal life; but it is the result, also, of success. In *Miracle de la rose* he had written with admiration and barely repressed joy about how radio messages managed to get through during the war despite efforts at jamming. Now he finds himself in somewhat the same situation; as a result of his persistence, his uncompromising determination not to lacquer his messages, his unwillingness to trim down the obscenities and unpleasantness of his works, he finds that he, too, is getting through.

He says in a brief preface: "One evening an actor asked me to write a play for an all-black cast. But what exactly is a black? First of all, what's his color?" For the rest of the play he gives an unmistakably clear answer to all these questions, putting the flesh of menace and implication on the skeleton of his definitions. The whole tone of the play is craftily enraged; its purpose goes beyond the simplicities of accusation into the complexities of finding means to leave the audience helpless. It is to depart from the theatre not simply convinced of its guilt but also of its utter futility. If the purpose

182

of *le Balcon* was to show us how much like its characters
we were, the purpose of *les Nègres* is to show us how
dangerously separated we are from *its* characters and to
what degree we, in thinking ourselves in the saddle riding
mankind, have instead become the mount. We shall
watch, however, not aware at the beginning that we are
to become involved. Our place will be very much like
that of the German soldiers in *Pompes funèbres* who,
mantled with haughty detachment, had watched the
amorous combat between Riton and one of their number. Genet described their situation in this manner
(p. 151): "The three soldiers silently watched this almost
motionless body to body contact. Their attention and
their silence were part of the action itself. They made it
perfect because they made it public and gave public
consent to it. Their attention—their presence in three
different corners of the room—enveloped the action."
Archibald, the factotum of these particular ceremonies,
suggests much the same sort of thing when he tells us
that the whites who are watching the play are to act on
its basis not out of indulgence but out of terror.

Here, then, we have stage action which is avowedly
stage action, but it is action dependent upon a thoroughly
different notion of theatre than that, say, which sparked
the drama of seventeenth-century France into greatness.
Here there will be no idealizing connection between the
theatre and the prevalent myths of the society whose
ideals it seeks to embody; the divorce is total, and the
purpose of the theatre will be to state the particulars of
the bill which legitimates the divorce. Archibald says
(p. 66): "This is the theatre, not the street. The theatre,
and drama, and crime." The theatre in question is, of
course, something more than the building in which *les
Nègres* is put on: the drama will be something more than
what happens on the stage; and the crime, by the end

183

of the evening, will clearly be the audience's. So that the movement can take place and the passage from theatre to crime be accomplished, the audience must be immediately involved in the action of the play. This is achieved through a simple device of having Archibald address the spectators directly and then organize his actors before the public's eyes to play the parts assigned to them.

What the audience is invited to see is the representation of a crime committed by the blacks, and, further, a representation of the punishment which befits the crime. But in seeing this the audience will see something more than a recreated delinquency: it will see also a presentation of a myth it wants to see, a myth which will confirm that the blacks are what the whites think they are and thus deserve to be treated as they have been treated. Archibald says, unctuously (p. 22):

> This evening we shall perform for you. But, in order that you may remain comfortably settled in your seats in the presence of the drama that is already unfolding here, in order that you be assured that there is no danger of such a drama's worming its way into your precious lives, we shall even have the decency—a decency learned from you—to make communication impossible. We shall increase the distance that separates us—a distance that is basic—by our pomp, our manners, our insolence— for we are also actors.

This statement is a deliberately murky invitation—unclear in the sense that Archibald's invitation and the organization of the actors in the early movements of the play merely suggest a solution it will take the whole evening to define in all its particulars. But the invitation, once issued, becomes something like the earlier dialogue of *JB:* it is designed to get us entangled, much as Nickles

184

and Zuss in the MacLeish play became entangled with their own speculations, until they were absorbed into impersonating and defending those speculations both for themselves and for the audience. What Genet's play involves us in has only the thinnest veneer of original action, but the veneer, until the moment when it begins to chip off, is enough to give the play one rhythm instead of several. With the early dialogue, the audience—whose brighter members will already have been upset by the tone of Archibald's remarks—begins to detect something resembling foul play; the furniture isn't genuine after all, but is only coated gumwood. The awakening of such detection initiates a certain amount of speculation: Are things going off as planned, or is the announced action getting out of hand and being replaced by something else that defies the limits of the written script and is out of Archibald's control?

This kind of impression is created by the basic mechanics of the play. The stage is divided on two levels. On the upper level there sit a Queen and her court, whose most remarkable members—since they hark back to *le Balcon*—are a general, an episcopus in partibus, and a judge. All of them wear white masks. Below them —and performing *for* them—are a group of blacks, the group which will enact the crime that has already enraged those who wear the white masks. The play-within-the-play, which was supposed to go off without a hitch, is soon disrupted by two elements. First, there is an undefined tension, expressed in argument between the two groups; secondly, there is an undercurrent of furtive movement among the blacks themselves; both elements will continue throughout the play until their final resolution.

These elements, like the upset they tend to create among the spectators, have nothing to do with foul play

or insufficient rehearsal. What they tell us is that everything we are seeing is illusion, since the real action—
one is reminded of the Queen in *le Balcon* who "em-
broiders and does not embroider"—is not this action at
all. The real action is going on off stage, and the purpose
of the action the audience is beholding is simply to serve
as distraction from that off-stage business. So long as the
audience is diverted—and theoretically it is diverted because it is seeing before its eyes what it wants and expects
to see—it is allowing the real action to take place. The
meaning of the play, therefore, is not in the action we
see, nor in the chain of events which forms the substance
of that action, but in the totality of the play as an object
designed to accomplish a very specific purpose. One is
reminded of certain Rembrandt or Whistler portraits
where the simple purpose of giving a faithful presentation
of lineaments is thoroughly suffused by the touch of
vision the commissioned artist brings to his work. Because of this touch, the portrait which was supposed to
be pictorial becomes commentary.

The object-play, then, represents two things: what
people think they see because they so choose to color
their eyes, and what is really there: the Negro as a re-
flective, astute, knowledgeable force who has learned to
use the white man's colorblindness to his own advantage.
But the object-play, as it unfolds, is also a symbol of the
danger, because the success of the play depends upon
its capacity to deceive the audience even as the audience
is given almost sufficient hints about what is going on.
The action taking place off stage is designed to advance
the Negro's cause, but its success is also dependent upon
the accuracy of the Negro's conviction that the audience
cannot possibly believe that the blacks are capable of
such cleverness and its resultant treachery. Bobo, a kind
of sorceress, says at one point (p. 88): "It's a Greek

tragedy, my dear, decorum; the ultimate gesture is performed off stage." But this simply isn't so; the definitive gesture is achieved in the theatre itself and is typified by what goes on between the stage and the audience; the definitive gesture in this case is going to be the act of theatre-going itself.

Much as one might multiply levels of irony in talking about Erasmus' *Praise of Folly,* where Folly mocks Wisdom and praises herself in order the better and more appropriately to establish convergent and divergent perspectives, so here the levels of irony are not those immediately apparent. The play is an attack on white people (by extension, of course, it is an attack on all who, not being with Jean Genet, must necessarily be against him); the center of the attack, the symbol of white people, are those who have come to see the play. And though they may laugh and act as knowingly as the most discerning initiates, they cannot possibly win, for if they had understood the furtive undercurrents of revolt at the beginning of the play they would have done something about the situation; and if they have not understood before one of the actors comes back to announce that the off-stage action has been carried on successfully, then they haven't understood at all. They may have learned—for the tone of a sermon is, after all, didactic— that the Negro is not what they have always thought him to be; but they have learned, too, that the Negro is so far removed from them now that not all the tolerance, nor all the good will in the world can bring the two together again. The Negro has chosen an independent path and has no intention of setting up guideposts to where this new roadway may be found. That the alienation is complete is suggested in the undelineated menace Archibald offers when, late in the play, he says, "solemnly" (p. 139):

187

> As we could not allow the Whites to be present at
> a deliberation nor show them a drama that does
> not concern them, and as, in order to cover up,
> we have had to fabricate the only one that does
> concern them, we've got to finish this show and get
> rid of our judges . . . (to the One Who Played the
> Queen): as planned.

To back up his remarks he can count on the memory
of one of the climactic moments of the play, which only
now can begin to assume sense for the audience. That
moment was the culmination of the supposed action
which was to be the core of the play. Through coaxing,
cajoling, and constraint Village has been brought to the
point of acting out in full if not presentational detail
his rape of a white storekeeper. The movement here,
characterized as it is by arguments over the accuracy of
his recountal, is of course a parallel to the whole relationship existing between actors and spectators during the
play. In the final phase of his explanation a transvested
Diouf gives birth to a group of white dolls who are then
pinned to the supports of the platform on which the
masked whites have sat during the performance. These
dolls, born full-grown (all eighteen inches of them) from
the womb of a transvested man on the verge of being
raped in accordance with Village's narration, are perfect
symbols of what the author thinks of his audience. The
dolls, once pinned to the supports, are the sole nonillu-
sory objects on the stage, since they *are* white and not
masked into whiteness; but they are objects which cannot act and whose creation henceforth will depend upon
the will of the Negroes. Remembering them, and listening to Archibald's remark, the audience cannot fail to
see the dolls as representatives of a white race petrified
into immobility by a fascination with its own myths; nor

can it fail to realize how thoroughly unrealistic has been the delivery, how unreal it itself consequently is, and how thoroughly it is now subject to whatever harm the Negroes may wish to do.

At the end of *le Balcon* the audience was left with provocative questions: are you better than these people, are your dreams less false? At the end of *les Nègres* the audience is left simply in contempt; it no longer represents a threat to anyone because it is itself threatened. This is made amply clear in production when, at the end of the play, the characters resume the positions they had at the beginning: the ceremonial is to be endless, the threat ever strong, and this effort to evoke endless cycles reminds one of Genet's own interest in the Roman Catholic Mass as a drama constantly enacted until it becomes the substance rather than a mere practice of the Church celebrating it.

What is the audience's reaction? On the basis of the statement Genet is making it might very well be indifference or dissatisfaction. To spend an evening in the theatre simply in order to be told that you're no good is hardly the basis for enthusiasm. Yet reactions to the play in at least three theatrical centers has been just that unexpected enthusiasm. Primarily, of course, critics and theatre-goers have no reason to expect or detect the kind of nasty joke Genet is playing on them; but this is not enough to explain such warm reaction to such unrelieved abuse. Rather it is the refreshing theatricality of the play that, carrying it far beyond the limited statement discursive reason can derive from it, makes it impose itself with unmistakable aesthetic authority. *Les Nègres* gets at its audience and the way it gets at the audience explains at once the important contribution it makes toward theatrical revitalization and the latest information it gives us about Genet's imagination.

The Imagination of Jean Genet

Dominique Fernandez, in an article in the *Nouvelle Revue Française* (January 1960), was quick to see the originality of this kind of thoroughly imaginative theatre, which gets at reality better by dispensing with it altogether, or, better, by dispensing with more conventional notions of verisimilitude and resemblance; he was quick to see, too, that Genet's theatre is very much like Claudel's in its determination to take the spectator away from his happier conventions in order to plunge him totally into a world which will make its own explanations. It is this kind of experience, a kind of confrontation with an imagination that is not afraid of itself nor concerned with the consequences of its own most exaggerated insights, that places *les Nègres* in a register of sophistication bound to appeal to those who patronize the off-Broadway theatre. It is obviously not the kind of diversion or commercial distraction about which I have written above; and, while it may mock and contemn its audience, it also presupposes a certain intelligence, a certain aesthetic attenuation on the part of that audience. The devices it uses go well beyond the more hackneyed emotional stimuli the commercial theatre has diminished into something disturbingly like the bell with which Pavlov summoned his dog to feasts of varying merit—at times, to no feast at all.

The basic inclination of Genet's imagination has become an adherence to ceremony, but, unlike his earlier works, where the possibility of ceremonializing his experiences was only a longing made pathetic by his inadequacy to achieve it, it becomes here a very genuine accomplishment. For all the digressions and deliberate confusions of its unfolding, *les Nègres* is none the less an unbroken line moving relentlessly toward a clearly sensed if not immediately perceived point. It has a rhythm keyed to the level of ceremony it seeks, and it maintains this rhythm by a quite uncannily structured exploitation of what common purpose its audience possesses. Thus at important points in the play we hear the strains of Mozart, witness a jazz dance, follow a procession organized to the music of the *Dies Irae,* recognize the distortion of certain litany invocations. The purpose is not blasphemy so much as it is tone. Since it would be impossible for a single man writing for a society highly diversified in its beliefs and nonbeliefs to create and maintain a private ritual, these borrowed ceremonies, possessed by sophisticated people as part of their aesthetic information, give the necessary familiarity which allows an astute author to blend them to his purpose. This sort of procedure evidently is not without its dangers and ironies, since it presupposes an intelligence sophisticated enough to appreciate and value Mozart and, on the basis of this knowledge, to see the bitter commentary involved in a Negro group's using this music as part of a general devastating comment on Western ways. It is a curious thing, however, to ask that an audience be civilized enough to understand the materials which are being used to cheat, dupe, and insult them.

The attack is unrelieved; the whites are to be made uncomfortable and brought into intimate contact with the fact that this play is written against them and, in order to have its full polemical effect, can only take place if there is a white man in the audience; otherwise, as Genet points out in a note to the second French edition, the point of the play would be lost:

This play written, I repeat by a white man, is intended for a white audience, but if, which is unlikely, it is ever performed before a black audience, then a white person, male or female, should be invited every evening. The organizer of the show

191

should welcome him formally, dress him in ceremonial costume, and lead him to his seat, preferably in the front row of the orchestra. The actors
will play for him. A spotlight should be focused
upon this symbolic white throughout the performance.

But what if no white person accepted? Then let
white masks be distributed to the black spectators
as they enter the theatre. And if the blacks refuse the
masks, then let a dummy be used.

Contempt could conceivably go no further; and perhaps
that is the only purpose of the preliminary note: to indicate to the reader what he would feel were he a spectator
in the theatre. But the terms of the note suggest a recurrent limitation in Genet: he has not the taste to go
with his imagination. He makes enormous demands, on
the one hand, and then, on the other, tries to pretend
that the demands do not exist. To understand *les Nègres*
readily one must have a broad education and a deep
sense of theatre; equipped with these a spectator can
draw various rewards from attendance at the play. But
his sensibility is needlessly being demeaned by these suggestions, and his intelligence is being quickened by the
challenge of Genet's words to a realization that is going,
in turn, to undercut Genet's pretensions. That realization quite simply has to do with an awareness that Genet's
play is unquestionably a Western play, dependent for
its impact on a sense of Western theatrical and artistic
traditions. An African audience would be puzzled by it,
and white dummy or no white dummy, it would not have
the equipment with which to understand any more about
the play than that it was in some way an attack on
whites; but the device that would produce that understanding—the use of a white man or dummy—is perhaps

the cheapest within the play. Any Negro who does understand the play as an aesthetic moment would, of course, be so Westernized as to be subject to the same level of attack being directed at the whites.

None the less the play is a remarkable achievement, whose accomplishments may seem less extraordinary when reported on here than they are when seen on the stage. They are the products of an increasingly versatile imagination that has absorbed a tremendous repertory of dramatic ideas and usages. This achievement could not have been chalked up, if there had not been a rather fundamental revolution in Genet's attitude and the results of this revolution on his imagination. What was tentative in his earlier works has lost all hesitation to become sure; what was cautious in the structure and organization of *le Balcon* has now become audacious. "Slavery," Village says in an important passage of *les Nègres* (p. 54), "taught me dancing and singing." It is a statement resonant of other similar passages in Genet, for both Yeux-Verts in *Haute Surveillance* and Georges in *le Balcon* had talked about dancing. But dance for them was therapeutic and instrumental; it consoled them against the assaults of life and simultaneously presented them with a liberating device whereby they might abstract their experience into the kind of ceremony which would give that experience the independent existence it needed in order to be protected against the attacks from without the limits of their experience. With Village, and by metonymy with Genet, this changes so that the replacement quality of dance and song is suffused into its more challenging potentialities. Yeux-Verts danced to console himself against society, or, more generally, against opposition; Village dances because in his dance (which is *les Nègres*) he can offer society the kind of statement about itself it cannot itself possibly make.

193

Dance, then, with *les Nègres,* becomes a primary activity and is no longer simply a consolation or a recreation, in the theatre, of a moment of earlier comfort. It has moved away from whatever there was of escape in it to become a direct, insolent, thoroughly self-assured means of challenge.

Things cease to belong to
those who've been able to
make them more beautiful.
　　　　　　　—les Paravents

'les Paravents'

　　　　　　As an imagination moves
into assurance, it moves also into a diversity and dexterity which produce at least two consequences; there is
the tendency, first, to derive a certain amount of justified
pleasure from the possession of an instrument which
seems to annul the perplexities of life by offering a means
of presenting them in an object where they seem to be,
if not resolved, at least significantly conveyed. We may
not be able to demonstrate that love and hate are the
same thing, but we can learn how to show off one against

195

the other so that their simultaneous existence as part of a unified general phenomenon becomes clear to the reader: he sees both the unity and the contradiction, but he sees them shaped into a whole. There is, secondly, the temptation to filter the whole world's experience through the imagination, so that the notion that each writer ploughs only those fields of experiences which belong to him disappears to be replaced by a certain avidity either to see a fundamental similarity between those few fields and all the fields of the world, or else to want to possess all the fields of experience in order that they, too, can be subjugated to one special kind of ploughing.

Further distinctions arise here, for the writer who sees a total appropriateness for his vision does not necessarily believe himself compelled to make specific applications of that vision to every situation which may present itself to the contemplation or dullness of the billions of people who inhabit the earth. Shakespeare, Racine, and other tragedians do not compromise the human validity of their characters when they insist that these same characters are not the common run of humanity. In another direction, a writer may see a totality in his work which he knows has weight and valuable consequences immediately for him but perhaps only indirectly for others. The world of Proust is a complete personal world, established to answer the inquiries and meet the needs of an individual sensibility; what sense and purpose it may have for others depends either on their sensitivity to being touched by the presentation of the personal dilemma which has produced the personal answer or else their possession of similar inquiries and needs.

But the temptation to place the stamp of one's private vision or personal means of operation on all things is not happy with such limitations. The Dantes and Balzacs of this world, though they move often in quite different directions, do not easily yield to the notion of a genteel self-limitation. Satisfaction with ploughing, watering, and cultivating one small terrain is not their way of doing things. The particular, though it may indeed have been what first led them into the labyrinths of literature, is not what keeps them there. The troubles of Florence seen conjointly with the loss of the love of a cherished lady to death's unsettling anarchy; the growing domination of the Parisian capital as it reaches out its economic, social, and ethical tentacles to touch all of France; the awareness that the multiplicity of experiences in one life make that life a testable sample of the general complex which is all human experience—these are the notions which lead Dante, Balzac, and Jules Romains to undertake vast works, where their convictions buoy them through all the initial difficulties either to total assurance, frustration, or mediocrity. Dante soars at the end of his great poem, his wings growing as large as his vision and his art will allow; Balzac roars as the smell of death grows strong in his nostrils and his eyes grow sharp to every pocket of social life which he has not yet been able to probe; Jules Romains fades away, his multi-volumed work growing happily less multiple as people stop reading.

Part of the reason behind this movement toward generalizing the particular world would have to do with the nature of each man's vision, which is made up, not simply of the data of emotional reactions to a set of circumstances, but equally of an awareness of the intellectual or ideological consequences of that situation. Shakespeare's heroes may rage against the gods or men, but they rage usually in different terms so that those who would be convinced that all art is intensely personal, even in the ideas it presents, will continue their frustrated attempts to uncover the personal ideological bias which

197

is at the basis of Shakespeare's ideas. They will be doomed, of course, because they set out with the wrong destination in mind, paying too much attention to intellectual systems and not enough to the emotions which Shakespeare seeks to convey. What is common to his plays is an impeccable sense of humanity: its workings, its evil, its good, and the mixture all these together create and which we label human experience. The same is true of Racine and, if René Jasinski's book proves nothing else, it does show that efforts to systematize Racine's thinking as though it were a philosophical or autobiographical declaration end up by becoming statements about how Racine felt when confronted with specific situations.

This is not true of Dante or Balzac. They have, existing simultaneously within them, myriad forces, some of which have ideological roots, others of which have emotional roots. Dante's mind makes a connection between its interests in the government of Italy and the love his emotions bear to Beatrice as an unrequited offering. Each experience represents the apprehension and pursuit of an ideal; that ideal does not become unified until *la Divina Commedia,* where it remains a splendid panoply for all time. Balzac grows into a sense of the power of his apperceptions to create a vast work which will convey the feeling of all the powers and forces which compete in the world; as the enterprise grows he finds his mind turning to embrace institutions and ideas which will help reduce the evil his pursuit of his vision relentlessly uncovers. Where there is an important contrast is in the divergence between the lives of these men and their ideas. They are quite capable of accepting *in abstracto* principles which they may violate in life; a theory of sin eases if it does not eliminate the resultant contradiction. The times and individual lives may get out of joint, but Dante and Balzac are sure of how they can get reset. If they are convinced of anything, Shakespeare and Racine are convinced that the dislocations are recurrent—the evil lives on and all the systems in the world will not interrupt its determined pattern.

If the twentieth century, in its literature, has not lost the temptation toward total explanations, it has not found any vision powerful enough and possessed of enough self-assurance to impose anything that smacks of being omni-explicatory. The more insolent systems are the more idiotic, primarily because they seek to enthrone caprice, finding it as good an answer as any other. Surrealism and Dadaism would put things together for us, if we were willing to possess, as important objects, the goods they have assembled from potato sacks, cigarette butts, and other refuse of Parisian streets and poorly stocked minds. The contemporary Catholic writer is more concerned with the anguish which results from the possession of a system in a no longer systematized world than with the value of the system. The Becketts and the Ionescos and the Pinters are so fascinated with the triumph of indecision that they forget how much decision-making goes into the process of keeping body and spirit together before statements about indecision can be made. The result, of course, is that their register, if indeed they possess one, is that of Shakespeare and Racine, for we simply cannot take seriously the kind of statement that is denied so frequently if banally in our daily lives and that is more significantly denied by the process which leads us to read their books and attend their plays. Estragon and Vladimir in *En attendant Godot* have unquestionable difficulties; but their total possession of these difficulties is obviously not a mirror of the difficulties of their author; were it, we would not have the play.

The apparent absence of a Dante or Balzac from our

world may, however, result more from the temper of the public than from that of the writer. I have already alluded to divergences in belief so sharp within our contemporary civilization as to cut down seriously not the possibility of communication but that of conviction. We listen patiently and sometimes profitably to many voices, but we hearken to few where the formation of our convictions is concerned. Others can evaluate the pertinence of this to the best available approaches to reality; its value here is in its application to Jean Genet, who risks finding himself in the wrong category, lined up with the prophets of or witnesses to the absurd, dumped into the company of those who wish to communicate to us the impossibility of communication, assigned to the lists of those whose frustrated hopes and fuller suffering have created the literature of sociological protest. He is none of these now, though he has unquestionably passed through various degrees of cousinship with each of them at earlier moments.

Because there has been a passage, a voyage through many outlooks and even more points in emotional expressivity, it is not easy to assign Genet either to the company of the Shakespeares and Racines or to that of the Balzacs and the Dantes. He belongs, if we take the measure of his complete experience, to both. But he belongs to each at different moments. Racine and Shakespeare are his past: the febrile and fragile world of *Notre-Dames-des-Fleurs* and *Miracle de la rose,* whence emanated the insufficiencies and inconstancies of life in a world not of his own creation. Dante and Balzac are his present and seem likely to be his future: the world of discovery, of growth into a body of convictions that become as a whiplash to beat the world. Perhaps Jean Genet had not created it and suffered the results. That was in another country and the past, if not dead, is transformed by his capacity to dominate the forces of the world with the power of his understanding and the energy of his imagination, which feeds that understanding into a perpetually moving generator. *Les Paravents* is, I should imagine, the first product of this generator; it is assured as nothing else Jean Genet has done is assured; it is bold in a way quite different from the explicit sexuality of his other works; it is insolent in its method as other plays were insolent in their matter. But the method and the matter have achieved that marriage I have referred to elsewhere. The old families are broken up; man and woman have gone off, leaving their own kin, to establish a new unit. We, the old kin who threw rice cheerfully at the wedding, are now to find out that we have not been left so much as abandoned. Because of this *les Paravents* is both epithalamion and dirge. In it Genet limns the assorted lovelinesses of where he is; in it we see where we have been discarded. If *le Balcon* was designed to show us what our experience really is, and if *les Nègres* was designed to show us that that experience could not assure us victory or even a good defense, *les Paravents* is designed to show us not only that we have lost but also that we have been left behind as all rubbish should be. We have not been displaced so much as dispossessed. But, unlike the others, those who formerly seemed to wear the tatters of the dispossessed, we will find that our newly discovered condition offers us no promise, for the dispossessed are no longer being glorified. Instead what is being glorified is the process of dispossession itself.

While we can sense and eventually discover a rather direct line connecting *les Paravents* to *les Nègres,* we should not become interested too early in the existence of that line since, in so doing, we are liable to miss some of the marginal but vital curiosa which have to do with the existence of the play. I have said that it is both epithalamion and dirge, but I have not yet made mention of the fact that, like all epithalamia, it represents an achievement which has an immediate past history. In order to get to the writing of this play, Genet has had to stop and take breath, as he had in *Journal du voleur,* by surveying what he has achieved and assessing the fullest dimensions and consequences of this achievement. This examination is not the same sort of spontaneously dynamic process which had made *Pompes funèbres* the trigger for a cannon from which would be shot the missile that was *Querelle de Brest;* nor is it the kind of change in import which could be noted between the presentation of the Negro mentality in *Notre-Dame-des-Fleurs* and the later, more threatening presentation given the same phenomenon in *les Nègres.* In the earlier work, the Negro had been presented, and parenthetically at that, as one whose rage against the whites was expressed by his determination to insult them. Thus Gorgui had left his nakedness exposed because, ashamed of it as a result of what he had learned among white people, he wished to use it as a sign of defiance. He had not achieved the sort of knowledgeable scorn which was to characterize the Negroes of Genet's plays who are indifferent to anything a white world may want to say to them, think of them, or do to them.

Rather than these things, what Genet has had to examine is his role as a revolutionary, and the best available way of measuring that is to determine if the waves of shock sent out by his plays are still creating dramatic oscillations on the receiving equipment. The equipment seems to have built up overly responsive pulses; its components do not seem to have been quite so jarred as they should be. Other revolutionaries, seeing this as the surest indication that their ideas were becoming everyone's would be cheered. Not so with Jean Genet. For him success offers no sweet smell, but only a fetid stench; for him, too, revolt can have no surcease. It must be ongoing, essential, unchanging, and unconsoling. Though his recent plays, *le Balcon* and *les Nègres,* had either been hooted in or chased out of Paris, they had been performed with distinction and received with enthusiasm in other theatrical centers. They have even been awarded prizes in countries where, being few, such accolades have some distinction. Undergraduates attend his plays with baffled eagerness, graduates explore their meanings with a dedication somewhat less energetic albeit equally determined, and scholars write articles about him. It has indeed been a long way from the time when his works were discussed with deliberate indirection in the back pages of the *Partisan Review,* and, with *les Paravents,* Jean Genet seems to have decided that it may have been the wrong way.

The problem, quite simply, is that Jean Genet wants no part of it; he wants nothing to do with passing from the *enfant terrible* he was at the beginning of his literary career to the *enfant gâté* he seems to be becoming as the bourgeoisie, against whom he has directed his most acerbic attacks, assimilate his ideas, talk about them, and either accept or reject them. He wants no part of this because the very process by which he is spoiled is the process he has been attacking in all his later works: the presupposition that it is the bourgeoisie, the *decent* people, who rule ultimately on this earth and whose assent to any body of ideas is the modern world's imprimatur and canonization, without which no man can be assured he has made his impact. If Jean Genet has deigned to talk to this world, it has been with the clear intention of demonstrating how deep, lingering, and unchanging his hostility to it is. And his hostility, once the

203

hesitations and uncertainties of his early works had been overcome, has had little to do with opposition to a group which has made him suffer indignity and upheaval; it has had a great deal to do with the assertion of his values as truer, more spontaneously experienced, and more thoroughly lived than any the bourgeoisie can claim as their own. His ideas, his ways have not grown in any well cared for hothouse, subject to vague Mendelian selection patterns of a cautious middle class society. They are his, poured out from the crucible of his experience and, since no individual born to respectability can possibly have been shaped by the same potter's wheel, no such individual has the right to think that dialogue between him and the *original* who is Jean Genet is possible. It is not possible simply because the two worlds—ours and Genet's—are necessarily and essentially exclusive and therefore opposed.

In *Journal du voleur,* his most directly autobiographical work, he had expressed the ruminations of his mind and imagination at that moment when he was passing from petulance into assurance, buttressed with the conviction that his particular experience was not quite so peculiar as he had been led to think and might have applications to the experience of others. He had seen, too, that his glorification of the world in which he had lived was producing impact and thus could write with satisfaction not altogether devoid of smugness (p. 116): "This effort shall not have been a vain one for me. I am already experiencing its effectiveness . . . the world is growing uneasy. As that uneasiness grows, I know a strange peace."

The process of establishing this uneasiness had seemed to work with fairly capital success in *le Balcon* and *les Nègres;* indeed, whatever insufficiencies the plays manifested were the result not so much of what had been invested in them as of the unpredictable nature of the dividends. *Le Balcon* could not fall short of its mark since the very act of understanding it on the part of the individual spectator was to be the guarantee that the message had got across and told the spectator where his place was in the world of power: at the very bottom of a ladder whose upper rungs included what the reputable theatre-goer would have considered the pariahs of society, and at whose top was perched, with incredible assurance and the shrewdness which had made the assurance possible, Madame Irma—a brothel keeper of unusual distinction and disturbing wisdom. Much the same process had been detectable in *les Nègres;* here again the audience's capacity to understand was to determine the extent to which the impact of the play's attack would be most sensitively felt: as the actors arranged themselves at the end of the play to begin anew the deceptive ritual designed to allow the whites to believe what they most needed and thus wanted to believe, the whites could not forget that the ritual, already enacted, had been merely a lid placed over a rebellion seething elsewhere, outside the range both of the audience's consciousness and understanding.

The dividends I have written of paid off in peculiar ways. There was, to start with, the fact that the audience did not seem quite so appalled as it ought; it had learned to live comfortably if not acceptingly with what it was being told and perhaps had found the whole thing either an educational experience or, taking wing from the intensity of its understanding, a proof that the attack could not be directed against it. But there was also the problem that the subject matter might have itself been tending toward a new hierarchy of heroism, a freshly explored terrain of new kinds of courage, fortitude, and even rectitude. *Le Balcon* had managed to keep these assorted dangers in balance, playing Carmen's desires to be respectable against Madame Irma's unwaveringly deft knowledge in understanding that her world, the universe which came into existence each evening in the curious salons of her brothel, was the only real world, because in that world all the masks and disguises were dropped so that men might give vent to their primeval and spontaneous interests and desires.

The world of *les Nègres* offered neither the same kind of frank revelation, nor did it limn the praises of a static vision of the world whose terms expressed what was and not what might be. Aspiration, ambition—a desire to be something else—charged *les Nègres* with an almost evangelical tone. On the one hand, there were the whites who, to assure their own ends, had subjugated the Negro and made him express his existence only in their categories; but on the other there were these ambitious Negroes who wanted the world for themselves, so that they might have their day in which they would express their hopes for themselves and their race. What was troublesome to Genet here was that his vocabulary did not escape from that used by white civilization to express its own ideals and, with the existence of that verbal parallelism, the possibility of total rejection became increasingly difficult. The implication, borne out by each day's news from Africa, was also that what the Africans were aspiring to was the right to control their own world, but simultaneously to make of that world the same sort of thing the whites had made of theirs. The benevolent white spectator, who contributes to CORE, supports the NAACP, and, in his more disinterested moments, goes freedom riding, could therefore leave *les Nègres* assenting to what had been seen and even convinced that the over-all tone of the play was hopeful. But hope, feathery and tickling thing it may have been for Emily Dickinson, has no place in the world of Jean Genet, precisely because hope implies a clearly seen or desired objective, and that objective, more often than not, is one that has been elaborated by those whom Genet rejects and against whom he asserts the integrity and honesty of what he is.

In reading *les Paravents* one has the impression of discovering what must have been Genet's dejection over *les Nègres,* and one comes to suspect why it was that, midway through its production in Paris, he lost interest and turned instead to this latest work. He had come dangerously close to suggesting that reform could replace rebellion and in that proximity had flirted with the loss of the absolute division between himself and others he had made into the enduring mortar of his other works. In the earlier play he had suggested a dynamic process not terribly distinct from progress; such dynamism could only serve eventually as a subtle but powerful battering ram against the fortress of his own earlier arguments. What becomes ever more clear and perhaps even disturbing in Genet's work is its total and inelastic dogmatism, its inflexibility in developing and thickening out a very small ideological register which is meant to have application to all men; what also becomes clear and increasingly impressive is the extraordinarily dextrous and fertile theatrical imagination which transfuses these repeating ideas into something compelling and impregnated with forceful beauty. Both tendencies are apparent in *les Paravents;* the theatrical ingenuity saves the ideology from its tendency toward tedium and perhaps organizes it into an accomplishment as it probes the fog-bound surfaces of reality. There is something curious about this because, in order to understand and better appreciate the dramatic qualities of the work, one must have a rather deep familiarity with Genet's ideas; a significant part of the excitement is in watching what new emphasis he will find for them; yet simultaneously the ideas and

207

novel emphases would be unrelieved monotony if it were and in that jumble only one figure, Saïd, is worthy of technique. The result is that one can imagine, on the basis of the experience created by *les Nègres* and *le Balcon,* a production of this very complicated play that would make a deep visual impression on an audience without that audience's in any way being able to understand the full range of the play.

To say that Genet's play is about the Algerian crisis is to limit it too much. To say that it is about Genet's interpretation of that crisis in terms of his own beliefs about the world is to open a more explorable path into the jungle of his preoccupations. It is a more promising suggestion primarily because it gets us out of the realm of historical cause and effect, out of the problem of accuracy in representation, which has never been a mainstay nor even a fleeting concern of Genet's imagination. What the Algerian situation poses for the author is what *les Paravents* poses for the audience: a jumbled situation in which diverse and differently powerful forces are matched unequally one against the other, two against one, four against three—the combinations, given the size and variety of the dramatis personae, are limitless. It is a situation in which levels of motivation are not sharply differentiated because, as a result of interaction over the years, the natives and the settlers have got confused in their ideas and have variously lost their commitment to what they originally might have believed and defended. It is, then, a situation where there is flux in action and thought with a consequent irritation that both diminishes the sharpness of distinctions and increases the dangers of confusion for those involved in it. Others, looking at the play, might conclude that it is a pretty good sampling of any confused sociological situation; Genet, offering it to those who like to look at things in this way, is saying that it is precisely what it is, a jumble, and in that jumble only one figure, Saïd, is worthy of respect or, more precisely, of being taken seriously.

He is worthy of respect because he has none and wants less. Abjection is the halo of his glory; revolt solely for sake of being opposed is the marrow of his bones; progress—the movement by which he would either pull himself up by his own bootstraps or be pulled up by others—is the great danger, for it would bring about change, and he has no interest in being changed, since his every action is designed to underscore the sham of all current belief in progress. He is what he is, and to become anything else would be to lose that essence and the information it brings him about man's eternal immersion in vileness and of the consequent importance of remaining vile if one is to remain a faithful witness to one's situation. One is vile because baseness is the basic datum of one's existence. Movement out of it would imply acceptance of another world and an intuitive agreement to forget, as though it had never existed, the suffering received from that world, once new terms of coexistence are established and the suffering is exalted into some necessary early manifestation of the "historical process." It would also imply a willingness to tolerate the existence of competitive views; and that simply cannot be, for in the church of Genet's imagination one tolerates neither the error nor the man who perpetrates it. This does not necessarily mean that there can be no progress; what it does mean is that progress is for others and is the measure of their ungodliness. It cannot be a distinguished activity or goal for the Saïds and Jean Genets of this world. They will not be duped into having short-range memories because of the promise of long-term gains. The stakes are too high and their accumulating information about the value of their roles too precious to be marketed cheaply, if at all. Saïd makes no progress in the play, as in a certain way, Genet makes no progress in his ideas. But others do, and they do because of the fidelity, the stasis of the Saïds and Genets who hold firm and keep faith with their abjection, so that abjection, unforgotten, will be the constant prod to memory not to forget, so that it will be a constantly refurbished stream feeding hate and rebellion into those who, like themselves, have suffered at the hands of others. It is a new kind of muse they offer, and it has a more effective, more independent life than that most characteristic of other muses. It is self-creating and self-perpetuating rather than being a potentially limited and unproductive projection of an individual's melancholy over the more readily available forces of life. Its inspiration is not some body of ideals culled from a mishmash of eventual profit and advantage to be sought after; its inspiration is its filth and its rags and its slime. It is not Baudelaire's Jeanne Duval, glorified and ensconced in some immensely ornate bed; it is Jeanne Duval, the petulant and diseased prostitute. Others may indite beautiful sounds from its noises and think, dangerously, that the noises no longer exist. But Jean Genet will be there, unregenerate and unchanged, grumbling his anger and his rage and his bad news to all those who flirt with such cheap optimism until they are seduced by it.

And he will even help them toward their sentimental death or their compromised progresses; help them, if they are inattentive to the full impact of his statement, by allowing them to believe that the world to which the Algerians aspire is a world established on the same terms as theirs; help them, if they are Algerians who feel such an establishment is either possible or desirable, to think they are getting somewhere where it is profitable to go; help them, if they are men intelligent and sensible to

210

theatrical power, by giving them an inventive and moving evening in the theatre where they can mix, at will, compassion and amusement. But below all this will remain the one constant: Saïd's abominable situation which he and Genet jointly cherish and which is the only true root of any rebellion in Algeria or elsewhere. And above it there will float Saïd's most characteristic battlecry (p. 197): "To the old gal, to the soldiers, to all of you, I say shit."

        Saïd's cry, unsettling and impolite as it is, cannot escape from the accusation of childishness merely because it is uttered with such quiet fervor. Yet at the moment when it is made in the last pages of the play, it is obviously more than the predictable outpouring of a limited sensibility unwilling to submit itself to a redeeming growth process. It is also something more than sheer bravura: the marshaling of nasty and challenging words designed to raise a thick and menacing thumb to an ugly nose, thereby creating an action sufficiently repelling to undo whatever punishment we might think it legitimate to inflict. It is more than this because Genet's art does not need the vulgar gesture as a substitute for skill; where vulgarity is found in his plays, there is found, too, sufficient reason for its existence. The gesture is more than this, too, because of Genet's ideas. What he offered tentatively and in an exploratory way in his early works has by now been so thoroughly absorbed into the texture of his mind that he can no longer differentiate between what *is* and what he has fabricated in order to alter unpleasant essences. The world of *les Paravents* is Genet's world, entirely his creation and, as Saïd's cry indicates, entirely his possession. Its ceremonies and its liturgies are rituals whose rubrics have all been cultivated in Genet's imagination; it has an indigenous hierarchy and a thorough canon of practices and habits, each as well-organized and as highly charged with multiplicities of meaning as Dante's system of numbers in *la Divina Commedia*. Actions, which had claimed ownership on meaning only in his mind, have now become conventions of his theatre and, as a result, are offered to the public as pegs on which to hang significance. A policeman's vibrating thighs, the mention of a rose, the equation of the bordello with the world, a judge's indecision over the value of his function, a military officer's homosexual fascination with his subordinates—these are all reference points designed to awaken intuitively an understanding that has grown in the reader or spectator as a result of exposure to other of Genet's works. Both in intention and achievement the effort is not very much unlike Mr. Eliot's. Inspired by a concern with the dissociation of the common sensibility once brought to the act of reading, Eliot has tried to find a vocabulary and a register of images which, even as they make links between the present and the past of our civilization, would have significance for the reader and novel power for the further expansion of poetic insight and expression. Genet's effort is somewhat easier than Eliot's, of course, because it is personal and has not been concerned with doing some of the reader's work for him; but it gets to the same place: a world, totally Genet's, totally possessed of a vocabulary of signs and symbols which will convey the relative worth of statements made within that register. Saïd, rather than being a reversion to an earlier moment—the moment, say, of the nasty challenge Genet offered in *l'Enfant criminel*—is the latest manifestation of the fact that Genet's world view is constantly reaching out on the basis of its initial terms to become a total and, therefore, a self-sufficient world.

Eliot looks back to a blending of the classical and Christian worlds; Genet looks into his own literary past.

What is happening is that Genet is seeing more things rather than seeing earlier things more clearly. With each new revolution of his world view, new problems and possibilities arise, and these must be incorporated into his poetry where, as we have seen, he seeks to annul conflicts by catching them in their convergences. Saïd, as a force, is not something new within Genet's work; he seems novel because his place is being better defined and consequently sets off the terms of his existence more distinctly. We have seen him before as the commentator Genet, standing in the background of *Pompes funèbres,* directing and participating in the imaginative events assembled there. We have also seen him in *Querelle de Brest,* the young sailor who loitered perilously on the precipice of the Hangman-Erik-Riton dynamic but was saved from a plunge into that devouring ethic by his discovery of its existence and his realization that the man who knew of that dynamic could save himself from its inevitable destructiveness. In these works, as in the two substantial plays which precede *les Paravents,* the person or persons who possessed this vision somehow seemed outside the interplay of forces which make up the universe. They had their discovery, and their discovery gave them a heady sense of superiority; but the world continued to turn about them, within the range of their gaze but outside the range of their determining influences. They could stand back and comment; commenting, they could feel a certain sense of pronounced superiority; but they were not yet at that hub where are organized and sent out the waves of influence which govern the world. Observation led them to discover what they were and an interpretation that could be given to that essence; but it did not put them in charge of anything better than a brothel or a minstrel show. With *les Paravents,* and especially with Saïd, this obstacle is demolished. Saïd discovers nothing during the play; he need not. All about him he can see the world reacting to what he is, indeed to what he always has been and, watching those reactions, he is spared the sense of deliberate organization which was most characteristic of Madame Irma's bordello, and the sense of planned revolt and deliberate opposition which was the register of *les Nègres.* His essence governs the world, and it is up to the world to discover it. Saïd needs no such knowledge; he possesses it as he possesses his essence.

The advantages of this obviously go beyond Saïd's ambitions and into the heart of Genet's. In those earlier works he, too, had been the spectator—a commentator on the world's follies which he could label thus with ease because he had discovered their pretensions and madnesses, their illogic and their obtuseness. But discovery is not involvement and, if you have a world vision, there comes a point when possession of it is not enough; it must be generalized so that all will fall under its exfoliating shadow. It is, again, the situation of Lucretius, for that brave Latin, having discovered that life is all a shambles of independent and determined atoms working their productive wills against our sterile and wistful one, did not carry the bravery through to full consummation. The silence which would have been the last mantle, and the most colorful, of his courage would have been too much to ask; the good news about the bad news of our ultimate defeat at the hands of thoroughly materialistic forces could not be kept to himself. Whether it was generosity or nastiness which inspired *De rerum natura* is a question to be put aside when faced with the manifold beauties of that hearty yet heartless poem. What makes it a searchlight on Genet's intentions is its similar desire to involve the world in what it has discovered and, in the act of involvement, to show that there have been other kinds of involvement. Lucretius shows us that his kind of outlook is the ultimately productive one because it is rooted in a true apprehension of the authentic forces of universal movement; Genet, with *les Paravents,* will show us the same thing. Elsewhere he had been nothing more than the recorder of an ethical movement from which he had escaped and, in *le Balcon,* had as much as said this in the penultimate scene when the slave, talking to the young revolutionary who has come to impersonate the chief of police, speaks of his role as the bard of the oppressed and, through the oppressed, the oppressing. In a remotely similar scene in *les Paravents,* the Cadi, an Arab judge, will speak of the encroaching impoverishment of self-assurance brought on by the discovery that his function is dependent upon the existence of the slaves, thieves, whores, and Saïds of the world. The tables have indeed been turned, with great noise; the dispossessed are no longer alone in their awareness of the critical role they play in the world; those who have been newly dispossessed have also learned the lesson and, imbued with it, they are helpless, impotent—touched with putrefaction more than death.

Saïd is at the center of *les Paravents* as Christian is at the center of *Pilgrim's Progress;* and, as *Pilgrim's Progress* is intended to be a paradigm of the experience of everyman, so *les Paravents* is meant to be a paradigm of everyman in a twentieth century where revolution brings to the ascendancy the least likely forces. The comparison is not forced, for Saïd moves through the play, overturning obstacles, struggling against distracting forces, refurbishing his strength much as Christian does in his journey. Christian's categories are those of the religion whose name he bears; Saïd's are those of Jean Genet. But each has categories and the categories can be applied to every moment of experience in order to prove that it is the stalwart man who wins battles against the pretensions and weaknesses of this world. Admittedly, the ultimate goals and basic philosophies of the two are quite different; but the movement is the same, as is the exclusive character of their mission. Christian may make it to salvation, and Saïd may make it to the purest haven of the dead—but their way is not one which can be easily or even voluntarily trod by whoever happens along. It takes determination, a recognition of the fact that the virtues which accompany the journey are not the most pleasant or commonly desired; it takes a strong back and a hard skin to resist the insults and jeers met along the way. In both works, then, we are dealing with exceptional men, whose merit derives from their discovery of and persistence in pursuing a difficult ideal, but an ideal whose mastery assures them a personal triumph.

There are differences, the most illuminating one being found in the point of view. Bunyan's hero is evidently a hero as is Genet's. The old Genet magic is needed here, if only because the true shock of discovering that Saïd is at the center of the world can best be registered if it is conveyed through the discovery of others. It is a jolt to learn that Saïd is the source and most reliable manifestation of the world's energies. It is a shock quite simply because Saïd is one of the least pleasant fulcrums ever given so crucial a role. He is sloppy, crass, obscene, cruel—the storehouse of unpleasant adjectives can hardly convey the gathering of disagreeable elements which are the composites of his character. He is loathsome to almost everyone: his fellow Arabs, the European settlers, and the audience. He is unpleasant to everyone without exception: his mother, his wife, and the others already mentioned. Nothing redeems him, primarily, I gather, because redemption would imply a renunciation of some part of what he is in order to accept other standards; and, if nothing else, *les Paravents* is bound to show the uselessness of those other standards.

Pleasantness, however, is another one of those words which belongs to our vocabulary, and we have been seeing how little applicable our vocabulary is to the universe's true realities. It is, too, a word which suggests, not a victory, for that would be just another term for self-congratulation, but a distillation of a true force into a truncated force. We say something is pleasant in order to express our relief that we have found some source whose waters cover, if only momentarily and inadequately, the full force of what really surrounds us. We lose something in the process, and what we lose Saïd possesses knowingly and craftily. As he makes his progress through the play, he emerges, clothed with his abjection and his general horror, as a tremendous dominating force, the extent of whose powers cannot be measured because we have no yardsticks capable of determining the length and breadth and depth of what he is. By the time we find out, it is too late to do much about it save to notice, sadly, what we have lost, how we have lost, and how there is absolutely nothing left to us.

We first meet him as he makes his way, accompanied by a mother whom he insults and vilifies, to his wedding with Leïla, an unkempt and unwanted young woman he is marrying reluctantly—but as the result of a clearly free and personal decision. We follow him through a sampling of the kind of events which are the pattern of his life: he is insulted by other Arabs, put into his place by the European overloads, mistreated by the civil governing authorities, and imprisoned. Since prison, to the

The Imagination of Jean Genet

mind of Jean Genet, is one of the locales where we encounter an honest representation of reality, it is not surprising that Saïd's encounter with it is the beginning of
new revelations about him. For him, his incarceration
is a beginning; it is much the same for us. Once it is before us we start to learn that this reviled and rejected
individual is reviled and rejected because those who surround him are beginning to discover how serious a threat
he represents. He who had been a pariah and therefore
safely classified in his proper place has become a power;
his name is on every tongue, manifestations of acts influenced by his existence can be seen throughout the
land as houses go up in flames, murders multiply, and
orchards are turned to ashes. He is mystery and might
in addition to being other ungentle things I have mentioned. The might, because it springs from the mystery,
creates the menace. For how do you deal with a force you
cannot easily locate and whose dimensions cannot be
accurately calibrated? One of the prison warders is the
first to grasp the fact that the dimensions are truly outside the competence of available measures, when he says
plaintively and yet with puzzlement in an apostrophe to
Saïd and Leïla (p. 82):

> What with always yelling and screaming at you,
> because of you I have godawful nights. Let the night
> get some rest. The night needs silence too. From
> one end of Moslem soil to the other there's nothing
> but muttering in the shadow, cracking of branches,
> cigarette lighters sputtering, olive trees blazing,
> prowlers who leave behind a smell of burning, re-
> bellions . . . and you two, you two, in your rags . . .
> you never . . . stop . . . singing . . . . (He dozes off.)

This fragment is rich in revelation; as the chants of
Leïla and Saïd break through the warder's sleep they

quicken his subconsciousness to the expression both of the danger the couple represents and the loss that danger will bring about. Somewhere within him the warder, like all the others Saïd encounters, had known this and yet, as his knowledge finds words to express itself, he can think of no solution except to go back to sleep. His sleep is the mark of his inaction; but it is also a sample of what will be the reaction of all the others who will come under and succumb to Saïd's menace. Obviously this is a change for Genet in the presentation of his protagonists. In *Journal du voleur* he had spoken of the need to create heroes because they could not be found in reality; in *Notre-Dame-des-Fleurs* he had spoken of the corresponding need to imbue the unpleasant with a certain aesthetic and moral force in order to make it imposing. These ideas, like the good things in the country song, are past and gone. They are past and gone because they have become unnecessary. As the structure of the play shows us, we are not here involved with an effort on Saïd's part to find his place in the sun. He has that place; he holds onto it firmly, securely, and quite instinctively. What we are concerned with here is the discovery by others that he does possess a stunning place, a dazzling brilliance, and a blinding force. Saïd, I have already remarked, does not move in this play; he moves into the consciousness of others and leaves them stricken. Once there he makes them and us aware of just how unbudging he is. This intransigence, in addition to telling us much about why he is the most privileged among men, also serves as a good technical device for the exploration of the other forces surrounding him as they move from confidence into paralysis.

If you were looking, as was Lot, for an ever-diminishing number of honest men, you would, in the direction of your search, come across different quantities of honesty and learn to appreciate otherwise unnoticed subtleties in the possession of virtues. If you are Jean Genet, looking ever, always, and in all directions for the most powerful, determined and unabashed adherents to evil, your experience will not be so totally different from Lot's as you might suspect. The number of unpleasant characters available will be, in the nature of things, limited; and their unpleasantness, as it grows more discernible, will make very small potatoes out of them when they are held up against the bigger spuds unearthed by diligent spading. With his Algerians, Genet removes the lid from an even deeper abyss of hostility and opposition than he had expected, and with his discovery there comes a need to shake up and rearrange former hierarchies. The old mainstays of his earlier works must abide by the new protocol, as the Hangman had abided by Erik and Erik had abided by Riton; in so abiding, they expressed their commitment to the triumph of evil and their recognition that greater victors than they are winning greater victories than theirs. In *les Paravents* what this means is a regrouping of forces we have seen in other works, and with that regrouping, a new designation of value and power to those forces. As the old moralities fall away, disempowered by the resilience and determination of Saïd, new emphases are enunciated.

Those who escape the least scathed are, of course, the Arabs; that is in the nature of the new reality. Ties of blood and a common past put them and Saïd into fairly much the same category, though room is left for him to emerge at the top, much as Querelle and Irma emerged in earlier works. But even the Arabs are not spared the consequences of whatever bad faith or fraudulent ambitions have come to sully the purity of their commitment to abjection. To the extent that their commitment is to getting someplace where they will be able to exercise the power now exercised by others, and in the same way, they fall victim to Saïd's and Genet's wrath. But to the extent that they share his commitment to the maintenance of a condition whose triumph is bound to reduce former worlds to the ashes of their pretensions, they share in his kingdom and are placed among the blest. Thus his mother, identified throughout the play as La Mère, and his wife Leïla move along with him into expressions of self-assurance and conviction. They are his most vivid supporters and their support teaches them lessons about the value of being immersed in the filth surrounding them. It is the coating which protects their skin from ever becoming too thin to continue with the mission. La Mère has been put on this earth with one purpose: to understand and sustain her son as his essence develops into revealing itself as the governing force of the world. She has this single goal in life and she pursues it with a determination that shuts her off from the insults of others and the distempers of a dusty, disturbed life. She is invested with the kind of generosity which allows her to say (pp. 113–14): "Go further, Saïd. Demolish yourself, demolish your wife, but carry on."

Wherever she travels, La Mère carries this sense of dedication with her; she braves the reproaches and condemnation of her countrymen, because she sees in them the evidence of the success of her mission. She is an agent provocateur who reads in every pained and embarrassed face the signs of the successful maintenance of her mission. The limited consolations she draws from Saïd's activities are enough for her if only because the fulfillment they promise more than compensates her for the burdens and difficulties met along the way. Her exclusion from the company of the Arab women who

221

have come to lament at Si Slimane's tomb—he is a dead hero of the revolutionary movement—is an indication not so much of her proscription as of her possession of a knowledge these other women of restricted vision have not been invited to contemplate. Rage, she says at one point, has been the encircling condition of her life; as such it will conduct her inevitably among the tombs and into the halls of death; but rage is the prelude to victory, is indeed an attitude toward life which is better than the sheer indifference visible elsewhere. Her rage, more openly expressed than that of her son, is directed against those who, having caused it in the past by their mercenary and thoughtless activities, seek now, as things change and the spheres of power tilt toward new poles, to make adjustments. To a man who promises to withdraw his charges against her son, she answers (p. 36): "Your complaints are complaints for all eternity." The suggestion disturbs the plaintiff who recognizes in it La Mère's fundamental attachment to her shame as the weapon with which she will fight against all the forces which once triumphed in her country. It is her devotion to her rage which places her outside the limitations of those Arab women who think themselves better than she.

Leïla, though she suffers more intense vilification than La Mère at the hands of Saïd, none the less finds a niche for herself in the temple being constructed out of his ambitions and, safely perched, achieves an understanding which allows her the limited enthusiasm she expresses in the following lines (pp. 108–09):

> I want you—it's my ugliness, earned minute by minute, that speaks—to be without hope. I want you to choose evil and always evil. I want you to know only hatred and never love. I want you—it's my ugliness, earned second by second, that speaks

—to refuse the brilliance of darkness, the softness of flint, and the honey of thistles. I know where we're going, Saïd, and why we're going there. It's not just to go somewhere, but so that those who are sending us there remain tranquil, on a tranquil shore. We're here, and we're here so that those who are sending us here realize that they're not here.

Ultimately she becomes a martyr so that Saïd may have his cause. Like the mother she is an important prop, but she would never have become that prop if she had not got up from her peaceful riverbank to follow him in his effort to become "someone."

The other Arabs who figure in the play represent a wider range of commitment and motivation. There are those like Kadidja and Ommou, venerable and vengeful women, who serve the same sort of function as Leïla and La Mère, though in a necessarily more minor key. But there are those, already alluded to, who seek from Saïd's activities something that is not worthy of that mission. They fall outside the terms of the conflict, principally because they were never really aware that such terms existed, so concerned were they with the triumph of their private aspirations which they had modeled, more or less, on the example offered to them by the Europeans. Finally, in this register of forces, there are the dead Arabs: the old warriors who launched the battles of rebellion and who live on as active forces so long as the memory of their acts and the dedication of Saïd persist. It is, of course, the latter which is more important for, as we have seen, Saïd's persistence in being what he is serves as the fundamental clay without which there would be no sturdy vessels of rebellion. To the extent that each Arab force within the play recognizes either instinctively or eventually the central position of Saïd, the Arab world is united; the future belongs to those who, having remained faithful to their past, are in the process of destroying the past of others.

Those others are the Europeans, and they appear before us here in almost unrelieved unpleasantness. Their attachment to the land is crassly based on the hopes of financial exploitation and overly generous profits to be derived from the economy of poorly remunerated labor. When the attachment moves beyond the profit motive in search of something more lofty, it is expressed with stupid sentimentality: a man loves the country because in it he has cultivated roses to which he has formed a decidedly disturbing attachment. But the land is obviously something more than an object to which they can become devoted either for financial or for sentimental reasons. In their ability to oppress the natives they can experience a sense of their own superiority both as better organized powers and as automatically better human beings. Observing the Arabs they can come to the conclusion that here, in these masses of dirty and grubby people, is the proof of the need for one race to triumph over another. At one point Sir Harold says (p. 78): "If a Frenchman robs me, that Frenchman's a thief, but if an Arab robs me, he hasn't changed." Cruelty must necessarily flow out from such convictions; once its flow has begun it can pick up unintended debris. One can treat the Arabs harshly because one has become convinced that no other treatment will produce results; but the habit of cruelty becomes infectious and, in the resultant contagion, others fall under the influence of the disease. The same Sir Harold, talking about his determination to remain in the land, remarks quixotically that to save "my son's patrimony, I'd sacrifice my son."

This is the bravura of words, a phenomenon we have observed frequently in Genet. But here it has shifted locale, as have so many of the forces we have isolated and labeled in speaking of his earlier works. At an earlier moment such brittle confidence would have been the companion to the uncertainties of criminals and homosexuals, sent out experimentally to test the winds of opposition. Here, the bravura is shifted to the watch-dogs of society and is expressive primarily of their fearsome knowledge that their era is over, their hegemony is in crisis, their dissolution as a governing entity is approaching. When the confidence is dispelled it is replaced by obtuseness and silliness. Even as they talk, Sir Harold and his interlocutor do not see the young Arab who is setting fire to their orchards; even as they dress Saïd down, they fail to recognize that what he is is at the source of all the agitation which is ravaging the country-side and toppling their imported idols. M. Blankensee wears his pillow to give himself a broader girth, irrelevantly convinced that such padding and stuffing in some way make him imposing to the Arabs but failing to recognize that he, more than they, needs the sense of weight and importance the pillow gives him.

There was a time when Genet would have been kinder or at least left a hollow sounding in his work which would have allowed us to believe that he still considered the decent a threat because he was still convinced they held power. But there comes an end to all things, good or bad, and in *les Paravents* the Europeans are experiencing that end. Reluctantly, even stumblingly, they blurt out the obsequies on their own existence in this disturbed land. In the opening scenes of the play, these exclamations are put into tones of possible future danger: a recognition of the fact that the inch given will soon become a yard and a consequent decision to give nothing at all. By the end of the drama, when the various European forces who have played some part in the formation of the country as their colony seek to explain what has happened, they recognize with blinding clarity that, if they have met their end, it has been met only because they have organized the beginnings in such a way as to bring about, inevitably, this kind of conclusion. The image of the whites presented us in *les Nègres* would never have allowed for this kind of self-knowledge. Admittedly, the image was a projection of the way in which the Negroes saw the whites: deaf, blind, and mute to authentic realities. The whites here are more intelligent—to their ruin. They are possibly more intelligent because they have learned something from the total message found in the length and breadth of Genet's *oeuvre;* or perhaps it is only that, as death approaches, they have that effulgent understanding of all things that is said to be the prelude to the unending sleep. The missionary who, in his earlier incarnation in *les Nègres* had been nothing so much as arrogant and unchurchly, here is allowed to express his demise in almost moving terms, whence generosity is not absent. He says (p. 180):

> As the sea recedes, in like manner they recede from us, carrying away with them and on them, like treasures, all their wretchedness, their shame, their scabs . . . as the sea recedes, so we, receding into ourselves, recapture our glory, our legend. That which was detritus they carry away. They have run a fine comb over us.

Imbedded in these words is more than a passing hint that the refound glory and legend are valueless. The God the Christians were dedicated to bringing to the Arabs has been replaced by the god Saïd has become; the glory the military were to find on the battlefields and in the administration of the territory is fled and with it is gone whatever healthy sap was left in France. The tree is rotted because the army is rotted, stripped of those functions and powers which once made the army a source of attraction and admiration for Genet. It, too, that once had seemed an authentic locus of honestly admitted power, has lost out to the new wave, for if the Arabs, like the sea, have withdrawn, they will, like the sea, come back in a vast wave that will wash over the bones of those who, having been passed through their fine comb, have been left without either the energy or the conviction to survive.

Genet's attitude as he contemplates this revolt of the masses is about as far removed from Ortega y Gasset's spoiled-child laments as one could get. And though one sympathizes with the determination with which he insists that all these changes have their deepest roots in the injustice done to the now emerging forces, one is none the less struck by how much Genet's meditations on this phenomenon have altered what had formerly seemed rigid categories of his. There had been a time when Genet had unbegrudged admiration for the military; the litheness, trimness, and beauty of the soldier was obviously a goad to Genet's homosexual proclivities, as the force and belligerence of the army formed a fit object of observation for his fascination with power. Like every other force which approaches and touches Saïd in this play, the army is in crisis, ruled by its insecurities, aware that its moment of glory, long and vigorous, has ticked its allotted time out. This might be explained by a simple process of decay, the sort of explanation given to us in the pages of the *New York Times,* where we are repeatedly told that the French military, disgusted with their frustrations of the last few decades, have taken to insubordination and rebellion in order to feel alive. Genet would have some part of this, and the part he would have is what has to do with the sense of unsettlement that his military figures express in *les Paravents*. They see an end to a tradition, brought about by the sudden eminence of Saïd, and they don't care for it, though they are helpless to do anything about it.

What Genet sees is an end to an image, and this discovery introduces a fundamental change in his thinking. It is not the army which has changed, decay or no decay. Genet's picture of it is still the same. Wily sergeants know their lieutenants experience a homosexual attraction toward them and profit from the existence of this attraction, if only to give an outlet to their insolence; the lieutenants discover that general officers have the same sentiments as they toward the soldiers and thus can feel comfortable with the generals: their guilt is common, though their ranks be different. The army here is still organized according to the Hangman-Erik-Riton dynamic and thus still testifies to how it is that power goes about organizing and distributing itself in this world. But the important novelty is that this distribution and organization are no longer the manifestations of existent power. They have been an image—at times not a bad one, since they could make their impact felt on Jean Genet's imagination—but the world keeps spinning and that terrain which now has its face to the sun is a terrain which has been stripped of the old structures in order that new ones may be built.

What Genet had begun discovering in *Pompes funèbres* and brought to artistic objectivity in *Querelle de Brest*—the fact that the man who observes the workings of the dynamic is ultimately the most powerful—has become public policy. The nations of the world, grown fearful, court the African and Arab lands, make public statements about the indecency of poverty and hunger, and offer generous contributions to destroy their hold on the colonies they established. It would be an amusing and ironic spectacle, if it did not seem so evidently organized to show that Jean Genet, reviled and looked upon with curiosity these past two decades, has finally triumphed. His vision of the world, his insistence about what should be the true nature of reality, is no longer ascribable to hallucination or delusion; it has become the way of the world, and its prophet has no intention of letting it get away from him.

Those forces he had once admired and which he had projected as the most authentic centers of reality now also turn out to be illusions. The army may have expressed an accurate distribution of the conflicts which are at the root of all power struggles, but it expressed this distribution in a substitutional way. The bordello also may have been the place where people came in order to express their truest desires and thus their truest nature. But in *les Paravents* the bordello is as much in crisis as is the military. Here the bordello loses its function, or comes very close to losing it. If it had once seemed, in *Querelle de Brest* and *le Balcon,* the only place in the world where authentic motives and impulses could be expressed, it has outworn its function. Warda, the petulant prostitute, must die because, like the directors of so many sociological enterprises, she will not recognize the success of her undertaking. In dying, she misses the more agreeable destiny of those committee chairmen who write gracious endings to their functioning, pointing to their accomplishments to explain their demise. Warda, unfortunately, lacks this particular brand of perspicuity, watching in horror the transformation of the world into a whorehouse. There are, she would like to think, limits; but her thought, on this score, is erroneous. She underestimates the efficacy with which she has worked, and so she, along with the military, must join the lesser dead.

The Imagination of Jean Genet

Her mistake, like the army's, has been in failing to recognize the substitutional reality of the brothel. It was the best thing available so long as the true human forces were kept under cover and reviled. But now, as they fight through the night of opposition into the day of acceptance, there is no need for substitutes. We have the real thing; men are finally being looked at for what they are; the illusions and deceptive ambitions of the past have fallen away and the ideals and ideology established by Jean Genet are ruling in this world as well as in the next. If there are no punishments in Genet's other world, there are degrees of reward which we discover only in the last lines of the play. The final scenes have been set in the domain of the dead—an unidentified terrain one enters by breaking through screens which seem to be the fuzziness of bad explanations cushioning the tough skin of truth. Entered into this domain, the dead are confronted with understanding, perspectives are established, forces are identified and comprehended. Yet, at the end of the play, Saïd and Leïla do not enter into this region. We do not know where Leïla is, though we do know that she has died of fatigue and hunger. But we are told by one of the dead, with a snickering laugh, that Saïd, after having refused to identify himself with either faction of the Algerians, and after having cried out his insult to all, is "among the dead."

The announcement, made by Kadidja with laughter, is received by the other dead in an atmosphere of knowing complicity. One has a right to be perplexed and, as the house lights come up on this mysterious, snickering, and gnomic announcement, one has probably the right to be annoyed. We have been tossed and turned in so many directions, we have been asked to keep so much in mind, we have been presented with so much multiplicity and complexity that we feel we have a right, at the end of the evening—and it has been a long one, for *les Paravents* is a monumental play—not to be left with the discomfort of this laughter. And yet the laughter, because it is inconclusive, is the most appropriate conveyor for Genet's mood and the essential temperament of his imagination. For Saïd to have entered into the common lot of the dead would have seemed a recognition of the end to all struggles. The dispossessed, having found that their kingdom is the width and length of the world, are not to be allowed smugness. That the struggle is out in the open in no way means that it is over; the brothel's doors are only closed temporarily. Each victory is, in its way, a defeat, because it suggests an end and there can be no end. Saïd is life and breath and life and breath suggest something continuous, not the casual acceptance, once the first skirmishes in the struggle have been won, of vested interests and limited visions. In death Saïd is elsewhere, because the force he represents only seems to sleep, only seems to disappear from the earth. The others who have entered into the rebellion learn, in death's kingdom, that their influence will last on the earth only a limited time. The implication is that Saïd's influence will not know this severance because the force he has embodied is undying; like the seventeen year locusts, it will emerge again, its noise growing louder and more intense, its accumulated needs eating away at the trees of smugness that have grown up under the conviction that all the problems of the world have been solved; and, like the seventeen year locusts, it will always leave behind progeny. Abjection, in short, will not disappear from the earth and, if nothing else, Saïd seems bent on allowing no one to forget this, the most pervasive element of reality.

It will not disappear because its manifestations are too many, and cannot simply be limited to the responsibility of helping the underdeveloped to develop. It is one of the achievements of Genet's play that he has found a way of presenting this multiplicity of distempers in an imposing way—about which I shall have more to say presently—and thus avoided creating the impression that he is a social realist. That, I should imagine, would be about the last thing that would hold interest for him. Whatever social gospel may seem to be preached here is ultimately irrelevant to Genet's deepest concerns; whatever help he may have been giving to the cause of Algerian independence and the emergence of the underdog is incidental to his more fundamental preoccupation. Genet's interest is with the nature of man, not as it has been defined, but as he has seen it and experienced it. The forces he sees involved in the political situation caught in his play become a vast mock-up of the situation of every man in his dealings with himself and others. Some solution may be found for Algeria, and that solution may appear to be a victory. Other myths and other irritations persist. Men will go along thinking that there is such a thing as love, but Madame Blankensee, even as she administers to her husband's illusions, will shoot him; and the Arab husbands will one day be back in the brothel. Few are the men who will have enough sanity and determination to live, as Saïd does, with Leïla. Yet each effort to escape the kind of marital life they have will be a flight from reality. If Jean Genet has discovered nothing else, he has discovered this, that reality is an unpleasant, unsettling thing from which men seek always to escape. The fact of discovery places him in very good company indeed; the reality discovered, however, immediately separates him from this company and places him in a world quite exclusively his own. And, to all intents, purposes, and appearances, he could not be happier about the exclusion.

In the last few pages I have, on one occasion, made use of the word *oeuvre* in talking about the body of Genet's work; I have done this because the word catches well what is increasingly the most notable thing about his literary output: its unity and simultaneous growth, the combination of which are at the basis of Genet's importance as an imaginative intellect and artist. That one is unsettled and forced into opposition by the more forceful audacities of his work in no way changes the fact that his is an intelligence that is never at rest, whether in the enunciation of the latest developments in his ideas or in the increased versatility of his theatrical understanding and inventiveness. Genet's ideas may not be pleasant; they may even be very wrong; but they are alive and mobile, which makes them a good deal more arresting than the fixed, unchanging register of limited aesthetic insight in which so many contemporary French playwrights work. From having once been possessed by a basically incoherent grasp of the existence of forms, he has now entered into possession of a rich mine which he exploits for the ore which will become the tensile and strong metal of his own forms. Genet has organized a style for himself; but because he has organized it on the strength of a long series of performances, it is a style which in no way suggests the kind of manufacture which characterizes Cocteau or Hemingway. Rather it is a style which is open as his ideas are open to the needs created by a consistently developing understanding; and, most significantly, it is a style which dispels the sense of limits which might ordinarily be expected to develop out of principles as dogmatic as his.

There are several consequences of this, as a reader looks at the total *oeuvre*. One can, for example, in examining the stage directions for *les Paravents,* hear echoes from the earlier works. But there they were less

coherent, and here they are masterful; those early uncertain thrusts toward a viable and appropriate means
of expression, which studded *Notre-Dame-des-Fleurs*
and *Miracle de la rose,* have finally worked themselves
out into a coherent and powerful statement. One can
also look at the *mise-en-scène* of *les Paravents* and see
its close relationship to the *mises-en-scène* of *le Balcon*
and *les Nègres,* where a novel sense of theatrical reality
was gradually dismantling the traditional proscenium
stage in order to replace it with a stage singularly appropriate to Genet's plays. The two earlier plays were,
however, designed to make of the theatre a completely
original moment in time. Ideas of representation of some
commonly experienced or observed reality were cere-
moniously banished to make the act of theatre-going as
much an original and consequential activity as any other.
Les Paravents is not quite in this register; while it is intended to teach something, it makes no forthright effort
to involve the theatre-goer in the structure of the play.
Instead it is a ceremonial offering, proffered as an effort
to put things into accurate focus. As the ideological
structure of the play represents a sophistication of
Genet's ideas and therefore demands a knowledge on the
part of the spectator of the earlier expression of those
ideas, so the aesthetic pleasure of the play is more immediately experienced and absorbed if a theatre-goer
is already familiar with Genet's other plays.

That familiarity will clear away, with profitable dispatch, some of the more superficial impedimenta. Accustomed to Genet's love of puns, keyed to look for the
ultimate meaning of objects, habituated to the ethic of
a world whose ways are the opposites of ours, a theatre-
goer has absorbed a glossary of terms for these particular
liturgies. Brought out of his theatrical illiteracy by the
continued efforts of Genet, he can begin to learn more

difficult lessons. One of those lessons has to do with the complexity and simultaneous multiplicity of those levels which go into each moment of reality. In writing of *Miracle de la rose,* I pointed out that the physical structure of the prison—its division into units which run from the collectivity of the cell block to the isolation of the individual cell—suggested to Genet about the best model then available for what he considered the structure of reality. In that book he had only partially managed to convey the full sense of his discovery, limited by the inability to escape from his own participation in the events he was describing. As he recalled his life in the prison during those days preceding Harcamone's death, he had created a bare sketch of the forces that operate simultaneously in the world and had also managed—and this was something more of an achievement—to create the sense that these present events were experienced by individual consciousnesses which could reach back into their own past, or a common past lived with other individuals, even as they experienced the present.

The experiment was not totally successful in *Miracle de la rose,* because it never got far enough away from the impression of fantasy and hallucination. Since the facts of the book were the facts of Genet's life, and since *Notre-Dame-des-Fleurs* had warned the reader to be wary where the truth of Genet's facts was concerned, a reader could read the book as he might read any other fantasy, neglecting the incipient values contained in its structure. *Les Paravents* avoids this because the multiple situations it presents, and the manner it chooses to present them in, are patently part of the immediate situation it seeks to convey.

Genet conceives of the play being presented in an open air arena with a many leveled stage furnished with readily movable screens which will be used as evocative backdrops, but which will also be capable of receiving periodic, spontaneous designs made by the actors. The advantages derived from these two props need little commentary. The multiplicity of levels gives him a vast floor space with which to work and allows him to work it dextrously. Only one area of one level need be lighted at one time; but, at other times, many combinations are possible: corners of two separate levels can be lighted simultaneously to establish the connections or the contrasts between different aspects of reality; at the end of the play, all the levels can be lighted to demonstrate all the interrelations. The over-all results will not be unlike those sought after and frequently achieved by Reg Butler, Germaine Richier, and Alberto Giacometti in their sculptures. There is a broad terrain on which figures can be placed in whatever degree of prominence is most appropriate to the evocation of their importance at a particular moment. Simultaneously, careful emphasis can be given, through the use of selective lighting, to the special connections existing between particular individuals at various moments.

The screens are evidently more than easy props designed to effect theatrical economies. They are both standards and symbols. As their name indicates, they can be protective barriers against the real forces of the world, walls serving as masks or delusions; but they can also be the measure of the detachment from these genuine forces and can be enlisted in the effort to make ironic comments on that detachment. Genet, in his stage directions, makes mention of the imperative necessity of always offsetting the screens with some real object which "will confront the objects drawn on the screens with its own reality." But he also makes use of the screens to demonstrate how those who have a great need of them are unable to see what has been drawn on them by others; the screens, intended to offer protection against the discovery of the real forces of the world can be transformed into blinders which keep the eyes of certain characters from falling on the danger those forces now represent for them. Thus the Europeans can carry on a conversation without seeing the Arab hand which comes to draw the flames of insurrection on their screen. Thus, too, but with a somewhat different accent, the dead, before entering their kingdom, burst through the screens, thereby destroying their effectiveness in blocking off the harshness of truth; but even as they break through, they find that reality is not the unpleasant, unrelieved thing they thought it. Like Stendhal's Julien Sorel, after his encounters with what were supposed to be among the most mysterious forces of the world, they can comment: "Is that all it is?"

With this mobile and fertile machinery fixed on his stage, Genet can create a most imposing and arresting experience. He starts his play off with Saïd setting forth on that journey which will make him "someone," because on that journey he will become the center of everyone's attention. As Saïd moves through his experiences he touches on the private worlds of other individuals, which are flashed to us from those various levels, almost as though we were looking into the windows of a vast apartment house where only one apartment was lighted at a time. As more and more forces admit the triumph of Saïd's idea of things, we come to know more and more about what a cross-section of reality might look like. In the nature of the play, the stage must grow brighter, more and more levels must be illuminated until, at the conclusion, the whole scene is ablaze with light, all the forces are exposed in their influence on this final moment when, awaiting Saïd's arrival, every group which has participated in the play up to this moment—and, I

237

must repeat, in creating the influences which have made the situation possible—discusses its part. When Saïd appears, they discover that all their decisions to make adjustments to the situation bring them to naught. Though they have had influence on the existence of what they contemplate in looking upon Saïd, that influence wins them no reconciliation, brings them no occasion to participate in a perfect situation. The movement of time, of reality, is not brought to an end because we have seen as thorough a presentation of all the components of that situation as has been possible to Genet's imagination. In the trivial phrase, time marches on, reality keeps changing: it has no fixed points, though it may have the kinds of fixed dispositions the total work of Jean Genet has been defining these past twenty years into a system disturbingly rooted in the thirst for absolutes.

The unimpeded play of the imagination we see in this drama may, because it suggests a fascination with the endless fecundity of that imagination, amount to a danger for Genet. There are elements in *les Paravents* which might seem to bear this out, for here technical mastery and imaginative play become so pyrotechnical as to dazzle the spectator out of comprehension: it is a kind of theatrical Piazza Navona where there can be no possibility of questioning skill, no denial of the power created by such monumental energy, such imposing dexterity. But sometimes the forces of energy and dexterity are so overpowering we cannot assent and find ourselves wondering if there is, after all, something beyond technique in this vast assemblage of matter.

There is and there isn't. If one were to pay attention exclusively to the physical deployment of the play in its many directions, one could limit oneself to noticing how facile is the imagination which can handle so much and turn it in the direction of unity. But such notice is limited and fails to investigate the reason for the presentation. Behind these many screens, or surrounding them, is a way of looking at things that demands this sort of presentation. Even that is a cavalier statement, because it is only when we are confronted with the presentation, in other words only when all the work has been done, that we realize how appropriate it is. What Genet has done here is something eminently more important than the discovery of the best arena for the three-ring circus of his imagination. What he has done is to catch, with art and aptness, a contemporary problem better than any of his contemporaries. Of Durrell's effort I have already written. But Durrell and Genet are not alone in their concern with the many elements that go into the composition of any particular situation and that, more often than not, must in the interests of artistic economy be either played down or stamped out. For them—as for Eliot in *The Four Quartets* and *The Elder Statesman,* and the majority of the anti-novelists—the full sweep of things must be paid serious attention to if one is to know oneself and understand one's way of living. But no one has quite managed to get so pertinent and well-organized a method of presentation as Genet, nor has anyone managed to put it together in a way which demands our admiration as well as our understanding.

Eliot's effort is, of course, one of the more finely hewn monuments of our time; it has emotional strength and quantities of beauty for which the civilized reader is grateful. But it runs a serious risk of seeming disembodied. The personal range of that statement remains perhaps too personal; its synthesis is bound to lack appeal for intellects untouched by the grace which suffuses it and unfamiliar with the forces it points out. With Valéry's *le Cimetière marin* it shares a proclivity toward being valued purely because of the art with which it conveys personal anguish and the solution found for that anguish; all the drama is in the tension of the line as it gets itself straightened in the movement of the poem. The anti-novelists, with the possible exception of Mme Sarraute, so weigh us down with trivia as to drug us into believing that nothing important ever happens, no violent catastrophes of accident or emotion ever come to upset the dull range of quotidian existence; everything is muted and snipped into insignificant particles.

Jean Genet's statement is quite as personal, but it is also engaging. One may leave *les Paravents* disagreeing with what Genet has said, but one would be petulant and petty if one were to leave pretending that he has not done a rousingly good job of setting all the elements off as distinctly as possible. If Genet states things wrongly in this play, he at least makes an effort to state them fully, to get as many factors as possible assembled and to show them in as many concatenations as his imagination has been able to locate and translate. And he does it with an art which cannot be denied. His play offers a bit of everything, without in any way seeming scrappy. There is a vitriolic humor, an atmosphere of degradation conveyed through the most scatological vocabulary he has yet used in such heavy doses; but there is also a visual power as the stage lights up, bringing before our eyes, with just the amount of organization necessary, that complexity which flashes in variously intense lights from our subconsciousness to our consciousness and which, when added to the progress of purely chronological events, we would, were we reasonable, recognize as reality.

> For a long time I believed
> that poetry proposes con-
> flicts; it annuls them.
> —*Notre-Dame-des-Fleurs*

Conclusion

If they have done nothing
else, the preceding chapters have shown how difficult
it is to label Jean Genet or to find a place for him in any
known literary constellation. It is his distinction and perhaps his most notable achievement to have demonstrated
a free-probing, limitless growth and continuous sophistication in his apprehension of ideas that seems to make
it inadvisable to say anything definitive about him. The
shifting emphases noticeable in any comparison of *les
Paravents* with the earlier works, like the rearrangement

of what had seemed fixed categories, might easily lead a critic into suspending judgment until that convenient date when Jean Genet, dead or exiled from further literary endeavor, ceases to write. Confronted with the body of work we now possess and the growth it represents from insecurity into something close to unquestioning self-assurance, we are bound, I think, to seek some sort of perspective. It is not enough to say that Genet is elusive, especially when we have learned, at times to our intended confusion, that his slipperiness is sometimes the crux of his work. Nor is it wise critical or human procedure to take any later Genet work on its own superficial evidence, for we have seen how our engagement with those superficies is part of an effort on the author's part to involve us even more deeply in the unsuspected but deadly net of his imagination. Touch the visible leaves of any recent Genet play and you are bound to find yourself pulling at tough, resistant roots—into the depths of yourself.

Some notion of why it is we should seek perspective and what perspective it is we are seeking can be found in a brief review of the sort of progress Genet has made since the debut of his literary career. Starting out with a sense of the fragility of his own message, its potential for crumbling under the relentless criticism and hostility of those who might find its existence inestimably offensive, he has passed to a point where he now finds that the fragility had the deceptiveness of the finest crystal and, rather than being treated gingerly, deserves to be exhibited in its beauty and strength. Somewhere along the uncertain argument which yielded the conclusion, the question of whether it is really crystal we are looking at has obviously been lost. Genet insists it is and, like all good rhetoricians, his persuasiveness has its value, since it wins him not only friends but adherents. At one point he himself had seemed aware that the quality of the material could be brought into question and so had asked: "If my song be beautiful, dare you say its inspiration is vile?" The question, if not reasonable, was intelligent, wily, and fraught with those dangers courted by all efforts at seduction. The beauty is there, unquestionably, shimmering through a prose style that is one of the more distinctive in contemporary French, primarily because it is a style grown strong from its appropriateness for conveying the vision inspiring it. The beauty is also effective, evoking from some indiscriminate critics the not unimportant compliment of comparisons to Jean Racine. Genet is no Racine, and his style has nothing of Racine in it; but he is a magician with words as he is a necromancer with ideas, and the public's fascination with all manifestations of sorcery has in a way been enough to make them tend to agree with the terms of Genet's question. They will accept the beauty of the song, and, listening to its dulcet notes, forget that its bass counterpoint is the sum of almost all the unloveliness we possess either in reality or in fantasy.

Yet, even as the public moves into limited acceptance of those terms, Genet seems to be moving away from them. The question which he had asked in *l'Enfant criminel* moves into a declaration of a quite different order in *les Paravents* when the Cadi says: "Things cease to belong to those who have given them their beauty," thereby suggesting that the well-wrought presentation of an unpleasant situation does not necessarily assure the artisan that his accomplishments can be offered as his apologia. The inference to be made here is, of course, that Jean Genet no longer believes what he once sought to insinuate. There are possibly two causes for this change in belief. Either he believes that words do not change deeds that have entered into past history, or else he believes

243

that the public expression of those deeds represents their loss to the individual who has lived and recorded them; with their loss, there comes a loss of the uniqueness which their unpublished possession conferred on the possessor.

There is, however, more to the change of view than a simple choice between two explanations. What is involved in the elaboration of some explanation is an understanding of the operations of Genet's imagination, the consequences of those operations, and certain fears Genet may have developed over the loss in publication of what he has accomplished at such great cost. In suggesting milestones in the growth of Genet's imagination I commented on the deliberate voluntarism which characterizes it. His first works are studded with deprecatory statements explaining that, though the realm of truth is not the concern of his work, he feels no especial qualms about his cavalier treatment of real events; his interest is in personal consolation, in constructing barriers against the increasingly menacing thrusts of his solitude and sense of exclusion from those he has most wanted to be associated with. But in the very process of carrying out this apparently arbitrary shifting of real forces and real events he comes to believe that his understanding is now deeper than it formerly was and that the shifts in interpretation are the result of a penetrating insight into the components of the experience. Lamenting over the insufficiency of the obsequies of someone he has loved, he comes to believe that the obsequies really weren't so insufficient after all. If the right interpretation is given to the gestures visible at the funeral services, one can come to recognize those gestures as the most apt and most dignified. His erotic reveries and drives, originally the source of shame in *Pompes funèbres,* were transformed, through the alchemy of that book, into a perfect-

244

ly pertinent funeral monument because, in those reveries and the book which resulted from them, the most pervasive and valuable forces of the dead hero's existence were isolated and transmuted into undying art.

The literary chronicle, then, comes to be not so much a rearrangement of reality as a deep presentation of it; the historical process is not changed so much as adjusted under the burden of the more revelatory information which comes to the fore as one makes the effort to set things down. If that were all, one might accept it as one accepts a new interpretation of the Constitution: critically, and with an eye to seeing what value can be extracted from it for a better understanding of the total reality which led to its adoption. Genet, however, moves toward different conclusions. The literary work is not simply a rearranged and therefore a more authentic chronicle, it is also a living and growing force which makes a decided contribution to reality. It creates, Genet has said, its own space and that space, in addition to being infinite, is the sign of a most imposing victory. Not only is the literary work a triumph of skill over words and phrases, it is also a manifestation of a triumph of the artist over the limitations he has known in his personal experience. The work of art is his liberation from the insufficiencies he has known. Since, however, those insufficiencies were the brute matter from which the liberating work of art was formed, the process of liberation is also a process of justification for those insufficiencies. If Laura had not seemed unavailable, we would not have some of Petrarch's more splendid sonnets. If Jean Genet had not been a homosexual, a reject of society, we would not have his vision and the works it has produced. Art, then, while it does not justify the vileness, does imperil the common notion that being vile is a condition worthy of condemnation. When artistic objects have been brought into existence, they, rather than the life which served as matter for their creation, can be looked back upon; subsequent works can be produced out of or within the infinite space they create. The initial works become—though they are never recognized as such—buffers between later vision and the earliest lived reality and are, in this sense, something of what the catechism is to the believing Christian: a primer for the interpretation of reality, which the catechism both presents and explains, thereby establishing a system which on its own terms is perfect and which, within the same terms, allows room for the incorporation of all subsequent discoveries made about reality. Like the Christian, Genet, once he has his catechism in hand, is not concerned with going back beyond its terms to see if there may not be others. His imagination has furnished him with a text which seems to explain all things; brandishing it, using its terms as though they were the only terms, he will confront the world with a confidence strong enough to allow for the expression of his fundamental opposition and sure enough to allow him to issue challenges. He can work in this way without sensing his own dogmatism because his dogmatism has evident expansive qualities without in any way being threatened in its integrity by the expansion. In this way, Genet's statements can be excused from the accusation of contradiction; though the forces of the world, like the God of the Christians, are unchanging and immutable, they are always susceptible to better understanding. What differences exist between *Notre-Dame-des-Fleurs* and *Pompes funèbres,* between *Haute Surveillance* and *les Paravents,* result from those different apprehensions of the same core reality.

The whole enterprise was to be brought to success and better definition through the alchemy of art; the reader, exposed to the process, was expected to be touched as Genet himself had been touched. Once affected, he was to find himself believing that that which had been so touching must indeed be true. Here a critic finds the basis for an approach to a judgment on Genet. The artistic alchemy, which is intended to bring about such fundamental changes, may not be quite the thing Genet believes it, and this may explain the phrase from *les Paravents,* where it is suggested that the artist loses possession of the beautiful things he has created. While the alchemy of art can produce transformations, these transformations can have unexpected results, especially if the public for whom the art is intended accepts the contribution as part of its common patrimony without concurrently accepting the ideological assertions contained within the art. Genet's fear here is much like the Cadi's fear: that his function, like his message, may depend upon the understanding of the public he has sought to revile. Having hoped for escape from the watchful eye of the public, Genet may be finding that he is still encircled. A reader can well understand why this is cause for serious alarm. A critic's dismay will not be so pronounced. He sees in Genet's alarm the terms of Genet's dilemma: the conflict which results from the attempt to excuse the distempers of life by forging powerful artistic objects from their raw material. But the critic sees also the terms with which to express a judgment that, though it has two heads, is not another dilemma. The critic can only conclude that we must qualify Genet's pretensions as a discursive mind, all the while paying serious attention to his accomplishments as an artist. Or, to avoid any suggestion of a dilemma, a critic might state his bias this way: what we must do is see how the art gives the plays power enough to distract from the ideas. On the basis of this some comments can be made on Genet's stature as an artist.

The Imagination of Jean Genet

The young burglar, who serves as narrator to Alan Sillitoe's *Loneliness of the Long Distance Runner,* tells us at the end of his particular confession that he has written his narrative in order to demonstrate the sinews of honesty which have been threaded through the motivation of his actions. His literary effort (hardly disguised by its stance as autobiography) will be his testament, and its principal codicil will be designed to awaken within the Borstal governor, who has sought to make an honest young gentleman out of the narrator, a realization that honesty wears at least two faces and that the more agreeable of these two is the countenance of the narrator. What Sillitoe's protagonist calls honesty, Sartre and the anti-novelists would call the search for authenticity, by which they mean, though their label is not non-axiological, that they write barely and bluntly about what happens. They do this to bring us to an open recognition of such happenings, so that we may understand both what we are and what experiences really confront us when we come across those we consider alien to our ways. But they do it also in order to demonstrate the extent to which our behavior frequently makes us such inadequate examples of what our beliefs are supposed to be that the authenticity of those beliefs as sources of value for others is called into question. These ideals and standards are false since they are rarely observed and frequently worn only as hypocrisy's cloaks to hide habitual and evil action. Worse than that, they are excuses, escape hatches used to temper present evil with the promise of future or greater good. To catch the particulars of this disparity within literary works is an effort to see what really confronts us as we work in the world, to give us an accurate rather than an idealized portrait of what makes us tick. But the effort is also designed to show us something more profound: that our inadequacies and hypocrisies are often the inspiration of other men's behavior. Before feeling free to evaluate their way of life, we must first recognize that it is, if nothing else, an authentic reaction to what they see in viewing us. If they choose other modes of action or different ethical goals, it is because we have shown ours to be shams.

No one would, of course, question such claims, though after reading those lucubrations about a bar of soap in Mme Sarraute's *Portrait d'un inconnu* one might wish for fewer happenings and greater art. One reads Sillitoe, the anti-novelists, Sartre and Genet with a certain amount of weariness when they write about this sort of thing, for, thinking to shock us, they only invite us to be as amazed as they are by knowledge which most of us already possess but which they are just learning. No amount of head-standing, hurdles, or somersaults is going to change automatically opinions about situations evaluated time and time again in that highly critical phenomenon which is Western civilization.

That it is true that certain of those entrusted with the punishment of the criminal are themselves given to sadistic exercises, that many of the decent have indecent phantasms that would make the sexually criminal blush or gasp, that the criminals of Jules Dassin's *Rififi* are in their own way pleasant family men, that good citizenship is only a sublimation of baser instincts under the threat of power—all these are fairly meaningless statements when they are made as part of an effort to disillusion us with our meaningful institutions. But beyond the question of fundamental meaning, they are also naive statements, for they seek to tell us something we already know: that our institutions are not perfect, that our statements are not stamped with any special charm, and that our beliefs are subject to adjustment, change, and even corruption. The Western mind has always known this, though it has not always obeyed its own better instincts, with the result that much of our present intensified scepticism is to a great extent based on our fear of the dogmatic and intransigent moments which dot our history. But there is something chaotically primitivistic about going back to the jungle simply because we have either forgotten how long and tortuous has been the way out of it, or else because the length and burdens of the journey have made us so tired that we no longer care to thrash out new paths.

Sillitoe, Genet, and Sartre are ultimately touched with a sentimentality that can be the death of the best liberal causes, precisely because it is the kind of sentimentality which is bound at one time or another to meet some sort of crushing disappointment—whether it be in the streets of Budapest, the corruption of labor unions, the rape of a child by one of the unfortunates one has been defending as a victim of society's assorted cruelties, or the emergence of African nations as simply later manifestations of bourgeois society. The sentiment is born out of dangerous juxtapositions and blessed by overly ready empathy; it rejects the "there but for the grace of God go I" position as being too facilely generous and instead substitutes "there with the grace of my own works, I will go, triumphing over you," which is not generous at all. To do this, of course, takes one of two things, neither of which is terribly easy of accomplishment; either you reason your opponents into agreement or else you bludgeon them. Sartre has tried the former, Genet the latter.

There is a continuously startling lack in Sartre's book, entitled, after the play by the seventeenth-century French dramatist, Rotrou, *Saint-Genet, comédien et martyr,* and it is born from the absence of perspective Sartre shares with so many contemporary intelligences. Alien, by the nature of his rigorously *actual* philosophic commitment, from the statements of value made in earlier periods and never negated on their own terms, Sartre is obliged to look upon every phenomenon as having much the same potential significance as every other: the spontaneous painting of the child, the filagreed decisions of an extremely sophisticated will, the scandalous insanity of the Cuban revolution in its later phases, the physical mechanisms of sexuality—all these must be considered, at least initially, as being of par value. What results is a very curious structure indeed, the more curious the more one is committed to a belief in the at least pragmatic (or informative) value of the wisdom of the past. In the case of Jean Genet, Sartre is led to say some remarkably inept things, principally because, intuitively convinced that he is better off being on Genet's side, he forgets some other fairly obvious things, the main one being that sexual activity gives pleasure and that, in the experience of the West (as in that of the East), men have sought pleasure for the quite unvarnished reason that they get enjoyment from it. Reading Sartre's lucubrations, the man of reason, having passed through astonishment into impatience, concludes by being quite genuinely embarrassed that this mind, which places such emphasis on good faith, is not content to accept phrases like the following—"I was horny for crime;" "prostitution was a greater satisfaction to my nonchalance"—on their own terms in order to recognize the simple fact that Jean Genet enjoys sexual activity and prefers to have it in the company of men. Rather Sartre—and later on, quite possibly under Sartre's influence, Genet himself—would seek to show that we are in some way responsible, because we have forced Genet to seek revenge on us for the crimes we have enacted on his childhood. The critic here is reminded of a letter H. G. Wells once wrote to James Joyce, stressing that he and the Irishman could never really have a meeting of the minds, since Joyce was still scandalized by phenomena Wells had learned to live easily with. In terms of morality, Sartre is often more puritan than we; in terms of ethics, he is frequently a less good pragmatist; in terms of history, he is less given to an understanding of the sense of development underlying the establishment of all human institutions.

What Sartre seems to overlook is the fact that no amount of rottenness on the part of a "cruel" society must necessarily force Jean Genet into wanting to be a thief, traitor, and homosexual; it is a nice bit of transfer, but it is also—for all its thrilling pirouettes—a naive one that ignores a necessary and not too extensive investigation of the passions in an almost will-less person, and which ignores, too, some of the more persuasive statements on evil Sartre has himself made. Much of what there is of the pariah in Genet may very well be the end result of unwholesome social conditions, but the specific moment of sexual desire brought on by the proper complex of erotic stimuli is really too personal a thing to be blamed on the bourgeoisie who, after all, need not be blamed for every distemper produced in human experience. Genet enjoys the sexual act; he enjoys it, admittedly, under rather special circumstances. But the fact of enjoyment, like those circumstances, is an important motivating force in his life and in his works. Perhaps he has a valid grudge against society; but, accompanying it, he has his own kind of special pleading, and the goal of that pleading is a presentation of the pleasures of inversion and a rigid conviction, growing ever more strong, that if anything makes the world go 'round, it is the sort of power drive he sees expressed most frequently in sexual activity.

Mallarmé had hoped the world would be summed up

in a book, or, economy prevailing, in a word. If Genet could have his way, the world, like the final pages of *Pompes funèbres,* would end either in his triumph or in an enormous display of spontaneous sexual combustion. Looking back from the mid-point which is *Journal du voleur,* he writes frankly that "I have sought only those situations charged with erotic intentions" (p. 90) and admits even more bluntly that his efforts to attribute heroic qualities to some of those situations is the result of a quite *inauthentic* (the word is mine, not his) imaginative construct: "Unfortunately, heroism was what struck me as being most charged with amorous qualities, and since there are no heroes save those we create in our minds, I shall have to create them. . . . And only this book of love will be real" (*Journal du voleur,* pp. 106–07). What we have, then, is the expression, not only of a basic descriptive situation—*this is what I was* —but we have also the expression of intention of what he will do with that situation. Since the tendency toward romance is common to all of us and helps us to understand a character like Walter Mitty, this kind of intention does not startle. What does startle is the way it generalizes in Genet's work and moves from being a total explanatory force into becoming a kind of proselytism. In this sense it follows the over-all pattern of Genet's work, beginning with a certain nostalgia for past moments, moving into a sugar coating of these moments into something they were not, metamorphosing them into a kind of philosophy, and ending in challenge. Though the Negroes in *les Nègres* and Saïd in *les Paravents* may seem to be heroes whose existence does not depend on the creative energy of Genet's imagination, we have no guarantee that they have not been chosen because of the consolation he derives from believing that their ideals are his and that they are, therefore, the best embodiment of the kind of heroism which produces amorous charges. Nor have we any guarantee that Genet, in choosing them, is inspired by the same sort of generosity which may exist within us when, contemplating their movements on the stage, we are aroused to a sense of our own guilt in having allowed such privational situations as they have known to develop.

Genet's dramaturgy follows, too, a movement detectable in sexuality, for its dynamism brings it close neither to refinement nor to truth, but simply toward ever more dramatic fulfillments. Put more properly, the movement is one that seeks at once novelty and further audacity, the former because sexual practice qua sexual practice palls more often than not; the latter because, even as the practice palls, it suggests more audacious experiments, none of which, in the range of history, is really very novel. Sade, Lautréamont, D. H. Lawrence, John O'Hara, certain contemporary literary critics like Jean Paulhan, all serve as witnesses to this effort to avoid the final truth about sexuality: that ultimately it is tedious and, to avoid the tedium, one seeks to become more audacious: one day of Sodom is simply not enough, there have to be one hundred and twenty; one penis is not enough when you want to make love to all the beautiful young men in the world.

It is this sort of dissatisfaction which triggers Genet's imagination into making explanatory statements of the most remarkable and unbelievable kind. Our minds stocked with the writings of Adler and Freud—and with our own more open discussions of our own experiences —we are equipped to recognize an intimate relationship between sex and power and the drive for power that can often be at the root of all sexual activity. With Genet we are confronted by another of his queerer juxtapositions: sex and power are both manifestations of what might best be called *longing*—whether it be after the inadequacy of the past or for the promise of the future, whether it be for glory or for something to replace, if only imaginatively, the dissatisfactions of life. In this kind of structure, Hitler's murderous propensities are to Hitler what Genet's imaginative reveries are to Genet: ways of bridging the gap between the data of the longings and the limitations of physical equipment. Saïd's movements into the heart of reality are simply projections of Genet's frustrated desires for the true possession of a world he has made only in art. The important thing in either case is to satisfy the longing—at least for a time.

But the satisfaction of the longing introduces its own kind of dissatisfactions. One does feel a certain amount of shame in betraying a former lover, an even deeper gnawing over the sexual phenomena which accompany the realization of the betrayal (*Pompes funèbres,* p. 82). Again it is the imagination which saves the day, for the imagination not only establishes other kinds of juxtapositions—the Hitler-Genet relationship—it also roots out all the inadequacies of experience and makes of what may be messy and untidy a kind of abstract purity. Genet writes in *Pompes funèbres,* making a relationship between his imaginative projection of a tangled romance which never took place and an imaginary African tribal feast to which he, though white, would be invited because of an undefined cousinship between himself and the Negroes: "All the boredom of preparations was spared me, except the dance which helped the cooking along, aided good digestion, and gave the best guarantee of the virtues of the child who was burning. I danced, blacker than the blacks, to the sounds of the tom-toms; I made my body more supple and readied it to receive the totemic nourishment; I was sure of being their god. I was God" (p. 107).

The Imagination of Jean Genet

There is, of course, an enormous convenience to being God and more than a token deposit of consolation; both the convenience and the consolation can be seen in the structure of *Pompes funèbres,* with its dazzling concatenations of what has happened, what should have happened in a better world, and what is happening in Genet's imagination as he writes. But to be God is also to believe in one's omnipotence and, believing in this, one is hardly going to remain either silent or inactive. This is where the proselytism starts but, like so many things in Genet, the proselytism is hardly inspired by divine generosity. There is more than a drop of self-protection in Genet's sermonizing, and it is there principally because he is not God but merely has become God. If he has been able to pull himself into Olympus by his bootstraps, there is always the possibility that others will be able to do the same thing; and, if those others are not impeded, Olympus will become such a crowded place that one might be better off being a simple creature. Genet's later writings are evidently designed to preserve the privileged place he has found. He does this by changing constantly the data of his attacks or, in the case of *les Nègres,* suggesting ill-defined terrors against which the non-Olympians are quite unable to organize any opposition or resistance, primarily because the forces they would have to oppose do not exist as Genet would have us believe they do. The new African leaders may not like white men; still, they have shown little inclination to establish tribal living as a better kind of social structure than the one they have inherited from Western civilization.

Coupled with this staving-off action is the need to involve us just enough in Genet's personal theology to make us assent to his divinity. No matter how versatile he becomes in the deployment of his vast imaginative resources he seems never to lose his immediate concern

256

with keeping his audience or his readers in their places. If, benefiting from the privileges of deity, he decides to make the world an arbitrary external manifestation of his imaginative desires, he must insure himself against the danger of protest from discursive minds. The method he chooses, as I have indicated, is that of constantly reminding us that his early desires (which he had bypassed) are still ours, that his characters' practices are merely realizations of our fantasies and, finally, that our enjoyment of his work is the damning proof of why he is entitled to tower over us as our most fitting Jeremiah. Since he is firmly convinced of this, a mantle of sexuality slowly descends from the heaven of his creation to cover and eventually to stifle all other sophisticated efforts to explain the world.

In any evaluation of Genet we must pay careful attention to this obsessive aspect of his work and, before seeking to find some extraordinary contribution to thought in what he has to say, remind ourselves with needed frequency of how deeply his sexual obsessions are at the root, not only of his work, but also of his imaginative flights. Nor should we blind ourselves to the extent to which he seeks to involve others quite deliberately in this. Like Sade's, his books are a kind of contract of bad faith designed to enmesh the reader so deeply in guilt as to stifle all eventual protestations of innocence. Genet is admittedly a pornographer, but he is a pornographer with a purpose, and that purpose is perhaps best summed up in one of the counsels he gives to Abdullah: "Have a hard on and make others have one, too. The heat which shoots out from you and spreads is your desire for yourself—or for your image—always unfulfilled" (le Funambule, p. 196). Here the circle is brought to its full arc; we shall be stimulated, and in our stimulation we shall be brought, not closer to the person or fantasy responsible for the stimulation, but closer to ourselves, to the realization, never fully achieved, of what it is we seek from the erotic pot pourri which simmers within us. Genet, with this kind of circular reasoning, would enclose us in a world where he, because he has discovered these things and can address such revelatory remarks, rules as we shall never be able to rule. In learning why we are no longer to control the world—and, in reality, never have—we are not to learn any usable lesson. Dismay over the discoveries of such analysis will bring us nothing but intensifying dismay and intensifying dismay will guarantee our impotence.

Are we ensnared? Hardly, even though we listen with something resembling attention and, when the acting is good and the prose elegant, are moved. Or if we are ensnared, it is generally for reasons quite other than those which are fundamental to Genet's desires. *Les Nègres* furnishes an example of this. As a production it is one of the better things that has happened to our theatre, if only because of its courageous assertion of the theatre's indigenous power; as statement, couched in the pathos of protest against injustice by a people who have been oppressed and stupidly classified, it is moving. But as discourse, designed to carry Genet's philosophical rhetoric one step farther, it is a failure, if only because most audiences are quite unlettered in Genet's preoccupations and, devoid of the kind of information they would have to have in order to understand the subtler strands of its argument, persist in viewing it as they would view any other work of art, with sympathy, cooperation, and aesthetic intelligence. In other words, while it is his personal art which wins an audience for Genet in the first place, it is the wider reach of Art which defeats him in the accomplishment of his wilier purposes.

Art somehow remains outside the Olympus of Genet's

pretensions; it has, like certain of the institutions he attacks, lingered about longer than he, and it has taught people certain habits and attitudes that are not easily changed. Genet can only go as far in getting at his audiences as their aesthetic education allows; given his unquestioned gifts this is very far indeed, far enough to make the audience grateful to him for the aesthetic pleasure his highly endowed imagination is able to generate in its deployment of theatrical techniques, his exploitation of rhythm and ceremonial effects. But Genet tricks himself by believing that he is vastly more intelligent or more perceptive than his audience and that, because of this, he can transform the world of literature or the theatre into something more than *aesthetic* reality. This does not mean that he is straitened by the conventions or indeed that conventional limitations are inflexible. What it does mean is that he places the wrong value on talent. Where Genet does in effect err is in confusing flexibility with elasticity, in seeking to make the conventions do more than they possibly can. Pirandello is spared this embarrassment of means, because what he has to say is very directly connected with the nature of the conventions he is using. The substance of *Six Characters in Search of an Author* points this up well; Pirandello is fascinated by the exemplary value of theatrical conventions in symbolizing those dilemmas which arise in all thought about illusion and reality and the delicate line that separates them. Genet does not have this kind of finesse and merely wishes to use the theatre. His is the mistake of believing art can be used to stimulate feeling rather than to articulate it. He does this because he presupposes a power for art that is the wrong kind of power and also because of his underestimation of the diversified knowledge and experience of his audience. He is at once asking too little and too much, something

259

Sophocles would never have done. The public, appreciating the detailed anatomy of reality presented in *les Paravents,* will be able, using the same intelligence that goes into the organization of the appreciation, to see the insufficiencies of the play's deliberately circumscribed and curtailed cross-section.

An audience will watch Genet's plays as articulations of some part of experience; but if pushed into accepting his insights as the whole of experience, the same audience will, all the while treasuring the aesthetic pleasure derived from his works, reject the author's pretensions. Faced with this rejection, Genet might ask on what it is based, especially given our confrontation with the proofs he has offered. The answer, of course, would be that this is what we have decided and our decision, despite his impressive techniques and Sartre's impressive ratiocinating rhetoric, is somewhat more humble than theirs and has the added merit of being derived from a better kind of empiricism, since it is concerned with the enormous range of possible human activity and not merely with one aspect of that range, since it is concerned with the consequences and not merely with the nature of activity, with the race and what we have learned of it and what we hope for it, not simply with individuals and their complaints.

We need be neither so obtuse as Saïd nor so dogmatic as Genet, limiting ourselves to seeing only one solution, pretending that one can live reasonably with such unreasonable assertions. Exposure to the world of the homosexual, with its frustrations and disappointments, may very well and profitably show us that men's emotions suffer and their sense of integrity diminishes even when they are immersed in a world of vice and vitriol; confrontation with the Negro as an angry and rebellious individual may remind us that his anger and rebellion are the products of our greed and purblindness; immersion in the world of Saïd may lead us to understand that the distempers of life are the surest crucible of its adjustments. But this kind of involvement, whether on its terms or ours, is inadequate. The very process which awakens sympathy for the homosexual, guilt toward the Negro, and compassion for Saïd is a process which leaves us dissatisfied with Genet's hopes. History, experience, and self-knowledge tell us that the abject will not remain abject simply because they have found their bard.

I have suggested earlier that one of the reasons we should perhaps heed Genet's voice is because it is a sad sound pointing to some frightful dislocation in our times. I am suggesting now that the basic pretensions of Genet's work reject the value of our listening at all if the basic terms of our attention are to be circumscribed in pity or in any other emotion that seems to suggest our superiority. Yet we have little choice, for whatever value we may place on isolated voices or the extraordinary visions conveyed to us by movements like Surrealism is a value derived from and defined in terms available to a community capable of analytic discourse. It is a good thing possibly to take note of the demands Genet's imagination makes; it would be a disastrous thing to assent to the total implications of those demands—and the most appalled victim of the disaster would be none other than Jean Genet, since, in a world deprived of community and returned to primeval struggles, there would be no one to listen to his voice, record his protest, or offer him sympathy and even encouragement.

The critic, then, finishes his meditations on Genet's works by noting a crowning irony: these works will be appreciated and enjoyed to the extent that they do not accomplish what Genet wants them to accomplish. Genet's instinctive imagination—the apparatus which forms the terms of his vision of reality—will be rejected, and with it will be rejected his most cherished ideas. But his presentational imagination—the force which allows him to organize the insights of his instinctive imagination and to impose them aesthetically—may very well give his works endurance; it already gives them power as it gives the theatre refreshed vitality. His ideas are ultimately too limited to have much chance of winning assent, and the kind of gymnastics Sartre goes through in *Saint-Genet* are not likely to help change this. But since Genet avoids the kind of petulant insult that characterizes *Ubu-Roi,* where the prevailing voice is the whine of the child, and since his method of presentation is more often of high quality than not, he will have the paradoxical consolation of seeing that presentation admired even as his ideas are either rejected or compromised. Genet had hoped to use the theatre as the scholastics had used the syllogism: to build an inescapable structure which would be at once a monument to and a bastion for his vision of the world. What his hopes overlooked was the none the less evident fact that one can admire the technique and élan of a syllogism without giving the slightest assent to its basic premises.

What happens ultimately is that one accepts Genet's work imaginatively, as one accepts the works of Hieronymus Bosch or Henri Rousseau—as a vision impregnated with a power which the work itself generates, as a locus of beauty and dynamism which, either by changing or clarifying the enigmatic face of reality, becomes part of the turbulent stream of human endeavor and accomplishment. Though that stream be stocked with visions of the most diversified sorts, though its waters seethe with statements of the most contradictory and paradoxical kinds, its enormity and its challenge seem somehow to come under momentary control each time a new imagination comes to build a new dam. We know the dam will break under the pressure of new currents of vision and insight. But there is pleasure in observing its audacity, even in noting the various fissures and cracks in its architecture. For when the dam breaks under the burden of some new effort to direct the stream, we see, not the destruction, but the waves of the future in which we place our hopes.

New Haven—New York—Haines Falls
February 1961—February 1963

SELECT BIBLIOGRAPHY

Works by Jean Genet

Notre-Dame-des-Fleurs, Monte Carlo, n. p., 1944; Décines, Isère, 1948.

Chants secrets ("le Condamné à mort," "Marche funè-bre"), 1 lithograph by Emile Picq, Lyons, l'Arbalète, 1945.

Miracle de la rose, Lyons, l'Arbalète, 1946.

Pompes funèbres, Bikini (?), 1947; revised and corrected edition, 1948.

*Querelle de Brest, clandestine edition, n. p., n. d.; edition with 29 original lithographs (by Jean Cocteau?), Milan, n. p., 1947; new edition, n. p., 1947.

les Bonnes (first version), Lyons, l'Arbalète, 1947; *Revue l'Arbalète,* no. 12, 1948; *both versions, Sceaux, J.-J. Pauvert, 1954.

Haute Surveillance, Paris, Gallimard, 1947, 1949.

*Journal du voleur, Paris, Gallimard, 1948.

---

*Indicates edition quoted or cited in this book.

Poèmes ("le Condamné à mort," "la Galère," "la Parade," "un Chant d'amour," "le Pêcheur du Suquet"), Lyons, l'Arbalète, 1948; Décines, Isère, 1962.

l'Enfant criminel and *'Adame Miroir*, Paris, Paul Morihien, 1949.

*Oeuvres complètes, Vol. II (*Notre-Dame-des-Fleurs*, "le Condamné à mort," *Miracle de la rose*, "un Chant d'amour"); Vol. III (*Pompes funèbres*, "le Pêcheur du Suquet," *Querelle de Brest*), Paris, Gallimard, 1953.

le Balcon, 1 lithograph by Alberto Giacometti, Décines, Isère, 1956; new revised edition with a preface, 1960.

les Nègres, Décines, Isère, 1958; new edition with 33 photographs of the original production, 1960.

*l'Atelier d'Alberto Giacometti, les Bonnes (followed by a letter), *l'Enfant criminel, le Funambule*, Décines, Isère, 1958.

les Paravents, Décines, Isère, 1961.

Writings about Jean Genet

Abel, Lionel, "Metatheatre," *Partisan Review, 27* (1960), 324–30.

Bataille, Georges, "Jean Genet," in *la Littérature et le mal*, Paris, Gallimard, 1957, pp. 183–226.

Boisdeffre, Pierre de, *une Histoire vivante de la littérature d'aujourd'hui*, Paris, Le Livre Contemporain, 1957, pp. 277–80, 661–62, and passim.

Dort, Bernard, "le Jeu de Genet," *Temps Modernes*, 15th year, no. 171 (June 1960), pp. 1875–84.

Duvignaud, Jean, "Roger Blin aux Prises avec *les Nègres* de Jean Genet," *Lettres Nouvelles*, 7th year, no. 27 (October 28, 1959), pp. 24–26.

Elsen, Claude, "Mythologie de Jean Genet," *Cahiers de la Pléiade*, Spring 1950, pp. 51–57.

---

*Indicates edition quoted or cited in this book.

"Entretien avec Peter Brook," *l'Express,* May 19, 1960.

Esslin, Martin, "Jean Genet," in *The Theatre of the Absurd,* New York, Doubleday Anchor Books, 1961, pp. 140–67.

Fernandez, Dominique, "Claudel et Genet," *Nouvelle Revue Française, 8* (1960), 119–23.

Fowlie, Wallace, "Jean Genet," in *Dionysus in Paris,* New York, Meridian Books, 1959, pp. 218–23.

———, "The Case of Jean Genet," *The Commonweal* (October 28, 1960), pp. 111–13.

Goldman, Lucien, "une Pièce réaliste: *le Balcon,*" *Temps Modernes,* 15th year, no. 171 (June 1960), pp. 1885–96.

Grossvogel, David I., "Jean Genet," in *Four Playwrights and a Postscript,* Ithaca, Cornell University Press, 1962, pp. 133–74.

Guicharnaud, Jacques, *Modern French Theatre from Giraudoux to Beckett,* New Haven, Yale University Press, 1961, pp. 168–72.

Mauriac, François, "le Cas Jean Genet," *Figaro Littéraire,* March 26, 1949.

Pingaud, Bernard, ed., *Ecrivains d'aujourd'hui, 1940–1960,* Paris, Grasset, 1960, pp. 255–63.

Poulet, Robert, "Jean Genet," in *la Lanterne magique,* Paris, Debresse, 1956, pp. 160–67.

Pronko, Leonard Cabell, *Avant-Garde: the Experimental Theatre in France,* Berkeley and Los Angeles, University of California Press, 1962, pp. 140–54.

Rinieri, J. J., *"Journal du voleur,"* *Temps Modernes,* 4th year, no. 43 (May 1949), pp. 943–45.

St. Aubyn, F. C., "Jean Genet: A Scandalous Success," *The Hopkins Review, 5* (1951), 45–63.

Sartre, Jean-Paul, *Saint-Genet, comédien et martyr,* Paris, Gallimard, 1952 (Vol. I of the *Oeuvres complètes* of Jean Genet).

Zadek, Peter, "Acts of Violence," *New Statesman,* May 4, 1957, pp. 568–70.

Index

270